D1394488

GENERAL PHONETICS

GENERAL PHONETICS

By

R-M. S. HEFFNER

With a Foreword by

W. F. TWADDELL

THE UNIVERSITY OF WISCONSIN PRESS

Published 1950
The University of Wisconsin Press
Box 1379, Madison, Wisconsin 53701

The University of Wisconsin Press, Ltd.
70 Great Russell Street, London

Printings 1950, 1952, 1960, 1964, 1909, 1975

Printed in the United States of America
ISBN 0-299-00685-9; LC 50-14864

To the Memory of
Karl Friedrich Richard Hochdoerfer
and
Charles Hall Grandgent

FOREWORD

THE WRITING OF A GENERAL BOOK on phonetics is becoming a more formidable undertaking with each passing year. For phonetics, the study of the sound-continua habitually produced in human speech, is being blessed with additions of data through startling new techniques and devices (electronics, high-speed X-ray photography) and through an increased number of languages under observation. Lively controversies as to the classification and formulation of such data lend piquancy to the work of the phonetician.

Today, in the middle of the twentieth century, we have left the Eden of phonetic innocence. Our predecessors could postulate as self-evident a repertory of "sounds," of more or less complexity, and describe how they and their fellows produced these sounds by putting such and such vocal organs into this and that position. Today we know that setting up a repertory of sounds is itself a complex analytic operation. We know further that human speech is not a succession of sounds, each characterized by its specific position of the vocal organs; on the contrary, we recognize an act of human speech as a continuum, characterized by movements; and only by an artifice (a necessary artifice, to be sure) can a "position" be isolated for study. Even these isolated sounds and their positions, we now know, represent ranges of variation rather than fixed entities. Increasing intimacy of observation and increasing precision of measurement have shown how inconstant are the productions of "the same sound," and what very different sounds can result from "the same articulation." The corollaries are two: impressionistic description of a sound and of its production is unreliable; no small number of instrumental observations can be trusted as typical or average. The instrumental phonetician of today and tomorrow is in scientific conscience committed to the wide sampling and statistical integration which is the method of all biometric study.

Nor can the modern phonetician ignore the hierarchy of variations in the ranges he discovers and studies. The work which began, substantially, with Troubetzkoy and Sapir, has focussed attention upon speech as signalling, and constitutes a body of data and theory now known, with varying degrees of classical learnedness, as phonology, phonemics, or phonematics. Phonemic studies have occasionally added to the gaiety of life for the phonetician through their phonetic naïveté; but they have also added to the earnestness of his task. They have laid upon the phonetician the obligation to distinguish between "significant" and "merely positional" differences within and among the ranges of variations; the phonetician is finding himself forced to operate with significant phonemes and positional allophones. An act of speech is a physiological performance and an acoustic event, but it is also a socially effective signal; and the phonetician can neglect the signalling nature of the acts of speech he studies only at the peril of triviality and irrelevance.

Such are the vexations confronting the writer of a general book on phonetics. The task calls for a common-sense eclecticism rather than an attempt at universal completeness. This book is addressed to the serious student of human speech; it assumes an interest in phonetics (and an ability to read), but no specialized competence. The physiological apparatus is described in some detail, as is fitting; for the phonetician or phonemicist who isn't sure whether the vocal bands are 10 mm. or 50 mm. long can scarcely trust his inferences as to their behavior. The principal types of sound are described, with their variations and the occurrence of these in various languages. Considerable attention is given to the continuum of speech, with its essential durations and fluctuations in intensity and pitch.

This book is a picture of the state of phonetic knowledge today, valuable and interesting as much for its indication of the sources and methods and aims of phonetic study as for its descriptions and explanations. The seasoned phonetician who reads it can be promised a refreshing account of the noises people make when they talk, and how they make them. Lovers of adventure among phoneticians will find some excitement in suggested connections between the physiological production of sounds and their acoustic nature. And the beginner who studies it can be assured that he will know what phonetics is about.

W. F. T.

ACKNOWLEDGEMENTS

FIFTY-FOUR YEARS AGO Charles Hall Grangent, with the active and extensive collaboration of Karl Friedrich Richard Hochdoerfer, published in Boston the little book called *German and English Sounds*. Thirty-eight years ago I first came under the tutelage of Richard Hochdoerfer, and seven years later I first studied under Grandgent. Both men were great teachers and loyal friends. I learned much from each, and dedicating this book to their memory affords me some satisfaction, although it comes too late to gladden the heart of either.

In the nature of the case, some sections of this essay are in part compilations. I hope I have, in the notes, fully acknowledged every obligation, however slight, in that respect.

I cannot too warmly state my gratitude to my colleague W. F. Twaddell for his sympathetic and incisive criticism of my work as it took the form it now has. He has prevented a number of those slips which human frailty imposes upon us; and he has given freely of constructive suggestions which have led to improvements, notably in the interests of the readers of the book. My obligation to him for his Foreword will be apparent to all who read it. For all this my earnest thanks.

R-M. S. HEFFNER

Madison, Wisconsin
December 20, 1945.

CONTENTS

ILLUSTRATIONS

GENERAL PHONETICS

CHAPTER I

INTRODUCTION

0.1 *What is Phonetics?*

Phonetics as a science is an integral part of linguistics; phonetics as an art proceeds from the basic data of scientific phonetics. Linguistics is the scientific study of a language, or of languages; that is, linguistics strives to discover general truths and to formulate general laws relating to the growth and structure of its object, be this one or several languages. A language is commonly, and grossly, thought of as the sum-total of words and constructions, or combinations of words, used and understood by members of a considerable community. However, the only phenomenal existence which a language has, and therefore the only form in which it can be observed, is in the speech of individual members of the community, either as this is heard and understood or as it is more or less imperfectly recorded, for example, in the written word. The introspective contemplation of remembered language experiences is the contemplation of the speech of individual members of the community recorded in the memory rather than on paper.

Linguistics therefore has to study one kind of human behavior: namely, the systematic use of sound signals for the purpose of evoking appropriate or desired responses from the hearers thereof. Such sound signals can be shown to consist of individual sounds, or of sounds recognizable as recurrent, produced singly or in configurations. The fundamental task of the phonetician and the primary business of phonetics is to identify and to describe these recurrent sounds of speech. Phonetics, then, is the study of the sounds of speech: as a science it seeks to discover general truths and to formulate general laws relating to these sounds and their production; as an art it uses the basic descriptive data of scientific phonetics to facilitate the recognition and reproduction of speech sounds.

0.2 *The Sounds of Speech*

Suppose yourself to overhear the following conversation: Mr. A. "Oh, hello, John! Could you tell me where I can find a good dentist?" Mr. B. "Why yes, Henry, I find Dr. X a very good dentist." Mr. A has uttered a complex sound signal, or a sequence of sound signals, to which Mr. B has responded with a different set of noises which probably represent an adequate response to Mr. A's stimulating question. When we compare the two utterances we discover in the sound sequences a number of configurations which seem to be alike as we hear them and also in the manner in which

1

they are produced. These "sames" are (I), (find), (a), (good dentist). If we knew nothing at all about the English language we should not be able immediately to divide utterances into segments representing "sames" in this way. But by comparing these utterances with many other utterances and responses, we could ultimately make out the identity of the signal (I) and its distinctiveness from (find); and if we persevered we might discover that (good dentist) is compounded of two units (good) and (dentist).[1] These configurations or segments of utterances which recur in approximately the same physical forms and with the same values as stimulus-response (i.e., with the same "meanings") are called words, and there are a great many of them in any language.

Further analysis of English utterances would reveal that the segment (find) is itself a configuration, the constituent parts of which recur in other arrangements. We can isolate the first part by comparing the effects of substitutions made in utterances. If we substitute for (find) any of the words, *bind, hind, kind, mind, rind, wind, lined, pined, signed, vined*, the stimulus-response value of the utterance is changed each time, although these words are identical except for differences in the way they begin. Each of the initial portions or segments is therefore distinctive—that is, associated with differences of meaning. Similarly, if we substitute for (find) any of the words, *fanned, fend, fiend, phoned, fond, fund, found*, we produce a change in the meaning of the utterance. In these cases the initial and the final portions of the configuration are constant, while an intervening segment is different and distinctive in each instance. By repeating the process of contrasting meanings we can discover in the end of the word (find) two distinctive components which we call [n] and [d]. When we apply this kind of analysis more widely we discover that multitudinous observations of speech forms reveal only a limited number of distinctive components which recur repeatedly in many different configurations. Scientific phonetics begins by gathering the components distinguished by means of such analytical observation into classes; and it is a striking fact that no one language yields more than a few dozen discrete groups of distinctive constituent sounds.

0.3 *Genetic or Gennemic*[2]

The stimulus-response behavior which we call speech consists typically of a series of physical movements, initiated by patterned nervous impulses and performed in sequence by the vocal organs, so-called, in such a way that these movements result in audible agitations of the surrounding air. That is, speech movements produce sound waves. These sound waves in turn displace, in intricate and minute movement patterns, the tympani of the ears and the displacements ultimately produce nervous impulses which act as sound-signal stimuli and, when uninhibited, lead to a response. Such behavior can be studied in various ways. The phonetician, in his effort to delimit and to describe the several distinct constituent speech sounds, can examine the movements of the speech organs which produce the sounds (genetic investigation), or he may examine the sounds as acoustic phenomena after they have been produced (gennemic investigation). For some purposes genetic investigation is indicated, while for others gennemic study yields better results. Neither approach may properly be ignored.

0.4 *Phonemes*

The phonetician must first, by processes of analysis applied to the speech continua which are his raw material, identify, delimit, and describe, either genetically or gennemically, or in both ways, the three or four dozen recurrent segments which are recognizable as distinctively different from one another. Of course, in the reduction of these primary data to a limited number of classes he must neglect nondistinctive differences, although he should observe them. He may observe, for example, that the first portion of the word *keel* is different from the first portion of the word *cool;* but he will discover that the substitution of the one sound for the other never occurs as the sole cause of a change in the stimulus-response value of the sound signal, in the way in which such a substitution as that of [v] for [f] in *vine* for *fine, five* for *fife,* changes it. Hence the phonetician must include the two different initial elements of *keel* and *cool* in a single basic class. As soon as he has established a number of basic classes he is constrained to find a name for each, so that he may think about them effectively. It is inconvenient to speak or to think always in terms of the genetic or the gennemic descriptions of the classes. It is correct to say that the word *keel* begins with a voiceless, mediopalatal, moderately aspirated stop (the genetic description), but it is more convenient to say that it begins with [k]. In like manner, it is convenient to say that *cool* begins with [k], though this [k] sound is not identical with the [k] sound in *keel*. Thus [k] becomes the name or indicator for a class of observed behavior patterns. Some scholars, in order to keep the class, as such, distinct in their thinking from the phenomenal occurrence which would be subsumed under it, speak of the phoneme /k/ when they mean the class, and the sound [k] when they mean the phenomenal occurrence or event which would belong to the class. In this sense, one may say that the phonetician's first task is to sort out the recurrent sound segments of phenomenal speech and to assign each to one of a limited number of categories called phonemes.[3]

0.5 *Phonetics—Science and Art*

Science arrives at general truths concerning its object by the processes of analysis, classification, and synthesis. Scientific phonetics proceeds from

the analysis of speech events to the classification of their constituent parts
in sound classes or phonemes. It then undertakes further the analysis of the
class, or phoneme, by seeking to determine which of the objectively observed features of the recurrent sound segment are essential to its identification and which are adventitious. At this point, conflicts between the
requirements of phonetics as a part of linguistic science and those of phonetics as an art appear. We have seen that the difference between the sound
[k] of *keel* and the sound [k] of *cool* is nondistinctive and that the two sounds
therefore belong to the same basic class or phoneme. From the standpoint
of a linguistic description of the phoneme [k], the difference between the
two sounds is not essential but adventitious. From the standpoint of the
art of phonetics, this difference is quite as important as any other, and
scientific phonetics, if it is adequately to serve the art of phonetics, must
pursue its analysis of events beyond the mere classification of its data into
phonemes. Groups of recurrent sounds within a given phoneme must be duly
recognized and described. It may well be that scientific linguistics can content itself with the observation that the final sounds of German *ich* and
German *ach* are members of the same phoneme. Scientific phonetics may
not stop at such a point in its analysis of speech sounds.

0.6 *Descriptive, Historical, Comparative*

Phonetics, as the science of the sounds of speech, may endeavor to describe the sounds of a single language at a given time. Such an undertaking
is called descriptive phonetics, or synchronic phonetics, since all of its data
are contemporary with one another. Since the records of many languages go
back a thousand years or more, differences in the phonetic state of affairs
at different periods in the history of these languages are observable. The
science of phonetics here is indispensable to linguistic analysis, since it
alone can provide adequate explanations of the observable phonetic facts.
The study of these matters is called historical phonetics, or diachronic
phonetics. Finally, there are many reasons for comparing the facts observed
about the sounds of one language with those revealed by the study of one
or more other languages. An undertaking of this sort is called comparative
phonetics. A certain amount of comparative phonetics is practiced by
everyone who learns a language other than his native tongue.

0.7 *General Phonetics*

When one speaks of the phonetics of English, or the phonetics of French,
one means normally the descriptive study of the sounds of English or of
French. Such a study will include the analysis and classification of the
speech sounds of the language and perhaps some systematic consideration
of the distinctive features of sound which are employed in the language to

mark the several phonemes or sound-classes. For example, we find distinctive contrasts in English between *big* and *pig*, *dick* and *tick*, *gut* and *cut*, and we discern in the presence or absence of voicing a similar marking of the distinction throughout the series [b]:[p], [d]:[t], [g]:[k]. Something very much like this may be inferred for French from contrasting pairs such as *barque : parque, doux : tout, gare : quart*. The distinction between the French phonemes [b]:[p], [d]:[t], [g]:[k] appears to parallel that found in English. Moreover the phonemes themselves in each case comprise sounds which are gennemically and genetically much alike in the two languages. This sort of comparison can be applied to many other languages which have some or all of these contrasts. From observations of this kind has come the notion that a single systematic treatment of the science of phonetics might be so devised that the methods and principles of analysis and classification set forth should have universal validity. Apart from the difficulties entailed in observing all of the speech sounds used anywhere in any language and all of the criteria of discrimination effective in any language, this can be done, but the result will not be, as might be thought, a single, unitary system of classification equally applicable to the speech sounds of all languages. The difficulty lies in the fact that different languages mark the distinctive differences between their phonemes in different ways. English, French, and German and many other languages have but two series of stops, b, d, g, and p, t, k, whereas still other languages have three series of stops marked by differentiating features which are nondistinctive elsewhere. Thus the presence or absence of aspiration after p, t, k, is distinctive in some languages and nondistinctive in others, or the presence or absence of a stoppage of the breath stream at the glottis during the articulation of p, t, or k may or may not be the distinctive mark of a difference between two phonemes. If we were to subsume the English [k] phoneme, the French [k] phoneme, the German [k] phoneme under a quasi-universal rubric of a [k] phoneme *in abstracto*, we could not include under this class any of the analogous stops of Haida,[4] which has three "voiceless k" phonemes, one marked by weak energy and no aspiration, another by greater energy and aspiration, and a third marked by glottalization (see p. 136 below). Neither could we put English [k] under any of the classes required for Haida or Nootka. One must not, therefore, expect a general treatment of the science of phonetics to yield a universally applicable linguistic classification of speech sounds. Descriptive phonetics can discern mutually exclusive classes of speech sounds only within a single language.

Nevertheless, there are many fundamental facts and generally valid basic techniques which must be learned by any one who proposes to engage in the study of phonetics. These matters may properly be dealt with in a discussion not restricted for its data to a single language and still not obligated by its "title" to undertake an exhaustive comparative study of all languages. I propose, therefore, in the following pages to set forth in some detail how speech sounds are produced, what they are when they are produced, the manner of their production and their nature when they are combined in speech forms.[5] In the interest of simplicity I shall call this exposition General Phonetics.

Part I

FUNDAMENTALS

CHAPTER II

THE PHYSIOLOGY OF SPEECH

1.01 *The Problem*

When we speak and are understood we accomplish this most distinctively human act by causing our vocal organs, so-called, to execute patterned movements which result in sound waves. These our ear transforms into sensory impulses which we interpret as conventional signals.

Evidently the sounds of speech result from movements made audible and we must examine both the movements which produce the sounds and the sounds themselves. To examine the movements which produce speech sounds (the genetic approach), we must study the physiology of speech. To examine the product of these movements (the gennemic approach) we must learn something of the physical nature of speech sounds.

1.011 *The Sensory Basis of Speech*

None of the sounds of human speech is produced by an organ biologically designed for a speech function; all are heard by an organ indubitably designed for the hearing of sounds. Language is founded upon the sense of hearing; there is no organ of speech in the biological sense.

The medium through which speech sounds reach the ear is, normally, the air adjacent to it, and the pertinent vibratory disturbance of this medium is accomplished ultimately and principally by modifications of the speaker's breath stream. We shall begin therefore with a description of the mechanism of breathing and proceed thence to trace the breath stream from its origin to its emergence.

1.02 *The Lungs*

The biological purpose of respiration is to cleanse the blood of its accumulation of carbon dioxide and to provide it with fresh oxygen from the outer air. This chemical transfer takes place in the lungs, which are large spongy bodies composed of many small vessicles or tubes, called alveoli. Each of these alveoli receives its supply of air from a larger tube, called a bronchiole, and the bronchioles in turn join two larger systems, coming together in the left and the right bronchus respectively. The two bronchi, or bronchial tubes, unite at the base of the trachea, which is the sole passageway for the air from the throat to the lungs. Plate 1 shows the arrangement of these parts.

1.03 *Breathing Movements*

The lungs are incapable of movement by their own energy although they possess a minimum of elasticity which causes them, if they have been squeezed together, to expand sufficiently to open the alveoli to the access of air. The inflation and deflation of the lungs is accomplished by alternately reducing the pressure upon their outer surfaces until air from the

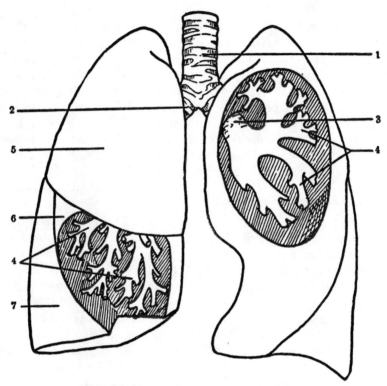

Plate 1. LUNGS, BRONCHI, BRONCHIOLES

1—Trachea. 2—Right bronchus. 3—Left bronchus. 4—Bronchioles. 5—Upper lobe.
6—Middle lobe. 7—Lower lobe.

outside is induced to flow in, and increasing this pressure upon their outer surfaces until the air contained in the lungs is forced to flow outward. Such pressures are called negative when they are less than that of the outer air and positive when they are greater than this. The "iron lung," or Drinker Respirator, accomplishes its function by enclosing the entire chest in an air-tight chamber and then, by pump action, alternately reducing the air pressure in this chamber till it is sufficiently negative to induce the outer air to flow into the lungs, and increasing the pressure in the chamber enough to force some of this air to flow out from the lungs again. Nature accomplishes this function by enclosing each lung in an air-tight chamber, the pleura, and then producing the required negative and positive pressures by movements of the thorax. Perforation of the pleura makes the production of the required negative pressure impossible.

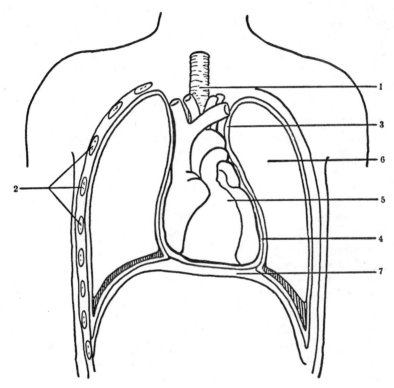

Plate 2. THORAX, RIB CAGE, DIAPHRAGM

1—Trachea. 2—Sections of ribs. 3—Outline of pleura. 4—Outline of pericardium. 5—Heart. 6—Lungs. 7—Diaphragm.

The thoracic cavity (Plate 2) in which the lungs lie is bounded above and laterally by the rib cage. The lower boundary is a large sheet of muscular and fibrous tissue, shaped like a tall dome with the concave side downward. This sheet is the diaphragm. It is attached in front to the sternum, or breastbone, and to the cartilages of the lower six ribs on either side. In the rear it is attached to the lumbar vertebrae. The diaphragm is the principal muscle of respiration. When its muscular fibers contract, the whole vault of the diaphragm is drawn downward until the pressure of its under surface against the viscera, supported by the walls of the abdomen, prevents further downward movement. This point is soon reached. Then with its center resting on the crowded viscera, the diaphragm, as it contracts further, lifts the front and side structures to which its margins are attached—the lower ribs and the sternum. These movements enlarge the thoracic cavity and thereby reduce the pressure per unit area upon the outer surfaces of the lungs. If the access of outer air is free as far as the trachea, the pressure on the inner surfaces of the lungs will be that of the outer air. Whenever, therefore, the movements of the diaphragm and rib cage so reduce the pressure on the outer surfaces of the lungs that this is lower than the pressure on their inner surfaces, air will flow into the lungs and inspiration will take place. When the pressure in the thoracic chamber is reduced, the air flowing into the lungs will force these structures to expand into the thoracic cavity until the pressure on the outer surfaces of the lungs is equal to that on the inner surfaces. When the muscles of the diaphragm are relaxed, the weight of the raised portions of the thoracic walls and the elastic push of the viscera and abdominal walls force the diaphragm upward. This reduces the size of the thoracic cavity and increases the pressure per unit area on the outer surfaces of the lungs. The result is that the air is then forced out of the lungs until the pressure on the inside surfaces is equal to that on the outside surfaces. If for any reason the movements of the diaphragm are restricted, the required negative pressure in the pleurae can be produced by lifting the walls of the thorax. Indeed these walls are usually lifted to some extent in conjunction with the depression of the diaphragm in all but very quiet breathing. Two types of breathing are usually recognized: the abdominal type, in which the diaphragm is the prime mover; and the thoracic type, in which the movements of the diaphragm are minimized and the movements of the upper rib cage are made more extensive. Posture, clothing, or custom may favor one or the other of these types of breathing.

1.031   *Rest-breathing or Speech-breathing*

The rate of respiration when the body is at rest is determined by the requirements of the blood stream. Whenever the content of carbon dioxide in the blood reaches the critical point, the nerves which cause the diaphragm to contract are automatically stimulated and new air is breathed in. On the whole, the normal rate of rest-breathing may be said to range from 10 to 20 inhalations per minute.

The normal cycle of events in rest-breathing may be regarded as a sequence of inspiration, expiration, and pause, although the pause may disappear altogether when the rate of breathing increases or when the relative speed of expiration is reduced. The pause is also a phase during which there is relative rather than absolute inertness. The body structures displaced by the movement of inspiration return during expiration by virtue of their weight and elasticity to about their initial positions. Expiration requires about the same length of time as inspiration; the ratio is something like 1 to 1.1. Then, before a new inspiratory movement is initiated, these body structures may still further compress the lungs in the pleurae, but at a greatly reduced rate. Occasionally in rest-breathing cycles complete equilibrium is reached, but such occasions are comparatively infrequent. In the breathing of different individuals these periods of relative inertness, or pauses, vary more noticeably than do the phases of inspiration and expiration. If we include the pauses with the expiration and thus differentiate only two phases—inspiration *vs.* noninspiration—the duration of the former is to that of the latter approximately as 1:2, when the breather is seated and truly at rest. Rest-breathing movements are slowest when the breather is reclining, and most rapid when he is standing erect.

The rate of respiration during speech is determined by the nature of the utterance. We speak in breath groups, that is, in more or less closely integrated sound sequences, between each two of which we take in a new breath. Hence the rate of speech-breathing varies considerably with the type of speech we use. Frequently this rate is slower than that of rest-breathing; more often, probably, it is more rapid. No phase of relative inertness, or pause, such as may be observed in rest-breathing, is to be found in speech-breathing. The movement of inspiration is greatly accelerated, being accomplished in one-half to one-third the time required in rest-breathing. The phase of expiration may be greatly prolonged. In normal conversation the ratio of the duration of intake to that of outgo ranges from 1:3 to 1:10, with occasional instances of ratios as high as 1:30 when the speaker has a great deal to say. This disparity results from the primary fact of phonetics, that most of the sounds of articulated speech are caused by impediments to the free outward flow of air from the lungs.

In rest-breathing the expulsion of the air from the lungs is usually due to the pressure exerted by the weight and elasticity of the structures displaced by the muscular act of inhalation. Forced expiration is possible and is accomplished chiefly by the contraction of the large muscles in the walls of the abdomen. In speech-breathing, when the rate of utterance is greater than 2.5 to 4 syllables per second, Stetson[1] finds that the abdominal muscles are fixated, or made rigid, so that they hold the lower edges of the rib cage firm. By this action they provide a resistant basis for the delicate muscular pulses carried out by the internal intercostal muscles. These pulses correspond to the distribution of energy over successive syllables, there being normally one such pulse for each syllable. Until and unless this thesis is proved to be untenable it will remain a valuable basis for the study of the problems of the syllable.

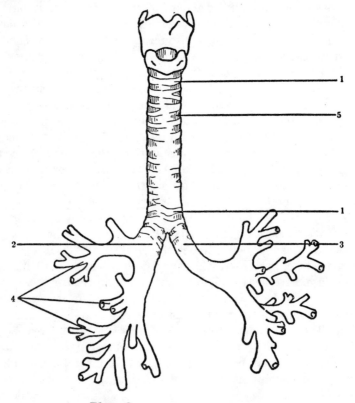

Plate 3. TRACHEA AND LARYNX

1—Tracheal cartilages (one near top, one near bottom). 2—Right bronchus. 3—Left bronchus. 4—Bronchial tubes. 5—Connective tissue between tracheal rings.

1.04 *The Trachea*

From the junction of the right bronchus with the left, a single tube leads upward to the throat. This is the windpipe, or trachea (Plate 3), which, like the two bronchi, is composed of a number of incomplete cartilaginous rings joined one above the other by tough and somewhat elastic connective tissue. The incomplete or open part of each ring is on the dorsal side, where the esophagus lies between the trachea and the vertebrae. In cross section the trachea is roughly circular except in the rear, where the open ends of the incomplete rings permit its wall to be somewhat flattened. Its diameter is from 2 to 2.5 cm., and its length is about 11 cm. Since the trachea and the two bronchi are never collapsed, but always open, they afford certain possibilities for resonance if the air in them is properly agitated.

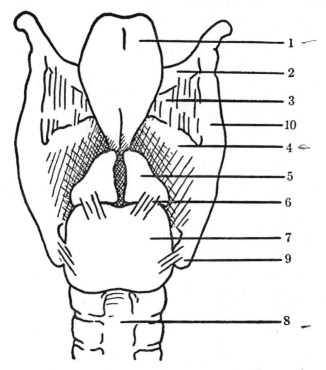

Plate 4. THE LARYNX FROM BEHIND

1—Epiglottis. 2—Hyoid bone. 3—Hyothyroid membrane. 4—Thyroid cartilage. 5—Arytenoid cartilage. 6—Posterior cricoarytenoid ligament. 7—Cricoid cartilage. 8—Trachea. 9—Inferior cornu. 10—Superior cornu.

1.05 *The Larynx*

The uppermost ring of the trachea differs from the others in that it is very much heavier and in that it is a complete ring. Its shape suggests that of a seal-ring with the wider part on the dorsal side. However, while its lower rim is approximately circular, the upper rim of this ring is distinctly oval, with the long axis from front to back. This ring—or cricoid—cartilage is the foundation of the structures which, as a functional group, are called the larynx. (Plate 4)

The largest cartilage of the larynx is the thyroid, or shield cartilage, which supports and protects the vocal bands and their adjusting mechanism. The thyroid cartilage stands in front of the opening from the throat into the trachea and gives to the larynx its distinctive outward shape which in men we recognize as the "Adam's apple." It is composed of two plates, or alae, joined in front like a snow-plow to form an angle of some 70 degrees. Each plate has two horns, or cornua, one projecting upward and one downward from its posterior edge. The lower horns are connected by a joint on either side with the cricoid cartilage, so that the thyroid may be tilted up or down slightly with reference to the plane of the cricoid cartilage. The upper horns of the thyroid are connected by a ligament on either side to the rear prongs of the hyoid bone, to which important muscles of the tongue are attached.

Sitting upon the heavy upper back rim of the cricoid cartilage are the two tiny, roughly pyramid-shaped arytenoid cartilages, which are so set upon the cricoid that their smooth adjacent surfaces may be drawn tightly together or slid apart laterally a few millimeters. The two arytenoid cartilages may also be rotated on these joints so that the anterior arms which project over the opening into the trachea, may be swung tightly together or as much as 8 mm. apart. These arms are called the vocal processes of the arytenoid cartilages.

1.051   *The Conus Elasticus*

From the upper rim of the cricoid cartilage a membrane of yellow elastic tissue extends upward more or less in the shape of a cone. In the rear it is attached on either side to the bodies and forward projections (vocal processes) of the arytenoids; in front the two edges of the membrane are joined together and to the thyroid cartilage, where the two plates meet. The edges of this elastic cone, or conus elasticus, as they extend from the vocal processes of the arytenoids to the angle of the thyroid, are called the vocal ligaments. (Plate 5)

In front the conus elasticus connects the cricoid with the thyroid cartilage at its angle, thereby closing the gap which would otherwise open between these two structures. Hence it is here called the cricothyroid ligament. It is through this ligament that the tracheal fistula occasionally used by instrumental phoneticians has been inserted.

1.052   *The Vocal Bands*

Above the conus elasticus, and running from the angle of the thyroid on either side to the arytenoid cartilage, is a pair of thin, but vertically broad, bands of muscle. Each is divided into two parts—an upper and a lower— by a recess, or ventricle, which undercuts the upper portion throughout most of its length. The lower portion of each thyroarytenoid muscle is attached to the vocal process of the arytenoid cartilage. The upper portion is attached to the body and the upper tip of the arytenoid. Indeed, some of the fibers of the upper portion of the muscle run on upward into the folds which join the artenoids with the edges of the epiglottis (i.e. the aryepiglottic folds). When contracted, the thyroarytenoid muscles tend to draw the arytenoids forward, at the same time tilting them towards the thyroid cartilage. This occurs normally during the act of swallowing.

The upper portions of this pair of muscles, with their covering mucous tissue, are known as the ventricular folds. Their function in most speech

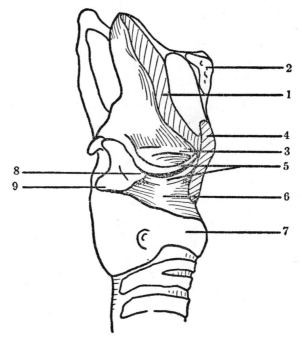

Plate 5. LARYNX SECTION, CONUS ELASTICUS

1—Epiglottis. 2—Body of hyoid bone. 3—Ventricular fold. 4—Thyroid cartilage. 5—Vocal folds. 6—Conus elasticus. 7—Cricoid cartilage. 8—Vocal process of arytenoid cartilage. 9—Muscular process of arytenoid cartilage.

is secondary and unimportant. When swollen or brought nearly together by excessive constriction of the interior musculature of the larynx, they cause a change in the quality or timbre of the sounds produced. When tightly closed they stop entirely the outward flow of air from the trachea.

The lower portions of the paired thyroarytenoid muscles have a name of their own, the vocalis muscles. These muscles lie on either side directly upon the upper surface of the conus elasticus from the thyroid to the vocal process of the arytenoid, and the two, together with their covering of mucous membrane, constitute the vocal bands. The term "vocal cords," frequently applied to these structures, is misleading. In cross section the vocal bands are triangular, being shaped much like the cushion of a billiard table, and only their median edges are free. (Plate 6)

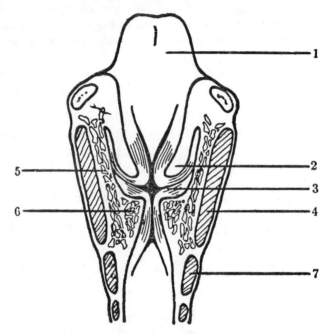

Plate 6. LARYNX SECTION, VOCAL BANDS

1—Epiglottis. 2—Ventricular fold. 3—Ventricle. 4—Thyroid cartilage. 5—Thyroarytenoid muscle. 6—Vocalis muscle. 7—Cricoid cartilage.

The space between the two vocal bands and the attached arytenoid cartilages is known as the glottis. It may be divided into two sections, the intermembranous part and the intercartilaginous part. The latter is the portion of this opening which lies between the adjacent faces of the two arytenoid cartilages. In men the intercartilaginous glottis is about 7.5 mm. long, while the intermembranous glottis is about 15.5 mm. long, making a average total length of 23 mm. for the entire glottis in men. In women the average total length is about 17 mm., of which some 11.5 mm. is intermembranous.

1.06 *The Epiglottis*

Just above the point at the inner angle of the thyroid plates where the conus elasticus is attached and where the vocalis muscle arises, the lower tip of the epiglottis is hinged. The epiglottis is a relatively large, leaf-shaped or spoon-shaped structure of cartilage and connective tissue. Approximately halfway up its anterior surface it is connected by a ligament to the hyoid bone, and also by the median glossoepiglottic fold to the base of the tongue. On either side of this fold there is a depression called the sinus glossoepiglotticus, or the vallecula. The edges of the epiglottis are joined to the tips and to the bodies of the arytenoid cartilages by the aryepiglottic folds.

There are no direct muscular attachments to the epiglottis, and it therefore moves only when pushed or pulled by neighboring organs, notably the tongue and the hyoid bone. In an earlier stage of its evolution it once was long enough to make connection with the now similarly degenerate velum, thereby providing a clear passage for air from nose to lungs independently of the oral pharynx. Contrary to common opinion it has no essential function in swallowing and may be removed down to its tubercle or cushion without its absence causing difficulties in swallowing.

Although it cannot itself be moved except mechanically by displacement due to the movement of other organs, the epiglottis may have some influence upon the quality of speech sounds, since it is in fact pushed far back over the opening of the glottis for some sounds, for example for the vowels of *far* and *ought*, while it is pulled forward out of the channel of the breath stream for others, for example for the vowels of *bee* or *bay*.

1.07   *The Intrinsic Muscles of the Larynx*

Four paired muscles and one single muscle make up the intrinsic musculature of the larynx. All but one pair of these are attached to the little arytenoid cartilages. These muscles can, by various combinations of their tension, cause the arytenoids and the attached vocal bands to assume a wide variety of positions. Typical among these are the following four.

1.071   *Exhalation*

When the intrinsic muscles of the larynx are at rest, the arytenoid cartilages are normally drawn apart at their bases. The vocal bands are in line with the bodies and vocal processes of the cartilages, so that the opening between the bands is triangular. This is the usual position of these bands during the expiratory phase of rest-breathing, and is indicated in Fig. 1 of Plate 9.

1.072   *Inhalation*

The posterior cricoarytenoid muscles pull from the back of the cricoid cartilage upon the muscular processes of the arytenoids, so that their contraction tends to swing the vocal processes of the arytenoids apart. This movement takes place at every normal inhalation. The action of these muscles is opposed to and thus can be controlled by the pull of the lateral cricoarytenoids and also by the direct pull of the thyroarytenoid muscles. The unopposed pull of the posterior cricoarytenoids widens the opening between the vocal bands to its maximum, as is shown in Fig. 2 of Plate 9.

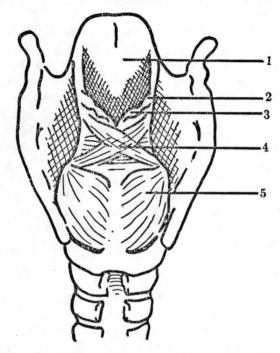

Plate 7. MUSCLES OF THE LARYNX FROM BEHIND

1—Epiglottis. 2—Cuneiform cartilage. 3—Corniculate cartilage. 4—Arytenoid muscle. 5—Cricoarytenoid muscle.

1.073 *Whisper*

The lateral cricoarytenoids pull on the muscular processes of the arytenoids from in front and from below. They oppose the pull of the posterior cricoarytenoids and tend to pull the vocal processes of the arytenoids together and thus to close the intermembranous glottis. However, they also tend to pull the bases of the two arytenoids apart, thus opening the intercartilaginous glottis. In this action they are opposed by the arytenoid muscle. Their action, when unopposed, results in a form of the glottis which is often, but by no means always, to be observed in vigorous whispering and which is therefore sometimes called the whispering glottis. This is illustrated in Fig. 3 of Plate 9.

1.074 *Voice*

The artenoid muscle has two sets of fibers. The transverse fibers connect the back surfaces of the two arytenoid cartilages, and their contraction

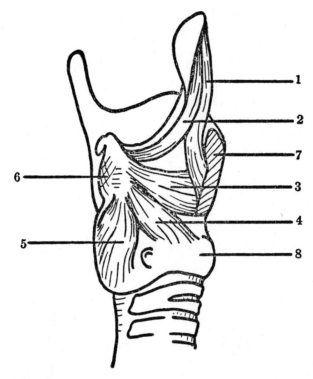

Plate 8. MUSCLES OF THE LARYNX FROM THE SIDE

1—Thyroepiglottic muscle. 2—Aryepiglottic muscle. 3—Thyroarytenoid muscle. 4—Lateral cricoarytenoid muscle. 5—Posterior cricoarytenoid muscle. 6—Arytenoid muscle. 7—Thyroid cartilage. 8—Cricoid cartilage.

tends to slide the bodies of the cartilages together. The oblique fibers of the arytenoid muscle run from the base of one arytenoid to the tip of the other, from which point some of these fibers continue upward into the edges of the aryepiglottic fold. Contraction of these oblique fibers tends to pull the tips of the arytenoids together. Both sets of fibers oppose the pull of the lateral cricoarytenoids.

The thyroarytenoid muscles, described in Section 1.052, tend when contracted to draw the arytenoid cartilages forward toward the thyroid notch. The lower fibers of the inferior thyroarytenoids tend upon contraction to bring the vocal processes of the arytenoids together. Also the contraction of the vocalis muscles, if unopposed, would pull the arytenoid cartilages forward on the top of the cricoid towards the thyroid cartilage. If the

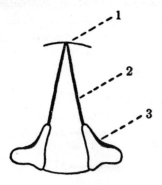

Fig. 1. Exhalation

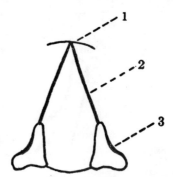

Fig. 2. Inhalation

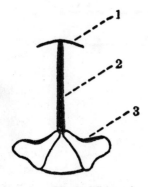

Fig. 3. Whispering

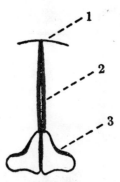

Fig. 4. Voice

Plate 9. POSITIONS OF THE VOCAL BANDS

1—Thyroid cartilage. 2—Vocal band. 3—Arytenoid cartilage.

arytenoids are held in position by the posterior cricoarytenoids, the contraction of the vocalis muscles tends to make the vocal bands rigid.

The action of the cricothyroid muscles is imperfectly understood. It is clear, however, that their contraction would tend to increase the distance between the angle of the thyroid plates and the arytenoids on the back rim of the cricoid. They may serve as opposers to the posterior cricoarytenoids and allow tension to be put on the vocal bands without displacing the thyroid cartilage.

When the bodies of the arytenoids are brought together by the contraction of the arytenoid muscles and prevented from turning on their joints by the opposition of the posterior and the lateral cricoarytenoid muscles, tension can be put on the vocal bands by the contraction of the cricothyroid and the lower thyroarytenoid or vocalis muscles. Strong contraction of these muscles effectively stops the flow of breath; moderate contraction of these muscles puts the vocal bands in the position to produce voice vibrations. This position is indicated in Fig. 4 of Plate 9.

It should be clear that by mutual oppositions in various degrees of tension these muscles can accomplish minute variations in the position of the arytenoids and in the tension upon the vocal bands. The accuracy with which we can intone a musical scale is evidence of the precision of these controls.

1.08   The Function of the Larynx

Biologically, the function of the larynx is to provide, and to protect, a mechanism for opening and closing the entrance to the pulmonary tract. The necessity for a means of closing the entrance to this pulmonary tract so that no air can escape from it or be forced into it is vital.

The ventricular folds or bands, when once brought together by the constrictive pull of the intrinsic musculature of the larynx, are forced more and more firmly together by increasing pressure of the air within the lungs. This mechanism is essential to normal elimination from the alimentary canal and it plays an important part in normal childbirth. The vocal bands are so constructed that when they are brought together by the constriction of the intrinsic musculature of the larynx their margins are more and more firmly pressed together as the pressure of the air outside progressively exceeds that of the air inside the lungs. If this mechanism did not exist, the nature and extent of our arm efforts would be drastically restricted. A great many of the muscular actions of our arms depend upon the creation of a partial vacuum beneath the vocal bands. Without these two valvular controls of the opening of the larynx the human animal would have very little power above the hips. He could not lift himself, or any other object of size, with his arms. These valves are shown in Plate 6.

1.09   Voice

If the free margins of the vocal bands are drawn together so that they make contact throughout their entire length, they will thereby stop the outward flow of breath. Unless the relaxation of the diaphragm and the fall of the rib cage, described in Section 1.03, is checked, the pressure of air in the lungs will increase as long as the glottis remains closed, or until equilibrium is reached. If the appropriate thoracic and abdominal muscles are contracted, this pressure can become quite high. It is possible, however, to control the contraction of the laryngeal muscles so that there will be a point in this rise of pressure at which the force of the confined air becomes sufficient to push apart the edges of the vocal bands. If, as is normal, the constriction of the intrinsic musculature of the larynx is insufficient to bring the ventricular folds together, the air from the lungs will escape into the throat when the vocal bands are thus pushed apart. Evidently, if air escapes in this fashion the pressure below the vocal bands will be reduced and the elastic forces of the bands will restore the closure. Then the pressure will be built up again sufficiently to blow the bands apart once more. If the muscular adjustments of the arytenoids are maintained, this alternate opening and closing of the bands may become periodic. The critical pressure and the period of this cycle are determined by the forces exerted by the muscles which move the vocal bands, by the elasticity of the tissues of which these bands are composed, and by the pressure of the air above the glottis. The area of the opening between the bands tends to decrease as the frequency of opening and closing increases. The whole action is in many ways analogous to the behavior of the lips in horn playing.

Each time the vocal bands part and emit a puff of air, this air moves that above it in the throat cavities. If there is a more or less free path to the open air through the nose or mouth, these movements set up alternate condensations and rarefactions of the air above the larynx. Whenever the alternate opening and closing of the glottis occurs more frequently than sixteen times per second the movements produce sound waves and hence a vocal tone. The known limits of frequency achieved in the human production of voice, or vocal tone, are from 42 (F_1) to 2048 (c^4) cycles per second. The normal range in calm speech for men is approximately from A (109 c.p.s.) to e (163 c.p.s.), while for women the range is an octave higher, or from 218 c.p.s. to 326 c.p.s. Public speakers and properly trained actors use a much wider range.[2] For example, the speech delivered by Prime Minister Churchill in Washington, May 19, 1943, moves for the most part between 115 c.p.s. (B♭) and 230 c.p.s. (b♭).

1.10   The Pharynx

Above the larynx, with its vocal bands, a more or less tube-shaped channel leads upward to the mouth and above this to the posterior openings into the nasal cavities. Disturbances in the breath stream will be carried through these channels as the breath flows out or communicated to the air which is in them. Down to the level of the tips of the arytenoids these channels are also parts of the digestive tube called the pharynx. One may, therefore, speak of them as pharyngeal cavities and divide the region into the laryngeal pharynx, from the cricoid cartilage to the hyoid bone, about 5 cm., the oral pharynx, from the hyoid bone to the velum, about 4 cm., and the nasal pharynx above the velum, also about 4 cm. in length. The size and the tension of the walls of each of these cavities, and therefore its characteristics as a resonator, are changed by the various movements incident to articulated speech. (Plate 10)

1.11   *The Hyoid Bone*

The hyoid bone, the upper boundary of the laryngeal pharynx, is shaped like a horse-shoe, with the closed arch in front and the open arms behind. It lies more or less parallel to and slightly above the plates of the thyroid cartilage and is attached to this cartilage by ligaments and by a membrane called the hyothyroid membrane. The hyoid bone is suspended by ligaments which come down from the styloid processes of the temporal bones. The hyoid is sometimes called the lingual bone, since it is the point of origin of some of the important muscles of the tongue.

In addition to and exterior to these tongue muscles, a number of muscles from above and from below are attached to the hyoid bone. (Plate 11) From above, these muscles (the digastricus, stylohyoid, mylohyoid, and genio-hyoid) can draw the hyoid bone—and with it the larynx—upward and forward or back, as occasion demands. The muscles from below (the sterno-hyoid, omohyoid, and thyrohyoid, with the help of the sternothyroid) can draw the larynx and the hyoid bone—and with the latter, the base of the tongue—downward and, if desired, backward. All of these muscles are involved in any vigorous lowering of the jaw.

These structures, the hyoid bone and the larynx, may be drawn back toward the vertebrae by two large bands of muscles known, respectively, as the inferior constrictor and the middle constrictor of the pharynx. The whole elaborate arrangement serves primarily the biological function of deglutition. The actions of these muscles become important for phonetics when they change the size of the pharyngeal cavities and the texture of the walls. (Plate 12)

The larynx itself may in speech be drawn forward as much as five or six millimeters from the position of rest and it may be elevated or lowered over a range of almost two centimeters in the production of various speech sounds. Since the length of the oral pharynx is about four centimeters, such movements of the larynx are of considerable relative magnitude.

1.12   *The Laryngeal Pharynx*

The lowest section of the pharynx, the laryngeal portion, is bounded behind by the wall of the vertebral column. In front its boundary is the epi-glottis, with those membranes which join this to the sides of the pharynx

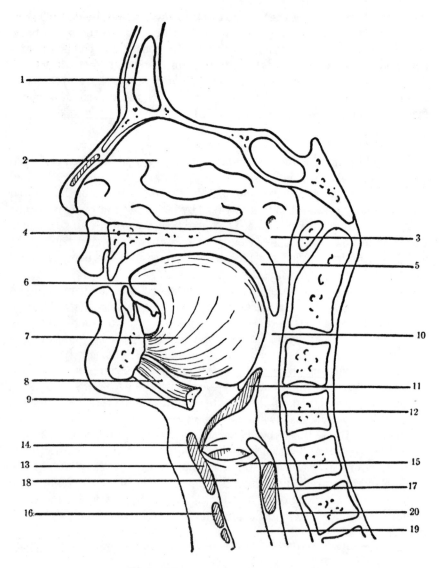

Plate 10. PHARYNGEAL CAVITIES

1—Frontal sinus. 2—Nasal cavity. 3—Nasal pharynx. 4—Hard palate. 5—Soft palate.
6—Tongue. 7—Genioglossus muscle. 8—Geniohyoid muscle. 9—Hyoid bone. 10—Oral
pharynx. 11—Epiglottis. 12—Laryngeal pharynx. 13—Thyroid cartilage. 14—Ventricular fold. 15—Vocal fold. 16—Cricoid cartilage (in front). 17—Cricoid cartilage
(behind). 18—Larynx cavity. 19—Trachea. 20—Oesophagus.

and to the base of the tongue. Vertically the laryngeal pharynx extends
from the cricoid cartilage to the hyoid bone.

By virtue of the membranous attachment of the epiglottis to the root, or
base, of the tongue, the front wall of the laryngeal pharynx is subject to

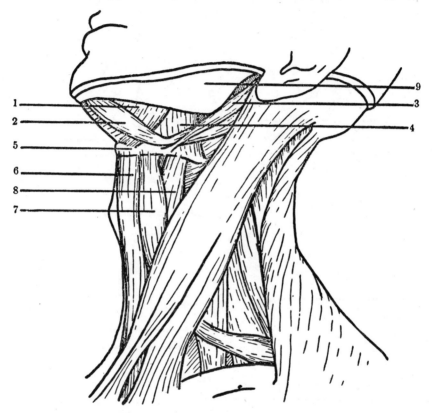

Plate 11. MUSCLES OF THE NECK

1—Mylohyoid muscle. 2—Digastricus. 3—Stylohyoid muscle. 4—Hyoglossus muscle.
5—Hyoid bone. 6—Sternohyoid muscle. 7—Omohyoid muscle. 8—Thyrohyoid muscle.
9—Mandible.

considerable movement incident to changes in the position of the tongue.
The lower end of the epiglottis is hinged to the thyroid cartilage at its forward angle just above the vocal bands. At this point, therefore, the diameter
of the laryngeal pharynx is essentially constant. The tip of the epiglottis,
however, may be pushed back by the tongue till the diameter of the pharynx
at that point is reduced to a mere 5 or 6 mm., as in the articulation of the

vowel of *far*. Or it may be pulled forward inside the curve of the hyoid bone until the diameter of the pharynx here is about as great as that at the lower end, say 20 to 24 mm., as in the vowel of *fate*. The capacity of the laryngeal pharynx, therefore, may vary from that of a cylinder 5 cm. high and 2.5 cm. in diameter, approximately, to something like half of this volume.

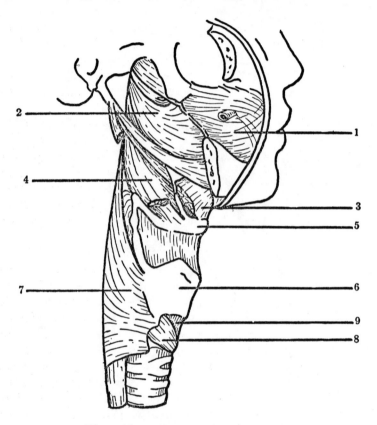

Plate 12. MUSCLES OF THE PHARYNX

1—Buccinator. 2—Superior constrictor of the pharynx. 3—Hyoglossus muscle. 4—Middle constrictor of the pharynx. 5—Hyoid bone. 6—Thyroid cartilage. 7—Inferior constrictor of the pharynx. 8—Cricothyroid muscle. 9—Cricothyroid ligament.

1.13 *The Oral Pharynx*

The oral pharynx, from the hyoid bone to the velum, about 4 cm., differs from the laryngeal pharynx in that it can be opened in front into the mouth, or oral cavity. Its front wall is the base of the tongue and its diameter from front to back may change very considerably from one sound to another as different speech sounds are produced. Its total capacity when shaped for the articulation of the vowel of *eat* is something like four and a half times as great as its capacity when shaped for the articulation of the vowel of *ought*.

1.14   *The Nasal Pharynx*

The nasal pharynx extends upward above the velum, or soft palate. This is the membranous portion of the roof of the mouth. It can be flattened somewhat by the contraction of a pair of small muscles, the tensores veli palatini, or it can be lifted and drawn back by another pair, the levatores veli palatini. It is drawn downward by two pairs of muscles, the pharyngo-palatine and the glossopalatine muscles.

The nasal pharynx is always open into the nasal cavities through the posterior nares (see Section 1.15), but it may be completely shut off from the oral pharynx by the elevation of the back of the velum. When raised and retracted, the back edge of the velum makes a tight closure against the rear wall of the pharynx. Here, under the mucous covering of this wall, the upper constrictor of the pharynx, when contracted, produces a swelling, called the cushion of Passavant, against which the edge of the velum is tightly drawn.

In normal breathing, with the mouth closed, the breath flows in and out through the nose, the nasal pharynx, the oral pharynx, the laryngeal pharynx, and the trachea. In the production of speech sounds, the nasal pharynx may be shut off from the oral pharynx, as just described, or it may be open for the passage of the vibrating breath stream. There appear to be three different ways in which the nasal pharynx participates in the articulation of speech sounds. The nasal pharynx may be the sole exit for the breath stream, as in the consonants [m] or [n]. It may be open but not essentially involved in the production of the speech sounds, as is the case when the velum hangs down inertly. Or the nasal pharynx may be involved with the oral cavity in the production of nasality, or nasal twang, as in the nasalized vowels of French. The volume of the nasal pharynx increases somewhat as the velum is more vigorously drawn down.

1.15   *The Nasal Cavities*

At the top of the nasal pharynx there are two openings, oval in shape and some 2.5 cm. by 1.25 cm. in area, one on either side of a vertical septum or partition. These openings are the posterior nares, and they connect the nasal pharynx with the nasal cavities. Each nasal cavity is more or less divided into channels by the protrusion into it from the sides and toward the median septum of three curved or turbinate bones called conchae, which are covered with a relatively thick coating of the mucous membrane.

The several channels are, however, interconnected vertically along the middle septum. The end organs of smell are located in the membranous covering of the superior turbinate bone—highest of the three conchae—and in its immediate neighborhood; this zone is therefore called the olfactory region. The rest of the nasal fossa, or cavity is then called the respiratory region of the nose. No part of the nasal cavity is subject to muscular movement, but the mucous covering of its walls is capable of very great expansion by the inflow of blood, so that it may swell up sufficiently to diminish very notably the size of the passageway for air through the nose.

1.16   *The Nasal Sinuses*

In the immediate neighborhood of the nasal cavities there are on either side four accessory cavities or groups of cavities: the frontal, the sphenoidal, and the maxillary sinuses, and the ethmoidal air cells. The frontal sinuses are cavities in the frontal bone near the medial line and under the arch of the eyebrows (the superciliary arch). The openings from the nasal cavities into these sinuses are through ducts of relatively minute diameter. The sinuses themselves vary considerably in size, but usually have a capacity of some 8 to 10 cc. The ethmoidal air cells are numerous small cavities in the bone between the nasal cavity and the orbit of the eye. They are arranged in three groups, each of which has a connection by means of a small duct with the nasal cavity. The sphenoidal sinuses lie within the body of the sphenoid bone, which is situated at the base of the skull, directly underneath and inward from the cheekbone. These are generally somewhat smaller than the frontal sinuses. They too are connected with the nasal cavities by ducts. The maxillary sinuses, which are cavities in the bodies of the maxillae, are the largest of the nasal sinuses. They are connected with the nasal cavities by one and sometimes by two very small openings into the lower part of the nasal fossae. Their capacity varies greatly in different individuals, but they may be said to average something like 15 cc. Because of the minuteness of their openings all of these cavities are probably unimportant as resonators in the production of speech sounds although they may have some effect upon general voice quality.

1.17   *The Isthmus Faucium*

The opening from the oral pharynx into the mouth over the arch of the back of the tongue is called the isthmus faucium. It is bounded above by the velum, below by the dorsum of the tongue, and laterally by the glosso-palatine arch, or anterior pillars of the fauces (see Section 1.18). This arch is formed by the bodies of the paired glosso-palatine muscles, which arise in the central line of the velum and run downward and backward into the sides of the tongue. (Plate 13)

Behind this arch is another, which forms the edges of the opening from the oral pharynx and which consists of the pharyngopalatine muscles under the mucous covering of the velum and pharynx wall. These muscles arise in the velum, behind the uvula, and run downward and backward inside the walls of the pharynx, where they join with the fibers of the stylopharyngeus muscles and thence are connected ultimately with the posterior border of the thyroid cartilage. Between these posterior pillars of the fauces and the glossopalatine arch in front of them lie the palatine tonsils.

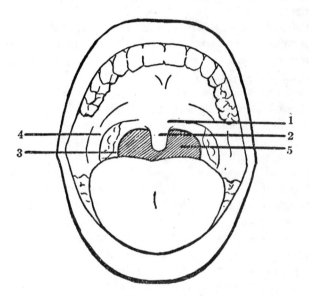

Plate 13. MOUTH CAVITY

1—Velum. 2—Uvula. 3—Pharyngopalatine arch. 4—Glossopalatine arch. 5—Isthmus faucium.

Biologically, the function of these two arches is to assist in the propulsion of a bolus of food from the mouth into the pharynx, and to aid in keeping it from reentering the mouth. In speech, the contraction of these arches reduces the area of the opening from the pharynx into the mouth, and by the same movement gives form to the front wall of the nasal pharynx. The contraction of the pillars of the fauces is a feature of the production of nasal vowels. However, a generally accepted genetic explanation of true nasality, or nasal twang, is not yet available. In any event it is evident that the mere passage of all or of part of the breath stream through the nasal cavities does not of necessity produce what we call nasality.

1.18 *The Tongue*

The tongue, when at rest, occupies the floor of the mouth. Its base forms the anterior wall of the oral pharynx. The upper surface, which lies below the velum and the palate, is called the dorsum; while the thinner and narrower extremity, which is directed toward the inner surfaces of the upper front teeth, is called the apex or the blade. The entire dorsum, the apex, the margins, and the front part of the under surface of the tongue are free of attachments to other organs.

The body of the tongue is a complex structure, with muscles on either side of a median fibrous septum. Spread thinly over the dorsum of the tongue, directly under the mucous membrane, is a layer of longitudinal and oblique muscular fibers, which when contracted tend to pull the tip of the tongue up and back and also to curl the margins upward. These fibers make up the superior lingualis muscle. On the under side of the tongue two thin, compact bands of muscle fibers extend from the root to the apex of the tongue, one on either side of the median septum. When contracted, this pair of muscles, the inferior lingualis muscles, tend to draw the tip of the tongue down and to make the dorsum of the tongue convex from back to front. Interlaced with the fibers of the genioglossus muscle are many transverse fibers inside the tongue, which run from the median septum to the margins and sides of the tongue. These transverse fibers, when contracted, tend to constrict the dorsum of the tongue, making it narrower, and by compensation, somewhat longer. In front, at the apex, another group of muscle fibers extends from the upper to the inferior surface of the tongue. These vertical fibers, when contracted, tend to flatten and to broaden the apex of the tongue.

The body of the tongue is moved by a number of extrinsic muscles. (Plate 14) The genioglossus muscle starts from the middle of the inside surface of the chin and spreads out vertically like a fan, so that its fibers are inserted in the under surface of the tongue all the way from the posterior boundary of the apex to the root. Indeed, some of the lowest fibers of the genioglossus are attached even to the hyoid bone. Directly below the genioglossus on each side is the geniohyoid muscle, a narrow band of fibers extending from the chin to the body of the hyoid bone in front. These muscles, when contracted, tend to draw the tongue and the hyoid bone forward toward the chin. For the most part, also, the pull of the genioglossus on the tongue is downward. From each side of the body of the hyoid bone and from each horn of that bone the broad, thin hyoglossus muscle rises almost vertically, to be inserted into the side of the tongue. When contracted, this pair of muscles tends to bring the back of the tongue closer to the hyoid bone, wherever that may be at the moment. From the styloid process of the temporal bone, on either side of the skull, a band of muscle fibers descends and divides into two groups at the side of the tongue. One group of fibers runs forward along the margin of the tongue and blends with the inferior lingualis muscle. The other group of fibers joins with those of the hyo-

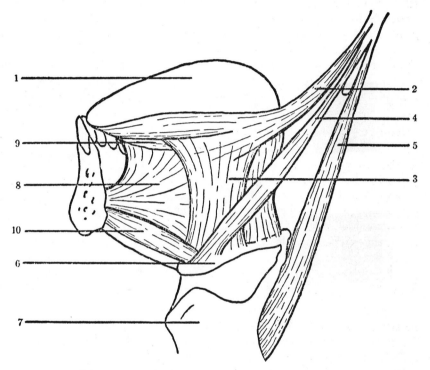

Pla e 14. EXTRINSIC MUSCLES OF THE TONGUE

1—Dorsum of the tongue. 2—Styloglossus muscle. 3—Hyoglossus muscle. 4—Stylohyoid muscle. 5—Stylothyroid muscle. 6—Hyoid bone. 7—Thyroid cartilage. 8—Genioglossus muscle. 9—Inferior longitudinal muscle. 10—Geniohyoid muscle.

glossus, behind. The contraction of the styloglossus muscles thus tends to draw the dorsum and the body of the tongue upward and back. To bring the larynx and the hyoid bone along with the tongue in this retraction, the stylothyroid and stylohyoid muscles may cooperate with the styloglossus.

As a consequence of its structure and its muscular attachments the tongue is exceedingly mobile. It may be extended beyond the teeth as much as two inches or retracted behind them as much as an inch and a quarter. It can be raised, as a whole or in different parts of its length, toward the upper teeth, the palate, or the velum. The tip of the tongue can be run backward along the palate, from the front teeth to the velum or even into the isthmus faucium. There are considerable individual differences in the freedom of movement in this respect. The upper surface of the tongue can be made convex or concave from front to back, or it may be made generally convex with a minor concavity somewhere along its dorsum, as in some of the "L" sounds. From side to side the surface of the tongue also may be either flat, convex, or concave, with a deep or a shallow ditch along the line of the median septum.

The tongue is often spoken of as the organ of speech and the very words "linguistic" and "language" attest the importance which has been attached to its speech functions. Biologically, however, the tongue is the chief organ of the sense of taste and a very important aid to the processes of mastication and deglutition.

1.19   *The Mouth*

The mouth is the cavity bounded in front by the lips, on the sides by the inner walls of the cheeks, and in the rear by the isthmus faucium. The floor of the mouth is continuous with the cheeks, embracing the framework of the mandible or lower jaw. It is largely occupied by the tongue. The roof of the mouth includes the maxillae, with the upper teeth, the hard palate, and the velum.

1.20   *The Mandible*

The mandible, or lower jaw, is the only movable bone of the face. It can be lowered so that the distance between lower and upper incisors becomes something like an inch and a half. It can be swung somewhat from side to side, the maximum movement to either side being about seven-eighths of an inch. It can be protruded slightly, say three-eighths of an inch.

The shape of the mandible is roughly that of a horseshoe with the extremities turned up. These extremities, the rami mandibulae, are thick and heavy. They are articulated with the base of the cranium. The horizontal, anterior arch of the mandible contains the lower teeth. (Plate 15)

The weight of the jaw is sufficient to lower it when the opposing muscles are relaxed. Hence, when we are adequately dumbfounded our mouths fall open. The downward movement of the jaw can be assisted by the contraction of a number of muscles connecting it with the hyoid bone, provided the latter is not allowed to rise. The digastric muscles, from the chin to the side of the hyoid, the mylohyoid muscles, which are broad sheets of fibers from the sides of the mandible to the body of the hyoid bone, and the geniohyoids from chin to hyoid, when contracted, tend to bring the jaw nearer to the hyoid bone. If at the same time the latter is pulled upon by the sterno-hyoid and omohyoid muscles, the jaw will be drawn down vigorously. Whether or not the whole head comes with it depends in part upon the action of the muscles which close the jaws.

The mandible is raised chiefly by a very strong and broad muscle on either side, which descends from the cheek bone to the body of the jaw. This is the masseter muscle. The temporal muscles, which pull on the forward prong or lever of the rami mandibulae, also assist in closing the jaws. The retraction of the mandible is mainly accomplished by the temporal

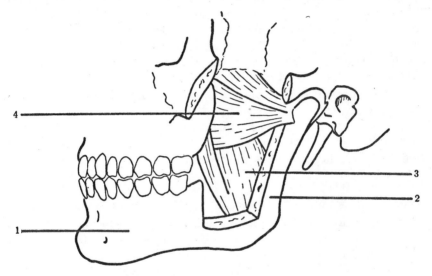

Plate 15. MANDIBLE

1—Mandible. 2—Ramus of the mandible (a part cut away). 3—Internal pterygoid muscle. 4—External pterygoid muscle.

muscles. The protrusion of the jaws is the result of the pull of the internal and external pterygoid muscles. These muscles, when contracted on one side and relaxed on the other, cause the sideward movement of the jaw.

1.201   *Movements of the Jaw*

The protrusion of the jaw is of little importance in English speech, although some speakers pronounce [z] or [s] with the lower jaw thrust forward a little. Sideward movements of the jaw are not infrequently observed in individual speakers, either as a mannerism, or as a means of compensating for malformations of the jaw arches or teeth.

The lowering of the mandible changes the angle which this makes with the maxillae. There has been much debate among phoneticians as to the importance of this jaw-angle (Kieferwinkel) for the formation of the several speech sounds, notably the vowels. There is no doubt that our lower teeth are normally much farther from our upper teeth when we pronounce the vowel of *law* than they are when we pronounce the vowel of *lee*, and there is no doubt that we can pronounce both vowels acceptably with the lower teeth completely in contact with the upper, or even with the jaw-angle as great for *lee* as for *law*. One must not conclude from these facts that the position of the jaw "makes no difference," until one proves that no compensatory changes in other movements are required when the normal jaw position is replaced by an abnormal one. One of the basic facts revealed by the genetic observation of speech sounds is that the same auditory impression can frequently be produced by two or more radically different sets of speech movements. It is better to describe what normally occurs when a given speech sound is pronounced than to attempt to determine what is essential and what is nonessential on the basis of incomplete and uncontrolled "experiments" involving undescribed compensatory adjustments. Satisfactory experimental answers to the questions raised by these and similar observations have not yet been given.

1.21   *The Teeth*

In the upper and in the lower jaw we have normally a symmetrical arrangement of four different kinds of teeth. Beginning in front, we observe, above and below, and on each side of the median division (1a) one central incisor, a broad, flat, and sharp-edged tooth, (1b) one lateral incisor, much like the central incisor, but not so broad, (2) one canine, a more sharply pointed and longer tooth, (3) two premolars, or bicuspids, which are broader teeth with more of a flat upper surface on which there are two peaks, (4) three molars, which are large flat-topped teeth with four peaks each. A complete set, therefore, comprises thirty-two teeth.

The lower central and lateral incisors normally slide in behind the upper incisors when the jaws are closed; and the bicuspids and molars bite with the forward cusps of the lower teeth fitting into the depressions of the corresponding upper teeth. Occasionally one meets the reversed arrangement and, with a slightly protruded jaw, the upper incisors close inside the lower. Frequently the position of the tongue in contact with the roof of the mouth is easiest defined in terms of the teeth adjacent to the point touched. The teeth form a part of the boundary of the mouth cavity and help to give this a firm and definite outline. The front teeth also permit the formation of a small vestibule between their outer surfaces and the inside of the lips, when these are protruded. This vestibule is characteristic of a number of speech sounds.

1.22   *The Roof of the Mouth*

The topography of the roof of the mouth is important because many speech sounds are best described in terms thereof. The inner surfaces of the upper incisors form what is called the dental region. Above this lies the narrow area of the gums, the gingival region. Above this is a ridge corresponding to the insertions of the teeth into the maxillae, the alveolar ridge or region. Beyond the alveolar ridge the roof of the mouth is formed by the hard palate, which is a more or less acutely arched vault of bone plates belonging to the maxillae and to the palatine bones of the skull. It is covered with a complex membranous structure, protected by mucous membrane and having peculiar corrugations in its anterior arched surface. There are very considerable individual differences in the height and breadth of the vault of the hard palate. Continuous with the hard palate and behind it is the soft palate, or velum. This is a movable fold hung from the back edges of the hard palate and terminating in the posterior pillars of the fauces or the pharyngopalatine arch. The velum is essentially an incomplete septum between the mouth and the oral pharynx.

The hard palate may be called the palatal region and the soft palate the velar region, although one may profitably distinguish between a prepalatal and a mediopalatal region. The latter term is slightly illogical, since it describes the back half, more or less, of the hard palate and this area is medial only with respect to the combined hard and soft palates. A more logical but less widely used terminology would distinguish, from front to back, the prepalatal, postpalatal, prevelar, and postvelar regions.

Just behind the anterior palatine arch (the palatoglossal arch), and in the central line, a small, slender, cone-shaped appendage dangles from the velum. This is the uvula. It contains a small muscle, the azygos uvulae, which manifests its presence by causing the uvula to curl up slightly as can be seen if one stares at it intently in a mirror. Normally, the uvula hangs inert and biologically useless. Phonetically it has achieved importance because we have discovered how to make trilled sounds with it. Hence we have uvular "R" sounds.

1.23   *The Lips*

A broad, relatively thin sheet of muscle, the buccinator, arises from the outer surfaces of the upper and lower jaws in the region of the molar teeth and extends forward inside the structure of the cheeks. The fibers of this muscle converge toward the angle of the mouth, which may indeed be regarded primarily as a slit in this buccinator muscle. The lips, however, are complex muscular structures composed of fibers from a number of the facial muscles joined together in a band, or girdle, surrounding the opening of the mouth. This band is called the orbicularis oris. When constricted, this girdle tends to purse the lips. In addition to this action the lips are subject to the concerted or variously opposed pulls of at least six bands of facial muscle fibers on either side.

The mentalis muscles run from the mandible, near the center, and take hold of the central portion of the lower lip and the integument of the chin. When contracted, they raise the lower lip; and if the contraction is extreme, they produce a considerable protrusion of the lower lip. The mentalis muscles are the primary movers of the lips in the articulation of the common labial consonants [p], [b], [m]. Their contraction is also associated with the facial expression of doubt or disdain which goes with such interjections as Hm! Pooh! Bah!

Apart from their closure and subsequent opening in the production of sounds such as [p], [b], [m], the lips also contribute to the articulation of other sounds by obstructing in one way or another the free outflow of the breath stream from the mouth. Three types of lip-opening may be distinguished: the lips may be (1) pursed, (2) spread, or (3) neutral. When the lips are pursed, the corners are drawn forward and nearer to each other while the aperture is formed as an irregular circle of the inner edges of the lips. There is usually, but not necessarily, some degree of protrusion involved in the pursing of the lips. When the lips are spread, the corners are drawn back and away from each other, while the aperture is formed as a slit or crack between the flattened bodies of the lips. When the lips are allowed to follow the movement of the mandible with no evident contraction of their musculature, their position is described as neutral. When spread, the lips may be close together, or they may be lifted and lowered respectively so that the teeth are bared and the aperture made wide. In either the spread or the pursed position the area of the aperture between the lips can be varied and controlled with great precision.

1.24 *Controlled or Ballistic Movements*

Muscles contract when end cells of the motor nerves which control them are stimulated: they relax when the stimulation ceases. Most voluntary movements result from the cooperative contraction of opposing muscles. These are called controlled, or tension, movements. Some highly skilled movements, however, seem to result from the reciprocal innervation of antagonistic muscles, in the sense that one set is relaxed in an orderly correlation with the contraction of the other and thus does not oppose the pull of the contracted muscle fibers. Movements caused by the unopposed contraction of a muscle or set of muscles are called ballistic movements. They may result from the maximal stimulation of all the motor units of the muscles contracted. Some of the movements of the muscles used in speech are controlled movements, others are, apparently, ballistic movements. No one can at will cause a given muscle to contract; movements, not muscles, are the units of neuromuscular behavior.

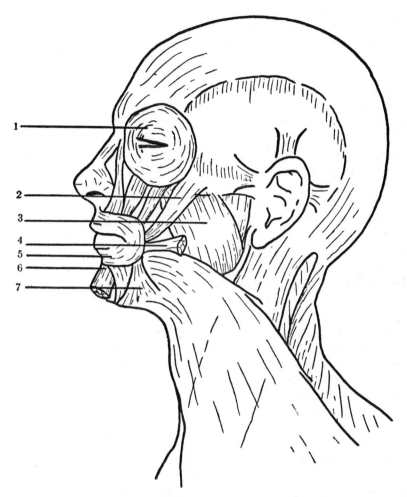

Plate 16. MUSCLES OF THE LIPS AND FACE

1—Orbicularis oculis. 2—Zygomatic muscle. 3—Masseter muscle. 4—Risorius muscle. 5—Orbicularis oris. 6—Mentalis muscle. 7—Triangularis muscle.

1.25   *The Motor Unit*

Every voluntary (striped) muscle is composed of an aggregation of muscle fibers arranged in bundles. Each fiber is a distinct unit, being either cylindrical or prismatic in shape; from nine to forty millimeters long and from one-tenth to one one-hundredth of a millimeter in diameter. The motor nerve which enters a given muscle is a bundle of nerve fibers, each of which is the branch (axon) of a single neuron, or nerve cell. The neuron is the functional unit of the nervous system. There are many millions of them in every human body.

Usually when a nerve enters the muscle sheath its several fibers disperse, each branching profusely, perhaps 150 to 160 times, until as a rule a single nerve branch enters a single muscle fiber. The motor unit for any muscular activity is a single motor neuron with the group of muscle fibers in which its extensions terminate. A statement showing which motor units are activated, where, when, and how many, would give a scientific description of any muscular movement resulting from such activation of these units.

1.26   *All or None*

Each muscle fiber contracts to exert the greatest pull of which it is capable with every nerve impulse which reaches it. The amplitude of the nerve impulse from any one neuron is also approximately constant. Any stimulation, therefore, results in full response, the reaction being in accord with the principle of "all or none." The time consumed by the building up and dying out of the electric potential characteristic of each nerve impulse is approximately 0.0035 seconds, and the nerve remains refractory to a normal stimulus for another 0.003 seconds or so before it will again efficiently transmit a new impulse. The rate of propagation of such an impulse along the nerve fiber is something like 100 meters per second in the best conductors, slower in the less efficient ones. Hence it is possible to feed nerve impulses through these nerve fibers at a very high rate. This rarely occurs in the efferent or motor nerves.

The relaxation of a muscle fiber requires much more time than does the restoration of the nerve fiber to full excitability. When nerve impulses reach a muscle fiber at a rate higher than its period of relaxation, renewed full contraction of the muscle cell is induced. A single nervous impulse results in a twitch of the muscle fiber; repeated nerve impulses, at a rate of from 40 to 50 per second will produce continuous maximal contraction of the fiber, or tetanus. Gradations in the "tone" of the contraction can be secured by sending nerve impulses at rates lower than this maximum, so that the muscle fiber can begin to relax between each two impulses.

However, since each muscle comprises a large number of single muscle fibers, each with its adherence to a particular motor unit, the strength of a muscle's pull may depend also upon variation in the number of motor units called into action by any given central excitation. Both the frequency of the nerve impulses and the number of motor units involved are usually factors in the quantitative description of the neuromuscular conditions cor-

related with the force exerted by the action of any muscle. In the case of
the muscles used in speech, the excitation comes from the central nervous
system and any given speech movement may be thought of as resulting
from the activation of a quantitatively complex spatial and temporal pattern of nerve impulses.

1.27   *The Motor Nerves of Speech*

Anatomically, the distribution of nerves to the muscles which produce
the sounds of speech is very complicated. The diaphragm is controlled by
the phrenic nerve, which is a spinal nerve but which is subject to voluntary
stimulation through a connection with a branch of the vagus, or tenth
cranial nerve. The muscles of the larynx are controlled by various branches
of the vagus nerve also. The muscles of the pharynx, constrictors as well
as the muscles of the fauces, are controlled by the glossopharyngeal, or
ninth cranial nerve. The velum and uvula are controlled, in part at least,
by fibers from the accessory, or eleventh cranial nerve. The muscles of the
tongue are controlled by the various ramifications of the hypoglossus, or
twelfth cranial nerve. The muscles of mastication, which raise the jaw and
move it from side to side, are controlled by branches of the trigeminal, or
fifth cranial nerve. The muscles of the lips are controlled by branches
of the facial, or seventh cranial nerve.

All this is a very meager sketch of a complex situation made doubly
difficult of analysis by the fact that each of these major cranial nerves is
connected with one or more of its neighbors through nuclei, like the nucleus
ambiguus, where branches of the glossopharyngeal, vagus, and accessory
nerves commingle; or in plexi, like the pharyngeal plexus, where two
branches of the vagus communicate with the glossopharyngeal nerve. It is
still impossible technically to follow out all of the connections of any one
single neuron. An attempt, therefore, to account for the complex muscular
behavior observed in speech on the basis of the number and distribution
of the nervous impulses which cause it is comparable with an effort to
account for the behavior of a chemical reaction on the basis of the number
and distributions of the protons, neutrons, and electrons involved. Perhaps
some day the necessary equations may be written, although many thou-
sands of nerve cells, each with a peculiar set of interconnections, appear to
be involved in the simple utterance of the syllable "Pshaw!"

CHAPTER III

THE PHYSICS OF SPEECH SOUNDS

2.01 *Sound Waves*[1]

When movements of the lips, of the tongue, and most importantly, of
the breath stream occur in speech, they create displacements of the air
which surrounds the speaker. These displacements result in alternate condensations and rarefactions of the air around their source, and the disturbances are propagated through the air very much as the displacement of
water caused by dropping a stone into a quiet pool is propagated outward
from its source until the energy communicated to the medium by the disturbing movement is exhausted. What travels is the disturbance, not the
particles of the medium, be it air or water. Such traveling disturbances may
be sound waves, that is, they may be audible. The actual movement of the
air particles back and forth about their centers of equilibrium may be very
minute, and still be audible if it is frequent enough. At a rate of approximately 2,000 per second, movements of as little as 10^{-8} cm. are quite
audible. In ordinary speech, the air molecules probably do not move much
more than 10^{-3} cm., or 0.01 mm.[2]

All wave motion depends upon the resiliency or elasticity of the medium
through which the wave travels. Sound waves are physical movements of
matter, usually of air molecules: they cannot exist in a vacuum. Air, like
water, can be compressed, but it cannot be twisted. Hence sound waves in
air, or in water, are longitudinal not transverse waves. The disturbance is
movement back and forth in the same line as that in which the wave is
propagated. A homely illustration of the longitudinal wave is the propagation of the bump from a switching engine down a long line of freight cars,
none of which moves appreciably from its original position. Still more con-
vincing as a demonstration of the propagation of energy is the return of
this bump from the free end of the train to the engine when the train remains standing still.

2.02 *Vibrations*

One can learn a great deal about the nature of vibrations from a few
simple experiments. Drop a book flat upon a table. The air is driven out
from the space between the falling book and the table, and as contact is
made, the last "layer" of air is expelled with some violence. As this air
moves away it is compressed by the pressure of its molecules upon those
nearest the disturbance and these in turn are compressed by being thus

pressed upon. The molecules of the book and of the table are likewise compressed somewhat by the impact. Then the elasticity of the air (a gas), and of the table, asserts itself; the compressed air expands back into the region of rarefaction from which it was driven, and the table expands as well. But this expansion carries the molecules of the air and of the table past their state of equilibrium so that a second compression in the other direction is achieved, leaving behind it again an area of rarefaction. Thereupon the expansion and compression are repeated in a vibratory movement which, in the case of the dropped book, will quickly subside into equilibrium because the vibrations receive no new energy from the source. The dropped book produces a sound when it strikes the table because the disturbance causes the air molecules to vibrate in this fashion and because these vibrations set up successive waves of energy in the surrounding air. The initial wave sent out is very much stronger than the one which follows it, and this in turn is stronger than its successor. Such a wave train is said to have a sharp decrement or to be strongly damped. (Plate 17, Fig. 1)

Take a toy whistle with rubber balloon attached. Inflate the balloon and allow the whistle to squawk. The air within the balloon is under the pressure of its own elasticity and that of the contractile forces of the elastic walls which contain it. It therefore exerts pressure upon the rubber membrane which partly blocks its outward flow. It pushes this membrane aside momentarily, and air escapes. This, however, so far reduces the pressure below the membrane that the elastic pull thereof momentarily exceeds the push of the confined air and the flow is stopped. But the contraction of the rubber balloon quickly restores the air pressure and the membrane is again momentarily pushed aside. This cycle of events is repeated as long as the quantity of air in the bag is sufficient to permit the compression required to displace the membrane. The rate at which these cycles of alternate release and confinement of the air take place depends upon the pressure in the balloon and the elasticity of the confining membrane.

Each time the band is displaced the air molecules above it are compressed by this movement, and as the membrane falls back, it leaves behind it an area of rarefaction. The air compressed by the outward push of the membrane now falls back into the area from which it was driven, and there it collides with the membrane. This alternate compression and rarefaction is repeated in more or less regular cycles for a time. Also each time the membrane is displaced, a puff of the confined air is emitted and this moving air also compresses that outside into which it is propelled so that another cycle of compression and rarefaction ensues. The two cycles occur at the same rate but not quite in the same phase. That is, the maximum compression caused by the moving membrane occurs slightly before the maximum compression caused by the emitted puff of air. We probably "hear" both

Plate 17. VIBRATIONS

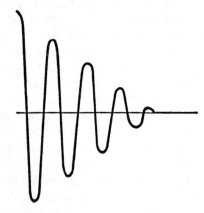

Fig. 1. Wave train with sharp decrement.

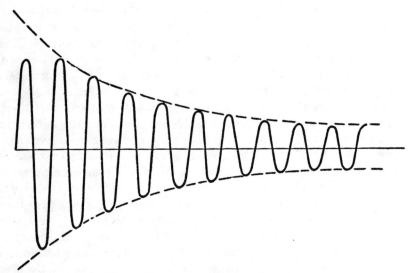

Fig. 2. Wave train with slow decrement.

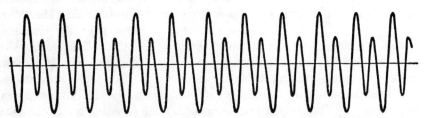

Fig. 3. Continuous wave.

disturbances, but that which arises from the puffs of air is likely to be the more vigorous. During the early moments of its operation such a whistle gives off a sustained sound of determinable pitch and hideous quality. The vibratory motions of the air particles around the balloon whistle's outlet are constantly and more or less regularly reinforced by new impulses from the moving rubber membrane and the emerging puffs of air. The waves of disturbances flowing from this kind of source will show considerable regularity of form as well as of frequency. The decrement of such a wave train is slow, and the waves may be for a time approximately continuous, though minute examination shows no two of them to be exactly identical in form and each exhibits a very complex pattern of energy. (Plate 17, Fig. 2)

Take an empty pint bottle with a small-sized neck and blow gently across its opening. With a little practice one can make such a bottle give off a more or less pleasing tone of definite pitch. The air within the bottle has been caused to vibrate by being compressed when blown upon and then rarefied when the elasticity of the compressed air carries its expansion beyond the point of equilibrium, despite the gentle pressure of the stream of air across the opening of the bottle. The pitch of the tone emitted is directly proportional to the area of the opening and inversely proportional to the square root of the volume of the container. The larger the area of the opening, the higher the pitch will be; the smaller the volume of the container, the higher the pitch will be. The vibratory movement of the air in the bottle is communicated to the air outside it through the walls of the bottle and by direct contact at the opening. The expanding air within the bottle produces compression of the air around the bottle, and the compression of the air within the bottle permits the outer air to expand in response to such compression and thus be set into vibratory movement. Vibrations of this kind cease when the driving force of the air stream across the opening of the bottle is removed; they are sustained while this force is maintained, and the sound waves which result will have a comparatively simple and regular form. (Plate 17, Fig. 3)

If you can find a tuning fork which gives the same tone as the bottle, or if, by pouring the right quantity of water into it, you can tune the bottle to the fork you have, you can make one more pertinent observation. When a vibrating tuning fork is held over the mouth of a bottle the natural tone of which is identical with that of the fork, the sound heard will be notably louder than that of the fork alone. The air in the bottle has been caused to vibrate at the same frequency as that of the fork, and we say that the cavity is resonant to the frequency of the fork. A tuning fork of different pitch will not cause this bottle to give off a tone unless indeed the pitch of this new fork is such that the frequency of one fork is a multiple or submultiple of the other.

There are two ways, then, to make the air in the bottle vibrate audibly. One is to excite it with a nonperiodic stream of air across its opening; the other is to impress upon the air in the bottle the vibrations of some other object (the tuning fork or the air around it), which are of the precise frequency to which the cavity is resonant, or are of a frequency which is a multiple or submultiple of that frequency.

2.03 Pitch

The pitch of a sound depends upon the frequency of the waves which produce it. Each wave of compression and rarefaction moves through calm air of moderate temperature, say 7° centigrade, with a speed of about 1,100 feet per second. If successive waves of compression and rarefaction follow each other at a rate of 110 per second, these succeeding disturbances of the air will be some $(1,100 \div 110)$ ten feet apart, and will activate the tympanum of a listening ear at a frequency of 110 impulses per second. The ear requires only three or four such successive impulses as an adequate stimulus for the perception of pitch.

When we distinguish broadly between high, low, and medium pitch, we are describing sounds due respectively to rapid, slow, or moderately frequent periodic disturbances. The lowest tone audible to the normal human ear is probably that due to vibrations at the rate of 16 cycles per second. Large organs sometimes have pipes that emit this tone. The highest tone audible to the average human ear is one due to vibrations in the neighborhood of 16,000 cycles per second although some ears perceive tones as high as 25,000 cycles per second. "Sound waves" of much higher frequencies are sometimes usefully produced; in the case of supersonic submarine signalling, the frequencies sometimes go as high as 50,000 cycles per second; for testing materials, as high as 2,400 kilocycles per second. Disturbances at frequencies below 16 c.p.s. are likely to be heard as recurrent noises rather than as a single tone. Indeed, it is probable that the pitch heard by many ears when activated by vibrations at 16 cycles per second is rather the pitch of 32 cycles per second associated with these vibrations. The lowest note of the normal pianoforte, when tuned to "international" pitch (a^1 = 435) is 27 c.p.s., and the highest note of that piano is c^5 = 4138 c.p.s. The lowest tone known to have been sung by the human voice is that of F_1 = 42 c.p.s. Most bass singers have difficulty with the proper intonation of "low D" = 73 c.p.s. The upper limit of the human voice is in the neighborhood of c^4 = 2,069. Lucrezia Agujari ("La Bastardella") is recorded by Mozart to have sung in his presence "C in altissimo," which is c^4, and the Associated Press on December 21, 1939, reported Susanne Foster, of Minneapolis, to have vocalized to d^4 = 2323 c.p.s. Nellie Melba's singing range was from 230 to 1,381 c.p.s. or from b^1 flat to f^3.

2.04 *Consonance and Dissonance*

When two tones of different pitches are sounded simultaneously, the air particles around the source of each are made to vibrate. Very quickly the two propagated waves commingle and the movement of any single air molecule becomes the resultant of the two forces operating upon it. The pattern of compression and expansion may then become quite complicated dynamically as the instantaneous energy from one wave is added to or subtracted from that of the other. The movements of the tympanum of the ear therefore are not the simple harmonic vibration caused by a single pure tone but represent a complex pattern of energy distribution in time. Sometimes the resulting sensation of sound is pleasant and we say that the two component sounds are consonant with one another. Sometimes the effect is unpleasant and we say that the two sounds are dissonant. Experiment has proved that these effects—pleasant or unpleasant—are correlated with the relationships between the frequencies of the component waves; in the sense that, when the ratio between the frequencies can be expressed by a small number, let us say, 4:5, the effect is pleasant consonance; whereas, when the relationship is one only expressed by larger numbers, say 16 : 15, which represents a semitone, the effect is one of dissonance. The initial chord from which the barber-shop quartet begins its labors is intended to be consonant, say 4:5:6 = do:mi:sol.

2.05 *Harmonics, Overtones, Partials*

The barber-shop quartet endeavors to produce harmony, i.e., to produce tones which are in harmonious relationship with one another. When they sing do : mi : sol, those tones are part of a harmonic series which can be described as the relationships of 1:2:3:4:5:6:7:8 and so on. If their *do* is "middle C" (= c^1 = 256), the frequencies of that harmonic series will be 64:128:192:256:320:384:448:512, or the musical tones known as C, c, g, c^1, e^1, g^1, b^1-flat, c^2. The lowest note of such a series is called the fundamental, the next highest is the first harmonic (128), the next is the second harmonic (192), and so on, of that fundamental. The tempered scale of the piano is slightly out of tune throughout, in order that equal intervals may be played in any key, or from any fundamental. Hence on that tempered scale the harmonics will be 65:129:194:258:326:388:461:517.

Simultaneous tones of various frequencies are produced not only by several vibrating bodies, but as a rule also by any single vibrating body. A strictly pure tone, i.e., a sound wave of a single frequency and simple harmonic motion, is very difficult to produce. The great organ pipe required to produce a tone at 16 c.p.s. will be somewhat more than 32 feet long if it is an open pipe; and when this pipe is being sounded, there will be in it not only the vibratory motion of the air particles at the fundamental frequency of 16 c.p.s., but also movements of the air particles at frequencies of 32 and 48, and perhaps 64 cycles per second. If the pipe is blown still harder, other frequencies may appear. The fundamental of such a pipe is C_2 (16 c.p.s.) the first harmonic is the octave C_1 (32), the second harmonic is G_1 (48), the third C (64), the fourth E (80), the fifth G (96), the sixth B-flat (112) and the seventh c (128). On the tempered scale, with $a^1 = 435$, the equivalent values would be 16, 32, 48, 65, 81, 97, 115, 129. Since these tones emerge from the same pipe, they are not only harmonics but also overtones of the fundamental note, and in this case the overtones are harmonic overtones as well. The difference between the sound of a^1 on the oboe and a^1 on the violin is not a difference of the fundamental pitch, of course, but a difference in the number of harmonic overtones sounded by each instrument and, notably, a difference in the relative energy of the several overtones. The violin a^1 combines with about equal energy the fundamental and the first and fourth harmonics; the oboe sounds predominantly the third and fourth harmonics, though its tone comprises as many as eleven harmonics in all.[3]

Many complex sound waves are found by harmonic analysis to have no power component at the frequency of the fundamental. The sound produced by these waves when heard has the pitch of the fundamental, but the energy of this component has been absorbed in the production of the other components and hence the fundamental frequency is not discernible as a power component in the analysis of the wave form.

Often the component frequencies of a given complex tone are not all in harmonic relationship with one another. In such cases they are commonly referred to as partials or partial tones. The lowest component is then called the first partial and the rest in order of their frequencies are called the second, third, fourth partial, and so on. This terminology is applied by many writers to harmonic series as well as to nonharmonic complexes. Hence the terms fundamental and first partial are synonymous. The second partial of a harmonic series is the same thing as the first harmonic of the fundamental of that series. The term overtone for upper partials should be used only of partials produced by a single vibrating body or instrument.

It is probable that more sound waves have been subjected to harmonic analysis in the past five years than in the whole century which went before. New techniques have greatly facilitated work with these problems. One change in terminology seems to be in a fair way to become established. Present-day acoustics students no longer speak of the first harmonic but say instead, the second harmonic. That is, harmonics are now named as multiples of the fundamental frequency: the second multiple is the second harmonic, the fourth multiple the fourth harmonic. What many books five or six years ago called the first harmonic or the second partial is now pretty generally called the second harmonic.

2.06   *Free Vibrations, Forced Vibrations, Resonance*

When a pendulum is displaced, it will, if left to itself, oscillate about its point of equilibrium for quite a while. The extent of its swings will gradually diminish as the energy communicated to it by the displacement is gradually used up in overcoming frictional resistances to its movement. Much the same thing happens to a guitar string when it is plucked. When we blow gently across the neck of a bottle and thus make it "sing," the air in it oscillates at the period natural to it by virtue of its volume and the area of its opening.[4] Each of these cases is a case of free vibrations. An initial displacement sets up a periodic motion, which ceases only when the energy of this displacement has been consumed. In the case of the pendulum and that of the guitar string, this takes some little time, and we say that the movement is only slightly damped. In the case of the bottle, the free vibrations cease when the exciting puffs of air are stopped. This vibrating system is highly damped.

Instead of blowing across the mouth of the bottle to excite the free vibration of the air in it we may hold a vibrating tuning fork over the mouth of the bottle. The energy of the fork's vibrations works directly upon the latent air in the bottle and forces this air to vibrate in tune with the vibrations of the fork. If the natural free period of the air in the bottle is within a tone or so of the period of the fork, the air in the bottle will vibrate audibly at the period thus impressed upon it by the fork. Such vibrations are called forced vibrations. The frequency of the free vibration of the air in the bottle is independent of the frequency of the puffs of air blown across its mouth; but the frequency of the forced vibration caused by the fork is always the frequency of the fork, not always that natural to the air of the bottle if this were allowed to vibrate freely.

Resonance occurs when the frequency of the source which causes the forced vibrations is the same as the natural frequency of free vibrations of the system upon which it exerts its energy. When the two frequencies are identical, the amplitude or extent of the forced vibrations may become very great. Resonant vibrations, then, are a special case of forced vibrations. They have the frequency of the exciting source and at the same time they oscillate freely at their own natural frequency, the two frequencies being in this special case, the same.

Cavities such as the bottle have their own peculiar ranges of resonance. By and large, any highly damped vibrating system is likely to respond to quite a number of different frequencies; though there is always one to which it will respond most vigorously. This is the resonance frequency (fR) of that system. For instance, a simple resonator with a resonance frequency (fR) of 430 cycles per second will probably give some response to excitations at any frequency between 383 (g¹) and 483 (b¹), or over a range of two tones or more. Its maximum response will be at (fR) 430. We speak of such a resonator as a broadly tuned rather than as a sharply tuned resonator. A sharply tuned resonator, on the other hand, refuses to respond to vibrations out of tune with its resonance frequency by as little as one-tenth of one tone.[5]

2.07 *Energy, Intensity, Loudness*

Since sound waves are movements of material bodies, these bodies, normally air molecules, possess energy. This is kinetic energy and it can be measured quantitatively in terms of ergs, like any other kinetic energy. It is conventional, however, to speak rather of power than of energy in such measurements; and it should be remembered that power is the rate of doing work, or the ergs per second developed or absorbed. The normal unit of power is the watt (10^7 ergs per second); but in measuring the power of sound waves produced in speech, a very much smaller unit, the microwatt (10^{-6} watt) is required, since the energy of the air molecules even in the most violent sounds is amazingly minute.

It is inconvenient to isolate a single air molecule in motion in order to determine its kinetic energy, but it is relatively simple and quite as satisfactory to measure the power developed per unit area, say per 1 sq. cm., of the sound wave. One can then ascertain, approximately at least, the total power developed by the sound waves emitted by a speaker by multiplying the power passing through a square centimeter at the distance of some 30 cm. from his mouth by the area of a hemisphere having a radius of this distance.[6] Evidently when we speak of the power of a speech sound in terms of a unit area of 1 sq. cm. we are, in effect, speaking also of the intensity of the development of this energy. This may be determined as an instantaneous value or as an average value over a period of time. Speech sounds, like many musical sounds, differ from one another in the distribution of energy among their partials, or in the intensity of the several partial tones.

Often it is desirable to compare the power of one sound with that of another. This could be done in terms of microwatts, but a different unit has been developed which represents, within the medium ranges of pitch and intensity, the minimum difference in power which is perceptible to the human ear. This unit is the decibel (db), and it resembles in a way a single degree on a thermometric scale. Before any statement of the power of a sound in terms of decibels can have meaning, a zero point, or standard point of reference, must be chosen. It is now customary to start such comparisons from the standard power of 1 microwatt per cm^2 = 0 db. The maximum range of speech power is something like 60 decibels, ranging from +20 db in loud speech to −40 db in a faint whisper. Street and crowd noises have a much larger upward range than this. The decibel meters which may be seen on many kinds of acoustic apparatus are microwatt meters calibrated to read in decibels.

It must be remembered that energy, power, or intensity described in terms of decibels is a property of the sound waves after they have been produced. There is little or no significant correlation between decibel values and the physiological energy expended by a speaker in producing these sound waves. Such correlation may be assumed only for the several values which may be found for the same speech sound at different times. If one pronounces the word *pat* several times, the several intensities found acoustically for the vowel [æ] will probably be correlated significantly with the quantities of energy one has expended physiologically in their production. But it is quite patently improper to reason from the fact that [æ] is by far the most powerful fraction of this word in terms of decibels to the conclusion that its production required the greater part of the total physical energy expended by the speech mechanism. The pattern of power development in terms of decibels, or the power pattern of the product, is by no means identical with the pattern of power development in terms of muscular activity, or with the power pattern of the process. This is a very inconvenient fact, because the measurement of the power in the product is very simple, whereas the measurement of power development in the process is exceedingly difficult and in many cases as yet technically impossible.

Loudness, which is commonly associated with the terms energy, power, and intensity, is a sensation and as such not subject to direct quantitative measurement. There is some relationship between the intensity of a sound-wave movement and the loudness of the sound it produces, but this relationship is anything but a simple one. Moreover, equal differences in intensity are not perceived to be equal by all of a number of observers. The sensitivity of the individual ear to loudness is quite varied. It is therefore difficult to make use of the quality of loudness in any careful description of sounds. Its use in gross descriptions is occasionally defensible.

2.08   Quality, Timbre

Within the normal ranges of pitch we learn to distinguish easily between the note of a flute and that of an oboe, a clarinet, a trumpet, a violin, or a violoncello. We say that the note of each instrument has its own characteristic timbre or quality. In a similar way we learn to distinguish between voices, so that we identify an unseen friend by the quality of his voice, independently of what he may be saying. Regardless of the fundamental pitch at which the various vowel sounds are spoken we identify readily those which we have learned. The vowel [o] of *boat* has a distinctive quality, different from that of the vowel [e] of *bait*.

These differences of quality or timbre are closely correlated with differences observable acoustically in the number, distribution, and individual intensities of the partials which accompany the fundamental vibration. There is a characteristic modification of the shape or pattern of each sound wave set up; for this shape, or pattern, is the result of the combining of the successive instantaneous values of a group of consonant or dissonant disturbances of various frequencies and intensities into a single complex wave form. Each such sound wave has its characteristic pattern; and the train of sound waves normally has a characteristic configuration also, due to the various decrements of the several components.

The complexities of the physical form of the disturbance we call a sound wave are difficult to observe directly as relationships within a longitudinal wave-form. Hence scientific acoustics usually translates longitudinal waves into transverse waves, either by mechanical or by electrical means; and then subjects these transverse wave-forms to mathematical analysis in order to determine the components which give the wave its characteristic form. This analysis is done either by applying Fourier's equation (or Vercelli's) to the geometric measurements obtained directly from the curves, or by the use of mechanical analysers which considerably lighten the labor of computation involved. Modern electronic analysers are even more efficient, and one can get from them the frequency, power, and duration of each component in a sound complex within a reasonable time. The results of the Fourier analysis and the mechanical analysers are satisfactory for sustained musical sounds in which inharmonic partials are relatively unimportant. The method has been objected to when applied to the analysis of speech sounds, because it has failed adequately to reveal the inharmonic or the transient frequencies which are present in the waves of some of these sounds, and which are shown by the modern electronic analysers. A great deal is currently expected of the device known as the sound spectograph, the use of which in phonetic research is described in Martin Joos' monograph, *Acoustic Phonetics*.[7]

2.09 *Noises*

The roar of traffic in a city street, the clatter of applause in the theater, the rustle of the wind through pine trees results in each case from exceedingly complex and rapidly changing vibrations of air molecules produced by large numbers of vibrating bodies. These various individual vibrations move in periods, or at frequencies, most of which cannot be related to one another in a harmonic series. If enough of the vibrations involved are consonant, we may be able to identify a "fundamental" pitch for the roar, or the clatter, or the rustle; but the predominant effect is completely inharmonic and unstable, and we call it noise. In a sense, a noise may be said to be composed of large numbers of constantly shifting dissonances. The difference between dissonance and consonance is one of degree rather than one of kind, and it is well known that some harmonic relations which we accept as consonant were, to the ears of our ancestors, very real dissonances. There is probably likewise merely a difference of degree between highly complex musical sounds and some noises. The twilight zone between the two effects has for some time been the favorite field of experimentation for some of our modern orchestral composers.

A noise may be sustained if the vibratory movements which cause it are persistently renewed or maintained. Other noises are "instantaneous," like the noise of an explosion or of a collision between two objects. The sound waves set up by a sustained noise are very complex and are constantly changing in form. Those set up by an instantaneous noise are equally complex, but show a sharp decrement (loss of intensity) and die out comparatively quickly.

2.10   *How Sounds Are Heard*

The end-organs of the cochlear branch of the acoustic, or eighth cranial, nerve are in the 15,000 or more hair cells of the organ of Corti, which is contained within the cochlea of the inner ear. The cochleae are completely imbedded in the temporal bone of the skull, on either side. In order to stimulate the end-organs of the sense of hearing, the energy of the sound waves must be transmitted to the hairs of these cells so that they move.

When a sound wave is set up in the vicinity of a sentient ear, some of the vibrating air molecules ultimately pass their disturbance along the canal of the outer ear to the tympanum, or drum membrane, to which the vibrating particles of air then impart their energy as they impinge upon its outer surface. Inside this membrane, in the cavity of the middle ear, a system of levers transmits the movements of the tympanum to another membrane in the vestibular, or oval, window of the inner ear. The lever system of the middle ear considerably increases the force per unit area which is exerted upon the membrane at the oval window over that which is exerted by the sound-wave on the tympanum. By way of the eustachian tube, which opens into the nasal pharynx, the air pressure inside the middle ear is kept equal to that of the outer ear. We increase the pressure of the air in the middle ear by forcibly breathing out while the mouth and nose are closed (either by

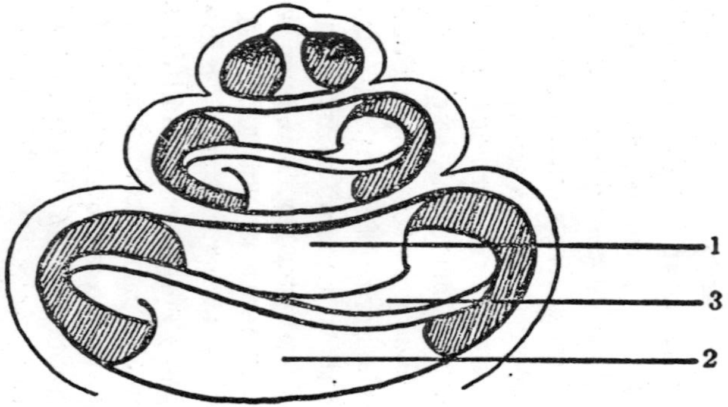

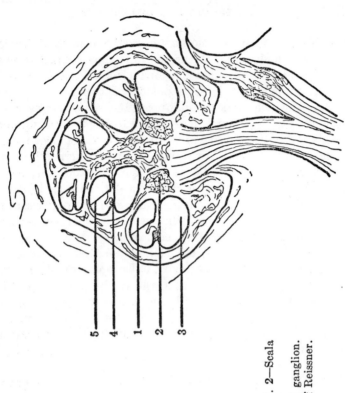

Fig. 1

Plate 18. INNER EAR

Fig. 1. Interior of the osseous cochlea: 1—Scala vestibuli. 2—Scala
tympani. 3— Lamina spiralis
Fig. 2. Membranous canals: 1—Scala vestibuli. 2—Spiral ganglion.
3—Scala tympani. 4—Basilar membrane. 5—Membrane of Reissner.

54

the lips and velum or manually). We decrease the pressure of the air in the middle ear by swallowing while the mouth and nose are closed. Such adjustments facilitate the free movement of the tympanum when the pressure of the outside air changes.

The part of the inner ear particularly concerned with the sense of hearing is the cochlea. This is a spiral structure of two and three-quarter turns around a central axis, resembling in form somewhat a common snail's shell, though much smaller. It measures about 5 mm. from base to apex, and the diameter of the base is about 9 mm. These dimensions are roughly those of a small Spanish peanut, or of a coffee bean, but the exterior shape of the cochlea is that of a cone. (Plate 18, Fig. 1) The interior space of the cochlea is divided by two membranes into three canals, the outer two of which (the scala tympani and the scala vestibuli) join at the apex of the spiral (called the helicotrema). The middle or cochlear canal contains the organ of Corti, with the hair cell termini of the auditory nerve. The organ rests upon the basilar membrane, which separates it from the scala tympani, and beneath the membrane of Reissner, which separates it from the scala vestibuli. Any movement of the liquid in either of the two outer canals will be transmitted through these membranes to the liquid in the central or cochlear canal and thence to one or more of the hair cells. (Plate 18, Fig. 2)

The disturbance of the air produced by the sound wave reaches the tympanum as a patterned disturbance of air molecules. It is transmitted from the tympanum to the oval window of the inner ear and to the liquid of the scala vestibuli by the mechanical movements of the system of levers of the middle ear. From the oval window to the hair cells of the organ of Corti the disturbance is transmitted by the movement of the liquid contained in the canals of the inner ear. Here the physical movement of the liquid, by moving the hairs on the organ of Corti, excites the nerve impulse which is the beginning of the sensation of sound.

The manner in which the movements of the membrane at the oval window are transmitted to the hair cells of the organ of Corti is not completely understood. It is clear enough that space patterns on the organ of Corti may be involved in the differentiation between two sensations of sound. Experiments and clinical evidence show that the sensation of sound at a very low pitch, say 64 c.p.s., arises particularly from the excitation of hair cells near the apex of the cochlea. Sounds of medium high pitch, say 1,000 c.p.s., excite particularly the hair cells near the middle of the organ of Corti, while those of a very high pitch, say 10,000 c.p.s., excite the hair cells near the bottom of the cochlear canal and close to the immediate source of movement at the oval window. The region of maximum sensitivity to difference of pitch lies roughly between the twelfth and the twenty-fifth millimeter of the basilar membrane as one measures from the oval window. The total length of the basilar membrane is about 31 mm., so that this area of great-est sensitivity is somewhat more than one-third of the whole. The sensations of pitch which come from this area correspond to frequencies between 2,048 and 512 c.p.s.

The transmission of the disturbances in the liquid of the canals of the cochlea is hardly comparable with that of a sound wave in open water, where we have to deal with wave movements traveling at known rates of propagation. Such waves have wave lengths ranging from 21 meters (for waves of 16 c.p.s.) to 34 mm. (for waves of 10,000 c.p.s.). In contrast, the cochlear canal is very tiny. The over-all length of the scala vestibuli or of the basilar membrane which supports the organ of Corti is about 31 mm. and its maximum diameter is about 3 mm. The total quantity of liquid in all three canals of the cochlea is less than 135 cu.mm., or about one-eighth of a cubic centimeter. The liquid of the scala vestibuli, which is directly agitated by the movements of the lever system of the middle ear, can flow freely into the scala tympani at the apex of the cochlea, and vice versa, because there is an elastic membrane over the round window at the bottom of the scala tympani where this gives upon the cavity of the middle ear. A push inward at the oval window easily produces a bulge outward at the round window. Repeated pulses on the oval window at low frequency prob-ably do just this. When the frequency becomes higher, it seems that the energy passes through the membrane of Reissner and the basilar membrane without displacing the entire contents of the cochlear canal, or at any rate with localized maximal displacements. These we know to be distributed according to their frequencies along the length of the organ of Corti.

It seems likely that the magnitude of the sensation we feel may be related to the number of hair cells thus activated. We may then think of a simple musical sound as causing a definite pattern of excitation along the organ of Corti, with an area for each partial of the tone and a relatively large number or a small number of hair cells excited in each area according to the intensity of each partial. This is no doubt a much over-simplified sketch of the result of a simple harmonious sound wave transmitted by the mechanism of the ear. What happens in the organ of Corti when the ear is exposed, let us say, to the stimulation of the first note of the first movement of Beethoven's Third Symphony is not easily imagined; but in some way out of the amazing complexity of tone and overtone we can with experience learn to perceive the whole orchestral tone and to judge its quality, and we can identify in the complex orchestral tone many of its individual components.[8] There seems to be little doubt that our acute perception of tones, noises, and the various qualities of sound which enables us, for example, to recognize persons by the sound of their voices, involves the existence of recognizable recurrent patterns, in space and in time, of the nervous excitation which is set up in these end-cells of the cochlea and conducted by the cochlear branch of the acoustic nerve to the base of the great brain. When we learn to match up the patterned nervous excitations thus set up in our ears by the sounds of speech with the patterned nervous excitations of the motor nerves required for the proper movements necessary to produce these sounds, we have effected an integration of the process of speaking with the product, speech, though of course the additional integration of imagery and "meaning" is required before we can be said to have learned to speak.

Part II

THE SOUNDS OF SPEECH

CHAPTER IV

CRITERIA OF ANALYSIS

3.01 *Is There a Norm?*

The first overt act of the normal infant is likely to be an inarticulate cry, that is to say, an act of phonation; but the ability to form speech sounds has to be acquired. The neuromuscular patterns which are necessary to the initiating of any speech movement are not innate; they are established by the process of learning. To be sure, the very existence of nerve-controlled muscle cells is a guaranty of movement; but every speech sound requires for its production the patterned correlation of the movements of large numbers of muscle cells, and these correlations are normally established by the conscious imitation of movements observed—i.e., seen or heard or both—by the learner. This process of learning, consciously engaged in, lasts for a very considerable period of time. As a process of "conditioning" it continues throughout the sentient life of the individual, since every experience of a speech sound, auditory or kinesthetic, may in some degree confirm or modify the sound's neuromuscular pattern peculiar to that individual. Consequently the several speech sounds produced by any speaker at any given time will be the product of the resultant neuromuscular patterns at that time peculiar to that individual. Such speech sounds are serviceable only insofar as they correspond adequately to those currently used in the same functions by other members of the linguistic community. By virtue of the very nature of the usual learning process, these sounds will tend to be those normal for the usage of the group.

We accept quite readily the doctrine that a given way of pronouncing a word may be said to be normal within a given linguistic community, and we describe such normal pronunciations in terms of the incidence of major and secondary stresses and in terms of a sequence of sounds. We have all experienced more or less lively debate over assertions such as this: "One should pronounce the accented vowel of the word *data* with the sound of *a* as in *state*, and not with the sound of *a* as in *hat.*" This kind of statement indicates the norm for the vowel by selecting a word which exhibits the sound in a form which every member of the speech group may be expected immediately to recognize and to accept. If now this statement be examined from the standpoint of analysis into stimulus-response relationships, the conclusion presents itself that "the sound of *a* as in *state*," is at once an adequate stimulus and an adequate response. One may quite as well say: "One should pronounce the accented vowel of the word *data* [e] and not [æ]." Here [e] and [æ] are the written notation for the speech sounds

61

"*a* as in *state*" and "*a* as in *hat*," respectively. The movements I make and the sounds I produce as examples of the pronunciations desired and rejected are likely to be accepted as normal vowel sounds appropriate to the context. The fact that a Nootka Indian, or a Hottentot may not so completely analyze his speech as do American speakers of English is not an adequate basis for the belief that such analysis as that just described is either unnatural or linguistically irrelevant. The normal speaker of any western European language, and of many others, can produce readily and upon demand any of the speech sounds which analysis shows to be regularly recurrent in his speech. To be sure, a speaker with no phonetic training can be misled into committing "egregious errors" in such an undertaking if conventional orthography is used in the experiment, but this does not invalidate the statement made.

The fact seems to be that for every speech sound which analysis shows to exist, let us say in English as spoken in a given American community, each speaker of that group has an integrated auditory and neuromuscular pattern which enables him at once to recognize and readily to reproduce that speech sound in a form acceptable as normal for the group. Where and how these patterns are retained by the individual no one knows. That they result from a learning process can not be doubted, and that the form of this process of learning determines the degree and the quality of the analysis exhibited by the individual and his group is self-evident. That the pertinent stimulus-response relationship in these cases involves equally the auditory and the neuromuscular patterns and that the latter are never activated without the activation of the former is clear. The reverse relationship, the activation of the efferent neuromuscular units while the subject is "passively" listening to speech of others, is obscured by our conventional inhibition of speech movements under such circumstances. There is now some evidence, however, that small action currents are set up in the neuromuscular units in such cases, and it seems therefore permissible to conclude that each such speaker as we have described has at his command a repertoire of integrated auditory and neuromuscular patterns which together are the determining or adequate causes for the movements and acoustic results characteristic of, or normal for, the several sounds of speech functionally valid in his speech community.

Clearly, we cannot now describe these integrated auditory and neuromuscular patterns scientifically in terms of numbers of nerve impulses distributed over various nerve channels and in accordance with a definite sequence in time. Neither do we at all understand the integrating process by which sounds heard are linked with movements made, to say nothing of the problem of the persistence of these patterns. There is no doubt that we remember neuromuscular and auditory experiences, but no one knows how we do it. Hence in our attempts to study speech sounds we are driven to the expedient of describing the movements of the muscular organisms which produce them and the acoustic phenomena which result. A good place to begin these descriptive efforts is with those phenomena which are conceded to be normal, in the sense just indicated.

It will, in any event, hardly be questioned that any normal speaker of any linguistic community can reproduce at will a generally acceptable pronunciation of any word or meaningful utterance which he has learned. It is self-evident that when an American speaker of English pronounces such a word as *crystallization* alone, or out of context, the form of the movements and the acoustic result may not be quite the same as those characteristic of any occurrence of this word in his discourse. We have as facts of experience the *lexical* pronunciation on the one hand and the *contextual* pronunciation on the other. It would seem a priori improbable that there is no definable relation between the two, since they are recognized as "sames" in the stimulus-response inventory of the linguistic group. It would add tremendously to the number and complexity of integrated auditory and neuromuscular patterns were it necessary that there be one such configuration for the lexical pronunciation and one or more others for contextual pronunciations of each linguistic form or word. It is an indisputable fact that patterned movements suffer modification under the influence of changes in the motor context[1] in which they occur. It is clear that a word like *crystallization* may be modified in different contexts so that it shows four instead of five syllables, since the vowel before [l] may disappear completely. Nevertheless, this reduced form is still equivalent as stimulus-response to the lexical or normal form. It therefore seems reasonable to conclude that the patterned innervations learned for this word by the normal individual are those which, when uninfluenced by factors of the general motor context (such as high speed, unusual stress, or lack of stress) will produce the form heard in his lexical pronunciation and that these same integrated neural patterns also control the innervations of the movements heard in contextual pronunciations. This seems true even though the execution of the patterned innervations is sometimes modified or prevented by the physiological limitations to the speed of movement peculiar to specific muscle groups, or by neural blocking. If any one pronunciation of a given linguistic form may be taken to represent the normal configuration of these integrated neural patterns, then it is the lexical pronunciation which is most properly to be so taken. It is thus not merely convenience which leads us to deal extensively with lexical pronunciations in our study of speech sounds.

3.02 *Speech Sounds as Events*

In their usual phenomenal form, speech sounds are recognizably re-current features of meaningful speech forms. The question of the relation of these recurrent features to the whole which they characterize is a difficult one. As a language is learned by the normal speaker, meaningful forms (utterances, words, morphemes) are the primary units and these forms are learned as movements. One learns "how to say it." The test of adequate learning is the ability of these movements to produce sound sequences which form an adequate stimulus-response unit in the meaning or function intended. Evidently, since in its practical use the stimulus is produced by one person and the response elicited in another, the auditory patterns must be adequately identical in the two individuals; the movement patterns can be different, if it is possible for the vocal organs to produce two sounds which pass for "the same" by two different movement complexes. Also, this adequate identity of any two auditory sensations does not at all imply physical identity but merely so much of similarity between the two sound-wave patterns as is required to stimulate the appropriate neuromuscular units in both individuals.

As language is used, it consists of a series of signals, and signals can be abbreviated or obscured very notably without losing their effectiveness if the level of presupposition or the nature of the context is favorable to such reduction of clarity. The test of the adequacy of the auditory stimulus is its capacity to excite those neuromuscular units in the hearer's body which would, if their action were not inhibited, produce the patterned movements appropriate to and integrated with the auditory patterns proper to the linguistic form intended by the speaker. Often when the obscurity of a signal leaves us uncertain of its intent, we find ourselves testing our under-standing of it by saying to ourselves or to others, "Did he say . . . ?" If the movements we then make correspond adequately with those we have heard, we shall ourselves recognize the two events as "sames," and any other member of the community, upon hearing both, would say, "Yes, those two people said the same thing." As a rule when we bring such a signal to full clarity in our own perception by reproducing it, we find our-selves producing the form in its lexical pronunciation. If the word *crystalliza-tion* be reduced in an actual speech context to the point where what we hear is barely adequate to produce the required neuromotor response—there being but four syllables let us say, and no vowel before [l]—we "recognize" the linguistic form, not by reproducing this reduced form but by reproducing the five-syllable form with the neutral vowel [ə] before [l], which we accept as intended by the speaker if it fits the context in which it occurs.

When we proceed then to analyze such a speech form as *crystallization* into the several regularly recurrent features which characterize it we shall divide the acoustic and the movement complexes into smaller recognizable units such as *crystal*, *-ation*, and *-iz-*, that is, into syllables or groups of syllables, and thence we shall proceed to identify smaller portions of the complex as "speech sounds," e.g., *-iz-* as "made up of" [ɪ] and [z].

When we have thus isolated [ɪ] and [z] from such a word as *crystallization* we have found two examples of speech sounds. We can reproduce them at will, and our reproductions will be accepted as adequate or normal by other speakers of our own group. To be sure, this same syllable *-iz-* would be analyzed as [aɪ] and [z] by some speakers of English, but this difference is a difference in dialects, and in this respect, at least, these speakers do not belong to the same group as those who analyze the form into [ɪ] and [z]. When we abstract the same two features [ɪ] and [z] from *business*, we have additional evidence of the reality of each of the speech sounds as distinctive features of linguistic forms. When we find in the form *things* a feature which closely resembles [ɪ] but does not sound quite like [ɪ] in *business* or *this*, we confront a problem of classification. We know by linguistic analysis that the difference between these two [ɪ] sounds is not used to differentiate one form from another; so we put the two sounds tentatively into a single class, which we call the vowel [ɪ]. We can go on in this way with the business of classification until we shall have found all of the various modifications of [ɪ] which our language uses. Thus a linguistic and a logical class may be established. What the situation may be as to the integrated auditory and neuromotor pattern in any individual speaker for whom these several varieties of [ɪ] may be usual is less clear. Does he have several different integrated neural patterns each corresponding to one of the variants observed; or does he have one neural pattern which, when combined with the others of the motor context from which our variants have been abstracted, will result by compensatory physiological adjustments in the usual variants each time? Here experiment with the lexical pronunciations of known words seems to indicate the probability that for most of our speech sounds each individual has learned a single integral auditory and neuromotor pattern. Unprejudiced subjects will respond with "the same" movements when asked to produce the vowel of *things* as they use when asked for the vowel of *this*. It is true that responses of this kind tend to be conditioned by peculiarities of the conventional alphabet. But if the inadequacies of this "key" be compensated for by other means of stimulation, the subject can be led to produce for each sound class a single patterned movement, and a sound which may be said to represent the integrated auditory and neuromotor pattern of this speech sound uninfluenced by variable dynamic and temporal factors inherent in any context in which the sound might occur. These responses appear to be adequate stimulus-response units in the language experience of the speakers.

It is clear that the [h] sounds of *he, hat, hot, hoot,* as they occur in these words are not identical each with the others, either as to the movements of the tongue or as to the acoustic product of the movement. But it seems likely that the [h] produced in isolation by any normal subject is the adequate representative of the speech sound [h], and that if we analyze it properly, it will reveal the essential character of the movements required to produce this speech sound. The normal speaker, if asked to pronounce [k], will produce a sound which is neither that of [k] in *keel* nor that of [k] in *cool,* but which is the representative of a patterned movement which may readily suffer modification in either direction under the influence of the different motor contexts provided by these two words.

There are some cases in which difficulty is encountered. For instance, the response which may be made by a native German speaker to the request to pronounce "ch" is unpredictable. He may say [ç] as in *ich* or as in the first sound of *chinesisch,* or he may say [x] as in *doch,* or he may balk, and ask which "ch" you mean. It seems probable that the learner here has developed two distinct neural patterns for two different "ch" sounds, despite the fact that the language does not use this difference as a mark of semantic differentiation. One may substitute any one of the variants of [ɪ] for any other without producing a form which would be challenged as unacceptable in the group usage; one may not substitute [ç] of *ich* for [x] of *doch* or vice versa and yet produce an acceptable linguistic form.[2] This is troublesome to those whose analysis indicates that the two sounds are conditioned variants of a single speech sound. Either the definition of the phoneme, or sound class, on the basis solely of the phonological opposition or semantic differentiation is not wholly satisfactory, or the speakers of German have learned to make a distinction between two sounds which is not "linguistically relevant." It is in any event a distinction indispensable to the acceptable pronunciation of the linguistic forms of that language.

No one disputes the thesis that the several words which compose any utterance are respectively the actualizations of complex integrated acoustic and neuromotor patterns, recurrent in other collocations with modifications of form due to differences in motor context. No one disputes the thesis that morphemes[3] such as *-iz-* or *-ation* are actualizations of complex, integrated acoustic and neuromotor patterns recurrent in many different motor contexts. No one disputes the thesis that within the complex, integrated neural patterns of words or of morphemes we are forced to discern regularly recurrent forms of movement and features of sound which, how-

ever much mutually overlaid by coarticulation or commingling, nevertheless resolve themselves in clear lexical pronunciation into individual
complexes recognizable and reproducible as speech sounds in isolation,
like the "*a* of *state*." The most reasonable explanation of this state of affairs
is that the larger complexes from which we thus isolate the sounds of speech
are indeed configurations in which these individual speech sounds have
been fused together by a specific motor context into a linguistic form which
is fully realized in lexical pronunciation but which may suffer more or less
notable modification under the influence of different motor contexts of the
larger units of the phrase or sentence.[4] It is of the essence of a configuration
that it is not merely the sum of its component elements but a unity into
which these have been fused. Since the controlling factors of these fusions
are principally variations of motor context and since the same components
usually behave the same way in fusions having the same contexts, it becomes important to study the form of the movements of the isolated real-
izations of these motor patterns and the behavior of their various features
in different movement contexts.

3.03   *Speech Sounds and Orthography*

Among the less grateful tasks of youth is that of "learning to spell."
One discovers that one must conform with "usage" and that under the
sanctions thereof each word has its accepted orthographic form. This accepted form, in turn, has two manifestations, which in the orthography of
by-gone days we may call respectively uncial and cursive, or in our present
practice, print and script. The distinction which interests us here is that
between a group of discrete symbols (uncial, print) and a fusion of distinct
symbols into a unitary configuration for each linguistic form (cursive,
script). The relation of the uncial or printed manifestation of the word-
form to the cursive or script manifestation is, from the standpoint of the
movement complex represented, analogous to the relation between a hy-
pothetically possible but actually nonexistent additive grouping of speech
sounds and the actually realized fused configuration of these sounds when
a word is uttered. But this relationship is analogous, not correlative; for
the muscles primarily involved in writing are not those primarily involved
in speaking, and the fusions therefore are determined by quite different
physiological factors.

There is an important difference between the written and the spoken form
of the word. The patterns of each (visual-neuromuscular:auditory-neuro-
muscular) are learned by the members of the speech community from their
fellows; but the pattern of the spoken form thus acquired is that of the
fusion (the configuration or Gestalt) while the pattern learned for the
written form is one of discrete symbols in a given sequence, and the graphic

fusion of script is secondary and individual. Presumably there was once for each individual community a time when the relationship between the component elements of the spoken form and the letters of the written form was clear and direct to those who wrote the forms. The physical preservation of written forms, however, has given rise to conservative practices in orthography, by virtue of which the graphic forms of many words have remained unchanged while the spoken configurations have undergone very considerable modifications. A simple illustration is the English form *knight*, compared with its cognate German form *Knecht*. English orthographic usage makes us write *kn* despite the fact that in the spoken form the pronunciation of the initial *k* has been given up (by assimilation). We still write *gh* despite the fact that the spirant [h] which was once pronounced before [t] in this word has long since disappeared from the spoken form. Many other influences exerted upon it since the Middle Ages have made English orthographic practice very irregular and in some respects very little related logically to the spoken forms it purports to represent. Everyone knows the uncertainty of the English graphic form *-ough* in such words as *though, through, plough, cough, hiccough, rough*. Only slightly less troublesome to the learner are such ambiguities as *doll*:*roll*, *home*:*come*, *sword*: *word*, *few*:*sew*, *break*:*squeak*, *paid*:*plaid*. In this respect English orthography is more obscure and less self-consistent than that of any other western European language, but every conventional orthography suffers more or less from this kind of inadequacy.

In order to be able to set down in writing our phonetic analysis of any speech form we need a means of graphic representation of speech sounds which will enable us to indicate each of such sounds without ambiguity. In order to be able to put these observations to practical use, we must have a graphic medium by which the pronunciation of words and phrases may be made immediately evident to persons who do not know how to pronounce these words when they find them written in the conventional orthography of the language concerned. Both the science and the art of phonetics require a more precise and unambiguous graphic system than is afforded by any of the conventional orthographies.

The problem is not new. In 1888 the *Phonetic Teacher*, which later became the *Maître Phonètique*, laid down this principle: "There shall be a separate sign for each distinctive sound: that is, for each sound which, being used instead of another in the same language, can change the meaning of a word." This principle, properly applied, would produce what, since the work of Henry Sweet,[5] has been called a "broad transcription" of the speech-forms concerned; it would give us a distinct symbol for each distinctive speech sound or sound class. It would not give us two distinct symbols for the two quite different sounds of [k] in *keel* and *cool*. If we wish to discriminate graphically between the variant forms within a given class of speech sounds we shall have to resort to further refinements of ortho-graphic representation and thus to what Sweet called the "narrow nota-tion." A narrow transcription, therefore, should tell us somewhat more than the broad notation does about nondistinctive differences. But both kinds of transcription are mere graphic representations which can indicate with precision, only analytically, the gross features of the elements found in the fusions characteristic of uttered word-forms. As a matter of fact, most printed transcriptions are in one way or another inadequate, in the sense that they are wholly unambiguous only to a reader who knows the precise regional dialect represented. Nevertheless, either a broad or a narrow transcription is usually a more consistent and rational representa-tion of the spoken form than can be achieved in the conventional ortho-graphy. The making of a good narrow transcription is also a most excellent exercise in phonetic observation, and this in turn is the rock-bottom founda-tion of all good work in the field of phonetics.

3.04   A Phonetic Alphabet

Since the late nineteenth century many different systems of phonetic transcription have been proposed. A convenient collection of those which have found notable acceptance in the practice of linguists was published by the German Government Printing Office in 1928.[6]

The basic cause of the conflict of opinion which has existed in this field of endeavor is the desire to create a universal phonetic alphabet, or a system of symbols adequate to represent in considerable detail the forms of any language in which linguists might be interested. It is evident that even the conventional orthographies of western Europe represent in many particu-lars an "international alphabet": an English [t] is not pronounced exactly like a French [t], nor like a Dutch, a German, an Italian, a Danish, a Swedish, or a Norwegian [t]; yet the same graphic symbol serves ade-quately in each language despite these differences. The r-sounds of the several languages are notably different one from another, yet the r symbol is adequate for each group. In much the same way but to a smaller degree the values of the phonetic symbols commonly used in our phonetic tran-scriptions are different in each of the different languages, but the glaring inconsistencies of the regional orthographies have been avoided and a form of notation achieved which is both a considerable aid to scientific dis-cussion and a very great boon to the teacher and the learner of strange tongues.

The most widely used phonetic alphabet at present is that of the Inter-national Phonetic Association (I.P.A.),[6a] or as it is more often called, "L'As-sociation Phonétique Internationale." In the lists which follow, the standard I.P.A. symbols are given with illustrative words from several different languages. It must constantly be remembered that the parallelisms thus presented are parallelisms of symbolic values and not of identical sounds. These symbols are unambiguous only with respect to the speech sounds of a single dialect; when applied to more than one dialect they represent similar, not identical sounds.

THE PHONETIC ALPHABET

The sound represented by the phonetic symbol is that which corresponds to the italicized letters of the words printed beside it. Only the more usual symbols are given in this list; special symbols are introduced with appropriate explanations later on. Forms in which the symbol indicated would be used only in a narrow transcription are set in brackets.

SYM-BOL	ENGLISH	FRENCH	ITALIAN	SPANISH	GERMAN
a		patte			
ɑ	father	pâte	casa	caro	Anna
æ	hat				
b	bat	bon	banco	buenos hombre	bitte
c	[keel]			[quince]	[kühn]
ç					[ich, Milch]
tʃ	choose		voce	chico	
d	deal	dent	dente	doble	Ding
dʒ	judge		magia		
e	date	des	che	queso	Ehre
ɛ	debt	dette	ecco vento	regla	besser hätte
ɝ[7]	hurt				
ə	data	le			eine
f	fate	fable	fatto	facil	fein, vor
g	goose	gar	vagabondi	guerra gallo	Gut
ɣ				rogar	[Waren]
ɟ	[geese]			[Guido]	[giessen]
h	he, who	[haricot]			Haus
x				jarro rojo	Dach
i	heat	qui	mi	chico	bieten
ɪ,	hit			[mirra]	bitten
j	yet	yacht	iato	hoyo labio	Jahr
k	cool	car	che amico	loco	Kugel

SYM-BOL	ENGLISH	FRENCH	ITALIAN	SPANISH	GERMAN
l	lip, loop	lapin	lacrima	lado	lassen
ʎ		[fille]	gli	calle	
m	me	madame	mio	madre	Mutter
n	net	nuit	netto	neto	nein
ɲ	[sing]	montagne	agnelli	pequeño	[singen]
ŋ	sung		anche	banco	Hunger
o	goat	faux	voce	adobe	Sohn
ɔ	fall	fol	cosa	corro	Sonne
œ		[feuille]			[Götter]
ø		deux			schön
p	pit	parle	pace	padre	Paul
r[8]		robe	rialto	roca / perro	rein
ɹ	red			color	
ʀ		[rue]			[Waren]
ɾ				pero	
s	see	sa	così	señora / rosa	lassen
ʃ	she	chat	scena / sciame		Schule
t	to	ton	tacco	tarde	tun
θ	thin			cerca	
ð	this			escudo	
u	pool	où	mulo	cura	Mut
ɷ, ʊ	pull			[lujo]	[Mutter]
ʌ	but				
β				cuba / doble	
ɥ		depuis / huit			
v	vine	vin	vino		Wein
w	we	oui	guerra / nuova	puerta / cuatro	
y		tu			Hüte
ʏ					[Hütte]
z	zeal	zèle	rosa / esiste	isla	sein
ʒ	azure / vision	agilité			

DIACRITIC MARKS

?	stopped beginning of vowels, coup de glotte (glottal stop)
˜	nasalized vowel
˳	voiceless
ˬ	voiced
.	tense vowel
˓	lax vowel
+	fronted, or palatalized
–	retracted, or velarized
ω	labialized
:	full length, long vowel
·	half length

3.05 *Classification of Speech Sounds*

From the utterances peculiar to any given speech group we can derive by analysis only a limited number of speech sounds, such as those represented by the phonetic symbols of our table. We can also distinguish certain regular features of the sound fusions of speech forms not appurtenant to any one of these speech sounds per se, but nonetheless characteristic of the form as a whole. Such features are accent by stress, accent by pitch, intonation, boundary markers, transitional sounds, and other phenomena of fusion. Every dialect has its own array of speech sounds which represent, or may be called, its phonemes, and each dialect has its own peculiarities in the use of such features of fusion as those just mentioned. These things must be sorted out and defined in the descriptive phonetics of each dialect. The classifications thus set up may not be applied directly to the sounds of any dialect other than that from which they are derived: one may speak of the English phoneme [t], or of the French phoneme [t], but not of the phoneme [t]. It is quite evident, however, that English, French, and most other languages use for their phonemes [t] speech sounds which, on the basis of comparison as to movement patterns and acoustic results, can be put into a general class which we may call voiceless dental stops, or "t-sounds." The construction of such general classes is one of the tasks of general phonetics.

The classification of speech sounds on the basis of their function in the movement of the syllable (Stetson) or on the basis of their relative sonority (Sievers, Jespersen) gives us two basic groups. The first is conveniently called the syllabics;[9] it comprises those sounds which occur usually as the most sonorous element of syllables or during the emission of the breath pulse of the syllable movement. For example, in the syllable *rat* the most sonorous element is [æ]. The syllable movement is released by [r], the breath pulse flows during the utterance of [æ] and the syllable movement is checked by [t]. Hence [æ] is the syllabic element of the syllable [ræt]. The syllabics most frequently found in western European languages are generally called vowels. The second group of speech sounds in this functional classification is called the nonsyllabics and comprises such sounds as the [r] and [t] of *rat*. The nonsyllabics most frequently found are generally called consonants.

Unfortunately, the terms syllabic and vowel are not synonymous, nor are the terms nonsyllabic and consonant. Some of the sounds commonly classed as consonants may, and frequently do, serve as syllabics. In Sanskrit, for example, the first person singular, perfect, indicative of the verb "to turn" is *va-várt-a*, whereas the first person plural of the same tense is *va-vrt-imá*; thus [r] is nonsyllabic in the singular form and syllabic in the plural form. In different motor contexts the same syllable shows [r] as nonsyllabic and [r] as the syllabic. Some of the sounds commonly classed as vowels are sometimes nonsyllabic in their function in the syllable. For example, the nominative singular of the Gothic word for "kingdom" is *þiudangardi*, while the accusative is *þiudangardja*. In the nominative, [i] is the syllabic element of the final syllable -*di*; in the accusative, [i] is nonsyllabic in this syllable, and under these circumstances is often written with a different symbol, *j*. Such interchanges of function for a single phoneme are not easily found in the modern European languages, and it may be disputed whether the speech sound represented by nonsyllabic [i] in French *nié* is the same speech sound as the syllabic [i] in *ni*. It may be disputed whether the first fraction of the English word *use* is the same speech sound as the first fraction of the word *youth*, and probably no one would agree immediately that the initial sound of these two words is the nonsyllabic form of the syllabic (vowel) of *eat*. Be that as it may, in every language there are a number of speech sounds which are regularly used as nonsyllabics, another group of speech sounds which are regularly used as syllabics, and a third group of speech sounds which may be used in either function. These sounds of twofold function have been called variously sonants, semiconsonants, semivowels.[10]

3.06   *The Syllable*

To divide speech sounds on the basis of their function into the two groups, syllabics and nonsyllabics, is to assume the existence of the syllable. Attempts to define the syllable by the investigation of acoustic records of utterances have been unsuccessful, and instrumental phoneticians have denied the reality of the syllable.[11] They do so because they cannot delimit the syllables on their records. As Jespersen long ago pointed out,[12] this is somewhat the same kind of reasoning as would lead one to deny the existence of two adjacent hills because one cannot satisfactorily determine how much of the intervening valley belongs to one and how much to the other. The fact is incontestable that the decibel (microwatt) meter of any properly functioning acoustic recorder will show definite "peaks" of acoustic energy which correspond in number and in sequence precisely with the enunciation of the sounds we have called syllabics. There is one such peak for every fraction of an utterance which we would call, in our traditional way, a syllable.

R. H. Stetson has set forth the thesis,[13] supported by extensive evidence, that the syllable is a motor unit; that is, that each syllable is basically a movement complex in which the larger, underlying movement is the breath pulse, or thrust of the chest musculature, which creates a compression of air in the lungs. The emission of this air is then started, controlled, or checked by movements of the articulatory organs. For Stetson, the non-syllabics are the factors which determine the character of most syllabic movements; the syllabic is a secondary element. But in any case, the syllable, in his view, is a reality and not a mere fiction. Unhappily, the underlying chest pulse can be observed only with the help of rather fussy laboratory techniques, and the practical phonetician who accepts the premise that the syllable is a reality will perforce operate, as his predecessors have operated, with the not wholly satisfactory criterion of sonority.

3.07 *Sonority*

Sonority is a quality attributed to a sound on the basis of its seeming fullness or largeness, and when attributed to speech sounds, sonority is correlated very largely with the degree to which the voice is audible. There is very little discernible difference between the sonority of any two speech sounds produced without voice. For this reason sonority may be equated more or less correctly with acoustic energy and its quantities determined accurately by electronic methods. This has been done, notably by the Bell Telephone Laboratories.[14] The results there found do not differ materially from those set down from aural observation by men like Sievers and Jespersen.[15] The gradations of relative sonority may be described as follows: (1) The least sonorous speech sounds are voiceless sounds like [p], [t], [k], or [f], [s], [h]. (2) Only slightly more sonorous are voiced sounds like (b), [d], [g], or [v], [z], [ʒ]. (3) Quite clearly more sonorous are the nasal sounds like [m], [n], [ŋ], and the lateral or "L" sounds. Here also belong the "sh" sounds [ʃ]. (4) Stronger than these are the "r" sounds. (5) Next come sounds like [u] or [i]; and then (6) the sounds like [o] and [e]; and (7) the sounds like [ɔ], [æ] and [ɑ]. Of all of these sounds [ɑ] is generally the most sonorous, though the difference as to sonority between [ɑ] and [ɔ] in American English is slight.[16]

One may test pragmatically the relative sonority of various speech sounds by combining them in small groups with others and observing the results in terms of the number of syllables heard. For instance, English [r] is more sonorous than English [l], because in a group like [kɑrl] only one syllable is heard; i.e., the sonority diminishes, without a new increase, from [ɑ] to the end of the word. The combination [kɑlr] will be heard as two syllables, because [l] is less sonorous than either [r] or [ɑ] and thus becomes a "valley" between two peaks of sonority in this group. There are two interesting variations of the word [kɑrl], however. On the one hand, the sonority of [r] may diminish till it is less than that of [l], in which event a dissyllabic form [kɑrəl] may result. On the other hand, in large areas of England and America the [r] before [l] has been completely lost; this word has become [kɑːl] and is therefore not a case here in point. Usually [l] is more sonorous than [m] or [n], as one can see from the English word [ɛlm], or the substandard form [kɪln], each of which is monosyllabic. Evidently, however, English [l] has a tendency to lose some of its sonority, or [m] a tendency to gain sonority because the dissyllabic pronunciation of *elm* [ɛləm] is widespread though clearly substandard. Each dialect has its own characteristics in this matter, although over-all, the sonority scale for most languages will approximate that given above.

Chapter V

THE SYLLABIC SOUNDS

4.01 *Vowel or Consonant*

The essence of a syllabic is that it shall be gennemically the element of major sonority in its syllable, or genetically the chief carrier of the emitted breath pulse of the syllable. More often than otherwise, these most sonorous elements are what we conventionally call vowels. Everyone knows what a vowel is; yet there is no really satisfactory way in which to discriminate either genetically or gennemically between vowels and consonants. The differences between the sounds usually comprised in these two categories resolve themselves upon analysis into differences of degree rather than differences of kind and thus into relative rather than absolute differences. Nevertheless, speech sounds like those just listed in groups (5), (6), and (7) of the sonority scale, or speech sounds like [u], [i], [o], [e], [ɔ], [æ], [ɑ] have certain common characteristics which have traditionally been and may still best be set forth under a single general rubric; and that rubric is, most conveniently, the vowels.

4.02 *The Vowels, Considered Gennemically*

Characteristic of the vowel sounds as a group is the relative acoustic prominence of the voice. That this is due to the comparatively free passageway provided for the glottal vibrations through the pharynx, mouth, and sometimes also the nasal cavities, is generally believed, and that these vibrations produce the quantity of sound they do is probably attributable to reinforcement of the fundamental tone by the action of vibrating air in the pharyngeal, oral, or nasal cavities. Concerning the physical nature of this reinforcement there have been two distinct theories. One holds that these reinforcements are due to the resonant vibration of air in cavities, the natural pitches of which are attuned to those of two or more of the harmonics of the voice note. The other holds that the reinforcements are due to the free (i.e., nonresonant) vibration of air in two or more cavities formed by the movements of the articulatory organs and that the tones contributed by these free vibrations need not be, and indeed usually are not, in harmonic relation to the fundamental voice note. The first theory has been called the harmonic theory, and in its essentials it goes back to Wheatstone and Helmholtz.[1] The second theory has been called, with less elegance, the inharmonic theory, and it goes back primarily to the research of Willis and Hermann. The difference between the two theories is less a difference in the observation of what is going on while the vowel sounds are being produced than it is a difference in the method of describing the movements in precise physical terms.[2]

Several facts become evident when one looks at the acoustic records produced by means of modern electroacoustic techniques.[3] First of all, one recognizes the fact that vowel sounds are not uniform throughout their duration. Three stages can be discerned with the naked eye: (a) a beginning stage, during which each period of the wave train is notably different from the next; (b) a stage of comparative stability of wave form; and (c) a final stage of more rapid change from one period to the next as the sound "decays." Acoustic analysis of the second stage of comparative stability has indicated that the fundamental tone of each vowel is reinforced in at least two frequencies;[4] some sounds appear to have three areas of reinforcement. Some investigators have sought to establish four areas of reinforcement as characteristic of each vowel sound.[5] Obviously, much of this investigation has concerned "sung" vowels, or vowels maintained for at least one second, often for as much as four seconds. When fractions of actual utterances are studied, one observes that the entire vowel duration is not likely to exceed 0.35 seconds and is usually much shorter than this. The lower limit for a fully stressed vowel is in the neighborhood of 0.10 to 0.15 seconds at the usual speech tempos. Consequently, students of the records of actual utterances find less evidence of the second or stable stage of the vowel wave train, and some find no two periods of the vowel sound to be quite alike.[6] In all of this kind of analysis, the factors singled out as characteristic of a particular vowel are but two, or three, or four of the much more numerous array of components which the acoustic spectrum[7] of the sound reveals. There one may see as few as six or as many as thirty-one component frequencies. Many of these components are evidently the causes of personal or individual peculiarities of voice, that is, of individual voice timbre or quality rather than essential characteristics of the vowel sound under scrutiny. Insofar as such individual qualities inhere in the physical form of the individual vocal bands, they may be largely eliminated from the study of the problem by resorting to the examination of whispered rather than of voiced vowels. Notable among the investigations of whispered speech are those of R. J. Lloyd and Sir Richard Paget.[8] Like other investigators, however, they find not only two, but three and even four components to be characteristic of some of the vowel sounds. The inadequacy of all of these descriptions of vowels in terms of formants has been flatly asserted by E. W. Scripture and Agostino Gemelli.[9]

It is expected that the problems which underlie these differences of opinion will be attacked with renewed interest by the men who are beginning to work with the sound spectrograph.

4.021 *Synthesis*

The natural way to test an analysis is to recombine the elements found to be essential or characteristic and thus to see whether the resultant synthetic product is the same to the ear as the original object of analysis. There have been many such experiments since those of Wolfgang von Kempelen's *Mechanismus der menschlichen Sprache und Beschreibung einer sprechenden Maschine* (Wien, 1791). The most satisfactory study of vowel synthesis made before the perfecting of the present methods of electrical analysis is probably that of Carl Stumpf, begun in 1913 and published in his book, *Die Sprachlaute* (Berlin, 1926). Since the development of electronic methods, we have had many analytical studies of speech sounds,[10] but the one conspicuous success with the synthesis of speech sounds is that directed by Homer Dudley in the Bell Telephone Laboratories culminating in the two devices known as the Vocoder and the Voder.[11] The former analyzes and synthesizes speech sounds automatically; the latter synthesizes speech sounds by manual operation. The Vocoder puts into its synthesized speech sounds approximately what an electrical analysis shows to be contained in the originals which are imitated. The Voder operates with much simpler arrays of component frequencies, but the sounds produced are recognizable as the speech sounds intended by the operator.

These devices are mentioned here because out of his work with them Dudley has evolved an explanation of the acoustic phenomena of speech[12] which accounts for many of the observed acoustic facts that have disturbed students of these problems for a long time. Fundamentally, his theory is an analogue of the theory of radio telephony by amplitude modulation. This latter process requires a constant wave train to be emitted from the "sender." Upon this constant wave train, or carrier wave, the message-bearing wave forms are then impressed by interference with or modulation of the carrier. The result is a carrier wave train within a superimposed "envelope," "form," or configuration, and it is this configuration which is "received" and interpreted. To explain the phenomena of human speech, Dudley posits two different "carrier" sources: (1) the vibratory buzz of the vocal bands, and (2) the hiss or random noise of the breath stream as this is variously impeded in its outward flow. For some sounds, notably the voiced consonants, both carrier sources are in action simultaneously. The movements of the tongue, the velum, the jaw, and the lips are by physiological necessity too slow to be heard as vibratory movements. What we hear is the modulating effect of these movements upon the steady source of sound, or upon the carrier frequencies of our speech. Stetson was very close to this explanation when he said:[13] "Speech is rather a set of movements made audible than a set of sounds produced by movements." The explanation offered by Dr. Dudley eliminates the difficulty of "wave-form changes" during the course of the stable portion of a speech sound since these changes are attributable to phase changes in the carrier, and the form of the carrier is unimportant to the integrity of the "message form." The proof of this pudding is in the articulated roar of the locomotive or of the dog's bark in our radio advertising.[14]

The components used by the Voder for the synthesis of vowel sounds are harmonics of the fundamental frequency or pitch of the sound. Vowels are produced by modulating the buzz or tone of a relaxation oscillator, by suppressing most and passing only certain of its partial tones. However, it is not just two simple frequencies combined with a fundamental tone which are heard from the Voder; rather, two or more groups of overtones receive reinforcement. Specifically, for example, if the vowel [u] of *pool* is produced by reinforcements in the neighborhood of 400 and of 800 cycles when the fundamental pitch is 100 cycles per second (or A_1 approximately),[15] the Voder will pass the fundamental and the second partial in one band with about equal intensities; it will pass the third and fourth partials, somewhat reduced in energy, in another band, and the seventh, eighth, ninth, and tenth partials, progressively quite materially weaker, in the third band. The naturalness of the resulting sounds has been found to depend not only upon the energy given to the several bands but in large measure also upon the variation of the fundamental pitch— and with it the frequencies of the harmonics—by means of a pedal pitch control. This is the converse of the repeated finding that the pitch of a spoken vowel often varies from one cycle to the next. Because of this shifting of the fundamental pitch one must not expect to define the characteristic components of any vowel sound as single frequencies but must rather indicate them as bands, or regions of frequency, within which major reinforcement of the fundamental takes place. Because also any vowel may be spoken at almost any fundamental pitch, these characteristic frequencies cannot be described as definite harmonic partials of the fundamental. Moreover, there is here, as with any other stimulus of the sense of hearing, a zone of tolerance within which the formant frequencies may vary without destroying the identity of the vowel sound. Finally, because of their function as modulators of the carrier frequencies of speech, by interference or impedance, these formants are adequately described only when we indicate their relative power, their relative phases, and their frequencies throughout their duration.[16] It may well be that an adequate description of the vowel formants will turn out to be a description of two or more resonance curves or, mutatis mutandis, resonators. There is some evidence tending to show that two resonators with peak resonances below 1,200 cycles per second are sufficient to determine the character of some vowels, e.g., the "oh-ness" or the "ah-ness" of a fundamental tone rich in the higher harmonics and thus analogous to the cord tone of the human voice.[17]

4.022 *Summary*

The results of the studies of the acoustic nature of vowel sounds may be summarized, perhaps, as follows. (1) In the phenomenal occurrence of vowel sounds, both harmonic and inharmonic frequencies are found. The wave form of a vowel sound is not a true periodic function.[18] (2) Efforts to discern amidst the complexity of the observed sound spectra of vowel sounds the minimum essentials—or that limited array of partial tones indispensable to the aural recognitition of the vowel—have resulted in the identification for each vowel of at least two formants, or bands of frequencies, within which reinforcement of the fundamental of the voice note is required. No one denies the existence of these formants; the adequacy of their statement as a description of the vowel is challenged. (3) All efforts at vowel synthesis result in the exclusion of inharmonic partials as nonessential to the sound and in the determination of two or more harmonic partials as formants, or indispensable components of each of the vowel sounds. (4) The precise pitch of these formants is less critical than the relationships between them or between their respective acoustic energies. That is to say, these formants constitute a configuration in time, of pitch, intensity, and phase, which is the essential form of each vowel. (5) This essential form is, under normal speech conditions, impressed upon a carrier wave, the precise acoustic nature of which is of secondary importance since it is the configuration of the modulating wave which is the critical acoustic element of the speech signal. (6) The characteristic vowel formants will be different in different dialects and a clear-cut discrimination of one vowel type from its fellows may be possible only within each dialect. There is no difficulty in distinguishing the [a] of French *patte* from the [ɑ] of French *pâte*; but there is considerable difficulty in distinguishing the [ɑ] of French *pâte* from the [ɑ] of American *father*, or even the [a] of French *patte* from some pronunciations of [a] in English *palm*. Unhappily the art of phonetics is obliged to concern itself with problems of this kind; while the science of phonetics may avoid them.

4.023 *Diagrams*

Various tabular representations of acoustic analyses of the syllabic sounds of several languages have been devised. The scheme used by Paget[19] is probably the one best known. More complex is the circular table proposed by Leo Barczinski and Erich Thienhaus,[20] who attempt in their tabulation to include four formants for each vowel. It is quite clear that numerical values thus selected as characteristic of a given array of vowel sounds represent deductions from a relatively limited number of observations and that considerable variations from these numerical values may be obtained for different speakers.[21] Also the tabulation of formant frequencies only, with no indication of their relative amplitudes or phases, gives a quite incomplete picture of the modulating factors characteristic of the vowel sounds. Hence such tables are bound to be unsatisfactory. Finally, it must be said that however indispensable this kind of analysis is as a function of scientific phonetics, the practical utility of these analyses is largely nonlinguistic. The interest of the Bell System Laboratories in these matters is basically that of the communications engineer, not that of the linguist, though a recent development has turned them to the problem of visible speech for those who can not hear.[22] No one can utter the component frequencies listed in these tables at will and as such. The component frequencies are produced only by producing the vowel sound of which they are the formants: that is, they are produced only by making the necessary movements of the vocal organs to say these sounds.

An interesting observation concerning the vowel formants was made by A. W. De Groot.[23] If one takes a series of data giving two median formant frequencies for each vowel and plots the lower formant of each as the ordinate (on the y-axis) and the upper formant as abscissa (on the x-axis), a configuration results which suggests a correlation between these acoustic data and observations which have been made of the positions of the vocal organs, notably of the tongue, when these vowels are produced. In the accompanying graphs I have modified De Groot's procedure and applied it to the data for the vowel formants given by Paget for his own vowels (Plate 19, Fig. 1) for the English vowels of Miss Somerville (Plate 19, Fig. 2) for the French vowels of Mlle. Coustenoble[24] (Plate 20, Fig. 1), and to data based on the average values given for the vowel formants of four male speakers as reported by Crandall and Sacia[25] (Plate 20, Fig. 2). The diagram for the "eight primary cardinal vowels" devised by Daniel Jones[26] (Plate 21, Fig. 1) represents the relative positions of the highest point of the tongue when the several vowels are uttered; i.e., it is a genetic not a gennemic diagram, as indeed, was the vowel figure of Wilhelm Viëtor,[27] which I have anglicized and somewhat abbreviated in Figure 2 of Plate 21.

It will be observed that the scaling on the graphs of Plates 19 and 20 is, so far as the numerical values are concerned, that of a figure in the third quadrant rather than the customary figure of the first quadrant. Since these numbers represent frequencies and since the resonant frequency of a cavity increases as its capacity diminishes, the ordering on the graphs may be thought of as representing cavity sizes. In this event the graph becomes a normal figure of the first quadrant, that is, a graph of positive

Plate 19. VOWEL FORMANTS

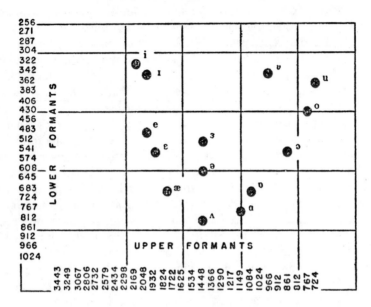

Fig. 1. Sir Richard Paget.

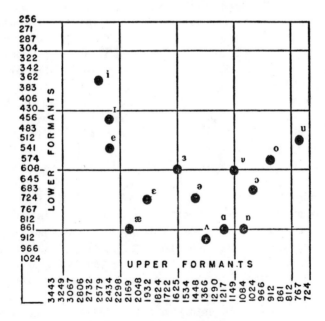

Fig. 2. Miss Somerville

Plate 20. VOWEL FORMANTS

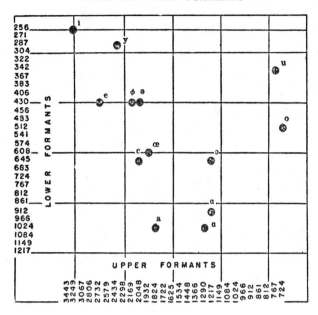

Fig. 1. Mlle. Coustenoble

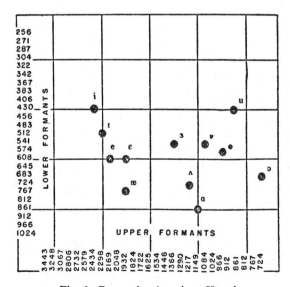

Fig. 2. Composite American Vowels

rather than of negative values. It also becomes a graph representative of physiological facts rather than a mere juggling of acoustic data if it can be shown that these formant frequencies are correlated with physical resonators which determine the character of the vowels. From the geometrical array of points determined by the lower and the upper formants thus graphed, it might appear that there may be a correlation between the

Plate 21. VOWEL DIAGRAMS

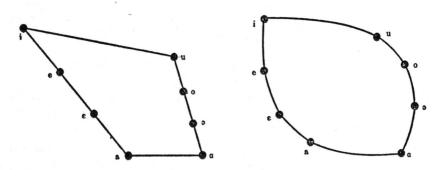

Fig. 1. Daniel Jones

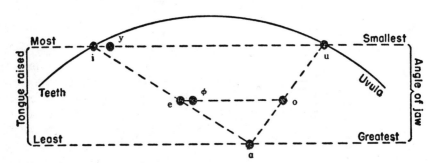

Fig. 2. Viëtor's Vowel Triangle

degree of tongue elevation and the size of the resonator producing the lower formant, in the sense that the higher the tongue is raised the larger this resonator and the lower its natural frequency of resonance will become. Also in the same way it might seem that there may be a correlation between the degree of advancement and retraction of the tongue and the size of the resonator producing the upper formant in the sense that the more advanced the tongue, the smaller this resonator, and the more retracted the tongue, the larger this resonator and hence the lower the pitch of the formant it will produce.

We know that a single frequency is a quite inadequate description of the kind of formant which acoustic analysis indicates to be operative in making the characteristic vowel configuration which is heard. Yet the possibility exists that as the peak frequency (fR) is an indicator of a resonance curve—though it does not describe this curve at all adequately —so these mean formant frequencies may be indicators of the total configurations of pitch, intensity, and phase which give the vowel wave its essential form. In any event, we find a point-to-point similarity of configuration between the graphs of acoustic data and the diagrams deduced from physiological measurements of tongue and jaw positions. Before we may discard this similarity as meaningless, we must examine the movements of the speech organs which produce our vowels.

4.03 *The Vowels, Considered Genetically*

The vowels are produced by articulatory movements of the organs of speech, which modify the vibrating breath stream as this passes from the glottis, through the pharynx, the mouth, and in some cases, also the nose. The nature of the vowel sound produced depends upon the behavior of the vocal bands; the size and coupling of the resonant cavities above them; and the amount of impedance, or damping, imposed upon the cord tone or voice.

4.031 *The Vocal Bands, Whispered Vowels*

Vowels may be voiced, murmured, or whispered. Whispered vowels are sometimes called voiceless vowels, since the voice or cord tone is replaced by a hissing sound caused by eddies in the breath stream as it rushes past obstructions in its path. It is evident[28] that the vocal bands behave variously when various vowels are whispered, and that there are other differences in their behavior when sounds are whispered softly and when they are emitted vigorously in a "stage" whisper. In the latter case, the vocal bands are notably closer together in their membranous portions while the bodies of the arytenoids are drawn apart. This produces a triangular opening with its base along the line of the cricoid between the two arytenoids and its apex at the point where the two vocal processes of the arytenoids are brought together in the median line. (Plate 9, Fig. 3) In the normal, or unforced, whisper this triangular opening is frequently not produced, and the intermembranous edges of the vocal bands are not brought quite so close together. There is, therefore, a slit-like opening between the bands for their entire length. There are also differences in the shape of this glottal opening for different whispered vowels. The margins of the vocal bands are displaced periodically, somewhat as they are in the production of voiced vowels, save that the distance between the bands is a little greater and the vibrations have much less amplitude; only the margins of the bands move appreciably, and these affect only the peripheral portions of the breath stream, which is not interrupted by their movements. The expenditure of breath in whispering is notably greater per decibel of disturbance caused in the free air at the mouth of the speaker than that in normal speaking. The sound produced in energetic whispering by the friction of the air against the intercartilaginous margins of the vocal bands is random noise, comparable with the hiss of air ejected from a narrow nozzle. The long sides of this triangular opening, indeed, are between 6.5 and 7.5 mm. in length. The vibrations of the thin edges of the vocal bands in moderate whispering may produce a periodic wave, or tone, but this is much less prominent acoustically than the fricative or random noise caused by the passage of the breath stream through the narrow slit of the glottis or through the triangular opening between the two arytenoids.

4.032   *The Vocal Bands, Voiced Vowels*

When vowels are voiced the intercartilaginous margins of the vocal bands are brought firmly together by contraction of the laryngeal muscles, and the fundamental tone produced is due to the periodic displacement of the wholly membranous portions of the vocal bands between the tips of the vocal processes of the arytenoids and the angle of the thyroid plates. The frequency of this tone depends chiefly upon the elasticity of the vocal bands, and this is conditioned (a) by the length and thickness of the bands, (b) by the amount of muscular contraction in the vocalis muscles, and (c) much less importantly, by the difference between the pressure of the air below the glottis and that of the air in the oral cavity.[29] The pattern in which the vocal bands move is a complex undulatory one, which is certainly different for different fundamental pitches of the same voice and probably different for each of the several vowel types.[30] The area of the glottal opening and the position of the epiglottis vary from vowel to vowel.[31]

4.033   *The Vocal Bands, Half-Voice*, Sotto Voce, *Murmured Vowels*

The vocal murmur, which is sometimes called half-voice, or *sotto voce*, is in a sense a compromise between full voice and whisper. It is produced by vibrations of the vocal bands; but these bands are then less elastic or more relaxed than when the normal speaking voice is produced, and the interarytenoid margins of the glottal opening are not brought firmly together, but kept slightly apart, thus never quite stopping the flow of breath. The subglottal pressure of the breath stream is somewhat lower for the production of murmured vowels than it is either for fully voiced or for whispered vowels. The vowels of weakly stressed syllables are sometimes murmured rather than fully voiced and may then be spoken of as reduced vowels. Reduced or murmured vowels have a tendency to lose their identity; whispered or fully voiced vowels are rarely obscure. This results less from the inadequacy of the vocal murmur as a carrier for the distinctive vowel forms than from the lax muscle tonus characteristic not only of the larynx but also of the other articulatory muscles when speech is murmured. These lax muscles fail adequately to give form to, or to provide modulation of, the cord tone. Evidently various degrees of this compromise between full voice and whisper are possible, and some languages use a kind of murmur in which the flow of the breath stream produces a notable fricative hiss in addition to the reduced cord tone. This has been called "breathy voice" and is found regularly interchanging with full voice, for example in the Madi dialects of the Eastern Sudan.[32]

4.04   *Vocal Resonators*

The vibrating breath stream of vowels, whether voiced, whispered, or murmured, enters the pharynx, and between the level of the glottis and the exterior of the lips (and nostrils, if the nasal cavities are involved) certain of the partials of the cord tone are reinforced while others are damped out. Damping is accomplished either by the absorption of the energy of certain partial tones when the vibrating air strikes against soft-textured surfaces, or by the neutralization of these vibratory movements by other movements set up in the spaces into which the breath stream enters. Reinforcement will occur when the vibrating breath stream of the vowel causes the air latent in spaces through or past which it moves to vibrate in tune with one or more of the partial tones which it comprises. Such spaces then become resonators and as such are comparatively broadly tuned; that is, they will respond to any vibrations relatively close in frequency to their own characteristic period.

Two types of action in such resonators must be contemplated: (a) selective transmission, in which some of the partials are passed through the cavity undiminished, while others are damped or reduced in strength by the vibrations induced in the cavity by partials selectively passed; and (b) reinforcement by the vibration of standing waves in the cavity, set up by one or more of the partials of the cord tone. By far the greater part of the total energy of any speech sound is in its fundamental and first harmonic.[33] For men's voices these frequencies are far below the critical formant frequencies which determine the vowel quality. However, the sensitivity of the human ear is considerably more acute within the range of the formant frequencies than it is within the range of the fundamentals and the correlation between the quantity of acoustic energy and the strength of the resultant sensation is not a linear one.

The search for resonant cavities which may be attuned to the appropriate formants of the several vowels, or for resonators which give the vowels their peculiar acoustic configurations has been resolute but inconclusive. The factors involved are chiefly (1) the volume of the cavity or resonator, (2) the areas of the openings into and out of the cavity, and (3) the number of cavities joined or coupled into a system and the effect of the coupling upon the individual resonance characteristics of the cavities involved. The relationships for a simple resonator with a single orifice and a short "neck" are approximately[34]

$$f = \frac{V_s}{2\pi} \sqrt{\frac{A}{LV_0}}$$

f = frequency, V_s = velocity of sound, A = area of orifice, L = length of "neck" and V_0 = volume of resonator.

4.05   *Three Typical Vowel Positions*

It is generally supposed that there is a position, or an array of positions, taken by the various organs of articulation which corresponds to and is correlated with the "steady" portions of the acoustic records of vowel sounds. Frequently in rapid speech there are no steady positions of vowel wave trains in such records, and it is probable that in such cases the "positions" described as characteristic of the various vowel sounds are simply limits of motion toward which the integrated, flowing movements of speech tend. On the other hand, there is no doubt that sustained vowel sounds mean sustained organic positions, and there is little to be gained by denying that a sustained [i] vowel is quite as much an [i] as the most abbreviated version one might find in rapid speech. The precise relationship between the two versions of the "same" vowel may require defining but there is in that fact no bar to the scrutiny of sustained articulations.

It is clear from the physiological descriptions typified in the cardinal vowel figure of Daniel Jones,[35] and it is also urged on purely acoustic grounds,[36] that the vowels [i] as in *beat*, (u) as in *boot*, and [ɑ] as in Midwest American *father* or *pot*, represent three extreme types of vowel sound: [i] has maximum front elevation of the tongue, [u] has maximum back elevation of the tongue, and [ɑ] has minimum elevation in either sense. (Plate 22)

The moving parts which can change the size of the pharyngeal and oral cavities through which the vibrating air of the cord tone flows are (1) the larynx, which may be raised, lowered, protracted, or retracted; (2) the epiglottis, which may swing on its hinge back over the lumen of the

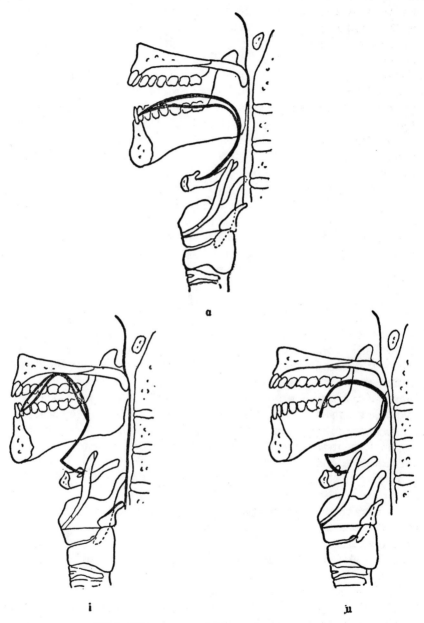

Plate 22. THREE VOWEL ARTICULATIONS

larynx, or forward away from that opening; (3) the tongue, the movements of which largely control the position of the front wall of the pharynx and the floor of the mouth; (4) the jaw, which may be raised or lowered; (5) the velum, which when raised enlarges the mouth cavity and shuts it off from the nasal pharynx and when lowered enlarges the nasal pharynx and couples this with the oral pharynx and the latter with the nasal cavities above it; (6) the lips, which control the area of the opening of the most anterior of the oral cavities. Not one of these parts is indispensable to the production of adequate or acceptable vowel sounds. (1) The larynx may be removed entirely, and intelligible speech can be produced by means of some other source of sound. The sound waves from an artificial larynx may be introduced into the oral cavity through a tube held in the corner of the mouth. One form of this device was built into a briar tobacco pipe.[37] (2) The epiglottis may be removed clear down to its cushion without destroying either the facility of speaking or the ability readily to swallow food. (3) The entire tongue may be removed and the victim can learn to produce satisfactory vowel sounds.[38] (4) The observed movements of the jaw, upon which the much criticized "Kieferwinkel" diagram of Viëtor is based, are evidently not essential to the production of the different vowels. Anyone can pronounce all of the vowels with his teeth tightly clenched. I can pronounce acceptable vowels of each type with my teeth propped apart 30 mm. When I increase this distance to 35 mm. I can no longer produce an acceptable [i] vowel. I make no pretensions to virtuosity in these endeavors. (5) The velum may be up or down without essentially changing the character of the sound produced,[39] except, of course, that one cannot produce the true nasal vowels with the velum fully raised. So far as our three typical vowels sounds, [i], [u], [ɑ], are concerned, the position of the velum is not critical. (6) The lips are usually spread for [i], and neutral but wide open for [ɑ], while for [u] a small lip aperture is normal. None of these lip articulations is essential, as one may observe by holding the lips widely apart or close together while producing the several vowel sounds.

If now we ask how we are able to produce the vowel sounds we wish when we thus eliminate one or the other of the movements normally made in their production, the self-evident answer is: by means of compensating adjustments of the movements of the other organs involved. If deprived of vocal bands we make a cord tone either with the ventricular bands, the lips of the esophagus, or by means of an external source of sound, or artificial larynx. If deprived of an epiglottis we may adjust somewhat the movements of the base of the tongue. There is no reliable detailed description of the compensating adjustments made by speakers who have lost their tongues. One can see for himself what adjustments of tongue movements he makes when he props his jaws apart and tries to produce the "high" vowels [i] or [u]. Movements of the velum may affect the timbre of the sound without changing its characteristic form. Variations in lip positions are made good by minor adjustments of tongue movements. Studies which show that this or that factor, ordinarily thought to be involved in vowel production, may be altered or eliminated without destroying the vowel quality are meaningless unless they at the same time describe the compensatory adjustments which are made elsewhere in the movements involved, or unless they prove that no such adjustments are made. Very little satisfactory work has been done in this field.[40]

On the other hand, whereas we may not say of any given articulatory movement that this must be just so and not otherwise if the desired vowel is to be produced, we may quite properly say of our X-ray pictures of speech articulations that these are the movements or the positions which occurred when this vowel was produced. If we had enough properly collected evidence of this kind we might be able to say with validity what is the usual movement or position of the various articulatory organs when the several vowels are produced. Phoneticians have not yet clearly enough realized that in these matters the statistical techniques of the biological sciences must be applied. Put baldly, we may not say that if one wishes to produce the vowel [i], one must raise the blade of the tongue toward the palate so that only a shallow but broad channel remains between the tongue and the roof of the mouth, while the main body and base of the tongue are drawn forward and up so that behind this shallow channel a large pharyngeal tube is produced. Meanwhile, one must draw the velum back, shutting off the nasal pharynx, and raise the jaw so that the teeth are perhaps 1.5 mm. apart; the lips may be either neutral or slightly spread. We may say, however, that most speakers appear to produce their [i] vowel in this way. We ought to be able to prove that statement statistically.[41] No single drawing of the position of the articulatory organs for the production of any given vowel could be said to have general validity, but much may reasonably be said concerning the various types of articulations usually correlated with the various types of vowel sounds. The description just given for the [i] vowel represents what one usually finds on the pictures of its articulation, minor variations excepted.

The vowel [u] is usually articulated by drawing the dorsum of the tongue back toward the isthmus faucium and up toward the uvula or velum, thereby forming a relatively narrow channel for the breath stream between the back wall of the oral pharynx and the upper surface of the dorsum of the tongue. The cavity below this constriction is notably smaller than that formed for the vowel [i], despite the fact that the larynx itself is lowered somewhat when [u] is articulated. The opening of this back cavity into the space in front of the constriction is a little wider than the opening from the back cavity of the [i] articulation into the broad but shallow channel between the tongue blade and the prepalatal region.

It is probable that the resonating system for the [i] vowel is most similar to a simple resonator of the bottle type and that the broad shallow channel is analogous in its function to the neck of the bottle.[42] The typical articulation of [u], however, produces rather two resonators, coupled by a narrow channel over the "hump" of the dorsum of the tongue. The individual frequencies of the two cavities thus produced are not just those of simple resonators, but each affects the other and both are affected by the conductivity (i.e., the area of a cross section divided by the length) of the opening between them, as well as by that of the opening at the lips and to a lesser extent, by that at the glottis.[43]

A striking illustration of the compensation possible in such articulations is offered by Grandgent's drawings of the front resonators for his own and Dr. Hochdoerfer's pronunciations of [u]. Grandgent's cavity is distinctly the smaller and on that account its resonance should be notably higher than that of Hochdoerfer, but the area of Grandgent's lip opening is very much less than that of Hochdoerfer, and on that account the resonance of his cavity should be much the lower of the two. I have no acoustic data for these two [u] sounds, but I know, from having heard them frequently and over periods of years, that both men pronounced what we should call a "close" [u], and this would indicate that the lower formant in each case was about the same.[44] (Plate 23)

On the basis of its apparent volume alone, the back cavity for [u] should have a resonant frequency much higher than that of the back cavity for [i], while the front cavity for [u] is very much larger than that for [i] and on that basis alone should have a much lower resonant frequency. As a matter of fact, the lower formant for [u] is, in general, about the same as that for [i], say 400 c.p.s. for [u] and 375 c.p.s. for [i], whereas the upper formant for [u] is maximally different from that for [i], say 800 c.p.s. for [u], and 2,400 c.p.s. for [i].[45] There is little doubt that the shallow channel of the front cavity for [i] (the neck of the bottle) is the usual source of the reinforcement of the high partials which give us the upper formant of this vowel. The lower formant for [i] would then appear to result from reinforcement or selective transmission in the large pharyngeal cavity behind the elevated tongue. If the same relation between cavities and formants exists for [u], the lower formant for this vowel should then also come from the back resonator, and this, since its volume is much less than that for [i] and its resonant frequency about the same, must get its lower pitch partly from the effect of the reaction of the front cavity upon it, but particularly from the conductivity of the connecting opening between the two resonators. This opening must have a relatively small cross-sectional area, or a relatively great length, or something of both, to reduce the frequency of the smaller cavity to about that of the much larger resonator for [i]. In the case of the disparity between the two front resonators we may at least say that this is in the same sense as the disparity between the formants, and the much larger resonator for [u] may be correlated with the much lower upper formant for that vowel. And, we may add, the high formant of the vowel [i] has considerable energy and appears to result

Plate 23. TWO ARTICULATIONS OF [u]

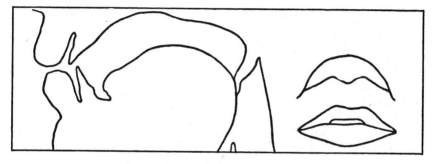

Fig. 1. [u] in English *pool* (Grandgent)

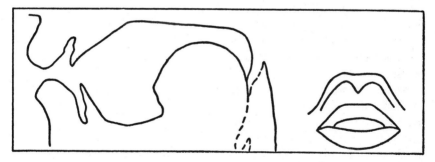

Fig. 2. [u] in German *Mut* (Hochdoerfer)

from standing vibrations in the shallow "neck of the bottle,"[46] while the upper partial for [u] is relatively weak, so much so in fact, that D. C. Miller did not include it in his characteristic curves of the vowels.[47] Hence it is possible that the action of the front resonator for the vowel [u] is of a type different from that of the front resonator for the vowel [i].

The articulation of the vowel [ɑ], as this is found in Midwestern *father*, *pot*, or as it is represented in French *bas*, *pâte*, or *part*, varies over a considerable range. The dorsum and blade of the tongue are low, or flat, in the mouth, not lifted or arched as in [u] or [i]. The constriction between the cavity of the pharynx and that of the mouth is made a little lower down in the oral pharynx and indeed only slightly above the tip of the epiglottis. As a result, the back cavity for [ɑ] is smaller than that for either [u] or [i]. The front cavity on the other hand is much larger than for the other vowels considered, but the lip opening is also large, and this prevents the resonance here from becoming as low in pitch as the volume of the cavity would otherwise make it. The formant frequencies for [ɑ] appear to be approximately 825 and 1,200 c.p.s.[48] In any case, the pitch of the back cavity is considerably higher for [ɑ] than it is for [u] or [i], viz., 825 c.p.s. *vs.* 400 and 375 c.p.s. respectively. In the case of a simple resonator in which only the volume was changed this difference would represent a reduction of the size of the resonator for [ɑ] to one fourth that of the resonator for [u]. Changes in the conductivity of the opening between back and front resonators which would result from increasing the area of its cross section or decreasing its length would tend also to raise the frequency of the resonator, thus making necessary somewhat less reduction in volume. The front resonator for [ɑ] has perhaps no greater volume than that for [u], but it has a much greater opening and its pitch is therefore higher, say 1,200 c.p.s. as compared with 800 c.p.s.

In the case of each of these three typical vowel articulations the acoustic data at our disposal in the various tables of vowel formants have been so far reconcilable with the physical facts as to the relative size of cavity and openings as shown by X-ray pictures that one may not deny the possibility that a significant correlation between the physiological and the acoustic data may be found. The problem is very complex because of the large number of compensatory variables which appear in the data.

When one studies the available evidence for the precise form of the articulations of the other vowels, one sees that the vowels [i], [ɪ], [e], [ɛ], [y], [ʏ], [ø], [œ], [æ], [a] appear to form a progression or series of stages different rather in degree than in kind, so far as the nature of the potential resonators is concerned. Similarly, the vowels [u], [ʊ], [o], [ɔ], [ɒ], [ɑ] may be regarded as a progression or series of stages. The evidence for the "uh-vowels," [ɜ], [ə], is anything but ample, but these vowels appear not to belong with either of the two foregoing groups, and so to constitute a group alone. It appears reasonable to suggest that in the series of vowels from [i] to [a] there may well be a correlation between the degree of fronting and the pitch of both the high and the low formants, in the sense that the more the entire tongue is drawn forward the smaller the cavity between the blade of the tongue and the palate, and hence the higher the high formant, while by the same movement the front wall of the pharynx is progressively drawn away from the back wall, thus yielding a progressively larger back cavity and a lower low formant. The case of the series [u] to [ɑ] is more problematical. There may be a correlation between the elevation of the body of the tongue towards the soft palate in the sense that the higher the tongue is raised the smaller the oral cavity becomes and hence the higher the pitch of the upper formant. The observed differences, however, are relatively minute and may readily be offset by changes in the lip aperture. The low formant is made lower for [u] however, not by the lifting of the body of the tongue, but by the lowering of the larynx. The differences here are of considerable magnitude and agree with the acoustic data in that the lowest formant appears to be correlated with the largest cavity and the highest of the low formants with the smallest pharyngeal cavity. If these or similar inferences can be at all maintained, we may not discard as meaningless the correspondence between the configuration of the vowel figure from physiological measurements and that of the vowel figure obtained by graphing the acoustic data. Until positive demonstrations are available we must leave a final decision on this point in abeyance.[49]

4.06   *The Classification of Vowels*

FRONT, BACK, CENTRAL

If we concede meanwhile that the series of vowels [i] to [a] as indicated by the acoustic data and as given by the descriptions of the articulatory movements do indeed constitute a group, we may properly continue to call this group the front vowels, since the most readily observed characteristic of each is the usual position of the front part of the blade of the tongue. The most clearly observable variable in the production of the vowels of the series [u] to [ɑ] is the narrow channel in the upper pharynx which is formed when the body of the tongue is drawn back. Hence these vowels may properly be called by their traditional name, the back vowels. The most evident characteristic of the "uh-vowels" is the neutral position of the body of the tongue with respect either to fronting or to retraction. Hence we may call these vowels, which are neither front nor back vowels, the central vowels.

HIGH, MID, LOW

Within the front series we recognize vowels of the type [i], of the type [e], and of the type [a]. In the back series we find vowels of the types [u], [o], and [ɑ]. The central vowels are of the type [ə]. Under normal conditions there is not only a distinctive tongue articulation associated with each of these vowel types, but also, in all probability, a distinctive laryngeal articulation peculiar to each type.[50] If names be desired for these three types within each series, we should retain the traditional terms and speak of high vowels [i] and [u], mid vowels [e] and [o], and low vowels [a] and [ɑ]. The high vowels then turn out to be those for which the lower resonator is largest, the low vowels those for which this resonator is smallest, while the mid vowels show resonators of intermediate frequencies. These facts are paralleled by and probably correlated with the facts as to normal tongue elevation, in the sense that the high vowels have the greatest degree of tongue elevation in their particular series, and the low vowels the least. Neither criterion gives us a definition of the boundary lines between mid vowels and high vowels on the one hand, or mid vowels and low vowels on the other, but the types are linguistically distinct, so that speakers of languages in which they occur will perceptually assign to its proper class any vowel that occurs.

NARROW : WIDE, TENSE : LAX, CLOSE : OPEN

Phonologic oppositions such as English *heat*:*hit*, *late*:*let*, *pool*:*pull*, *coat*:*caught*, or German *bieten*:*bitten*, *stehlen*:*stellen*, *Bruch* (Hose): *Bruch* (Brechung), *Schoß*:*schoss*, *Hüte*:*Hütte*, *Sohne*:*Sonne*, suggest that perhaps the vowels [ɪ], [ɛ], [ʊ], [ɔ] represent types distinct from [i], [e], [u], [o], despite the fact that it is customary to classify [ɪ] with [i], [ɛ] with [e], [ʊ] with [u], and [ɔ] with [o]. Sweet regarded [i] as the narrow form of the high front vowel and [ɪ] as the wide form thereof, because he thought that the body of the tongue was bunched for [i] and more flat for [ɪ]. He made the same distinction for the other vowel types in question here.[51] Later scholars have substituted the terms tense and lax for narrow and wide, and recognized that this tenseness applied not merely to the tongue muscles but to the entire articulating complex.[52] Still others have called [i], [e], [u], [o] close (fermées) and [ɪ], [ɛ], [ʊ], [ɔ] open (ouvertes). Still others incline to treat the second group as short forms of the first, which they then call long. Phonologic oppositions such as those cited prove the acoustic discreteness of the vowels involved, and there is nothing in the acoustic data which permits us to class [ɪ] with [i], or [ɛ] with [e], or to group any of the rest together. In fact, from the acoustic data we can really differentiate as discrete types only the front, the central, and the back vowels, or the vowels of the types [i], [u], and [ɜ]. The distinctions we have called high, mid, and low appear to reflect differences in degree only, and not differences of kind, so far as the acoustic data reveal the characteristics of the several vowels. When we examine the evidence for the tongue positions characteristic of the vowels we collide with disturbing facts such as E. A. Meyer's demonstration[53] that the elevation of the tongue for [ɪ] is often a good deal less than that for the vowel [e], or the observation of Henry Sweet,[54] that one may produce either the series [i], [e], [æ] or the series [ɪ], [ɛ], [æ] by continuously changing the tongue elevation without producing any of the supposedly "intervening" vowels of the other series as the tongue is raised or lowered. In short, the difference between [ɪ] and [e] or between [e] and [ɛ], or between [i] and [ɪ], is not due merely to a difference in the elevation of the tongue. The inviting hypothesis that there are in the several laryngeal articulations three types for each series, front and back, and that the laryngeal articulation, let us say, for the high category is then subject to modification by the tension and position of the tongue into two subtypes [i] and [ɪ], is apparently untenable in the light of Meyer's findings as to the breath consumption or "Luftfüllung" of the various vowels.[55] According to these studies [ɪ] and [ɛ] are produced with a wider glottis and a greater volume of air-flow than are the vowels [i] and [e]. This implies that the subglottal air pressures are less for the [ɪ] and [ɛ] type vowels than for [i] and [e]. However, these facts do permit us to apply the terms open : close or lax : tense to the two groups in the sense that the glottal opening and the air pressures are relatively open and lax for vowels like [ɪ] and [ɛ], while the glottal opening and the air pressures are relatively close and tense for vowels like [i] and [e]. We may retain the old terminology if we shift its reference from tongue elevations and tongue muscle tensions to laryngeal positions and air pressures.

We have then not only differences in tongue position but differences in laryngeal behavior which mark the differences in quality observed between [i] and [ɪ] or between [e] and [ɛ], or between [e] and [ɪ]. Nowhere do we find an adequate basis for classifying [ɪ] with [i], [ɛ] with [e], [ʊ] with [u], [ʏ] with [y] or [œ] with [ø]. The vowels [ɪ] [ɛ], and some forms of [æ] might be said to compose a series of high, mid, and low open front vowels as contrasted with the close front vowels [i], [e], and other forms of [æ]. Among the rounded front vowels [ʏ] and [œ] appear to be parallel [y] and [ø] in much the same way, but neither member of these pairs can be shown to be a conditioned variant of the other nor yet of any hypothetical type-vowel standing as the source of each of the members of the class. Nevertheless there is an undeniable, if undefinable, relationship which links the vowels [i], [ɪ], [y], [ʏ] together, just as it unites the vowels [e], [ɛ], [ø], and [œ]. The discreteness of the individual vowels in each of these groups is probably more definitely marked than that which can be found in the high back or mid back categories, although [u] vs. [ʊ], and [o] vs. [ɔ] are clearly marked contrasts. In the low categories, front and back, the corresponding differences are not generally significant linguistically, and hence are less readily observed. Despite our inability to give wholly adequate reasons, either acoustic or physiological, for the fact,[56] it still is a fact that [i], [ɪ], [y], and [ʏ] are to our perception [i]-type vowels rather than [e]-type vowels, and that [e], [ɛ], [ø], and [œ] are [e]-type vowels rather than any other type one may name. Practical phonetics here demands a grouping for which scientific phonetics has thus far failed to produce an adequate basis. Sweet observed: "A narrow vowel may be widened by trying to utter it as lazily and listlessly as possible, without altering the position of the tongue.[57] Meyer notes: "The [i] vowel, when unstressed passes, because of the reduced tension of the tongue muscles and the reduced tension of the vocal bands incident to the reduced stress, into the vowel [ɪ]."[58] Every one knows that the vowel [y] may most readily be produced by "saying [i] and rounding the lips," although it is clear enough that the actual tongue position for [y] is considerably lower than normally found for [i]. For reasons such as these, we shall discuss the vowels by types and try in each case to refer the characteristics of the individual vowels to one representative of the type which may be most generally known.

ROUNDED, UNROUNDED

On the basis of the behavior of the lips during their production vowels may be classified as rounded or unrounded. Unrounded vowels are produced either with the muscles of the lips quite inactive or neutral, or with the contraction of the several sets of muscles which draw back the corners of the lips and bare the teeth. This is called the spread lip position. The vowels [i] and [e] are frequently produced with spread lips. Rounded vowels are produced when the area of the aperture of the mouth cavity is reduced by contraction of the muscles of the lips. There are two types of lip rounding. (a) A long narrow slit is produced between the two lips by bringing the lips vertically nearer each other. This is called vertical lip rounding. (b) A horizontally short, more or less oval opening is produced by closing the lips from the corners toward the center until only a small aperture remains. This is called horizontal lip rounding.

Protrusion of the lips is often a concomitant of horizontal lip rounding. It is much less frequently found with vertical lip rounding. However, it is the size of the opening and not its shape which determines the acoustic quality of the sound, and lip protrusion is not essential to lip rounding. Lip rounding is by no means restricted to the production of vowels. Consonants and whole syllables may be accompanied by lip rounding, but its use as a distinctive feature of sound production is largely with syllabic sounds.

BASIS OF ARTICULATION

It is clear that there are certain general peculiarities of utterance which characterize the speech movements of whole groups of speakers. One of the most important of these is sometimes spoken of as the general basis of articulation. The matter deserves much more careful treatment than it has yet received. It has, however, been observed that in some dialects or languages the position of the tongue from which its articulatory movements start and to which it tends to return is relatively low and retracted, with the tongue surface quite broad. All of the movements of the tongue are made to harmonize with this habitual attitude, or "Indifferenzlage" of the organ, and the vowels particularly are then marked by dullness rather than by brightness of timbre. Some groups of speakers join with this generally low level tongue position a tendency to allow the lips to remain largely passive. In other regions the whole level of the tongue in its speech movements is higher and more in the front of the mouth. The tongue is more tense and the movements are quicker. Often in such cases the lips are notably active. French is a language which is usually spoken from a high and tense forward basis of articulation. German is intermediate between French and English in this respect, for English is spoken from a comparatively low and relaxed basis of articulation. On the whole, American English is even less energetically enunciated than British English. These are broad generalizations to which there are many individual exceptions. They are, moreover, supported only by the observations of men like Storm, Sievers, and Jespersen. No method of measurement has been devised which would permit the mathematical description of a basis of articulation.

4.07   Vowels of the Type [i]: High Front Vowels

We must recognize in the category of high front vowels at least two unrounded vowels [i] and [ɪ], and two rounded vowels [y] and [ʏ].

The high front unrounded close, or tense, vowel [i] is the sound of the stressed vowel in French *vivre*, *vif*, German *Biene*, and English *heat*. The lips, when they participate in the articulation of this vowel at all, are spread, the corners being drawn back to some extent. The apex and blade of the tongue lie parallel to and slightly below the curve of the hard palate. The velum is raised high, cutting off the nasopharynx from the mouth. French [i] is likely to be higher, more tense and close than German [i], while English [i] is usually less strongly fronted and less tense than either. Indeed, English [i] is often a diphthongal rather than a pure vowel. This means that the sound begins as a relatively lax [i] and becomes more tense or close as it develops, so that a difference of quality becomes apparent. One may transcribe this diphthongal sound either as [ɪi] or as [ij], according as one observes its initial portion to sound like the vowel of *fit* or like that of *feet*. The diphthongal form is most likely to occur when the vowel is final or when it precedes a voiced consonant. The pure [i] vowels of French and German are pure because the articulation is maintained without notable shifting during the brief stable portion of the vowel sound. One may say that the English vowel [ɪi] in many regions is diphthongal because it is slow to reach its full form [i], whereas the French and German vowels starting from a basis of articulation more tense and farther forward, reach their full form promptly. Whether it be [ɪi] or [ij], the diphthongal form of [i] results from increasing closeness of the articulation and not from its relaxation.

The high front rounded close, or tense, vowel [y] is the sound of the accented vowel of French *ruse, russe,* or German *Lyrik, Bühne.* This vowel is not a part of the normal English vowel system. In German as in French the lips are usually strongly rounded. This does not of necessity imply the pursing or protrusion of the lips, but means always that the aperture at the lips is made quite small. Indeed, the protrusion of the lips for [y] is considerably less general than it is for [u]. The velum is high, as it is for [i]. The tongue position in French is approximately the same as that used for [i], and there is no notable difference in this respect between the long vowel of *ruse* and the short vowel of *russe.* In German, [y] in words like *Lyrik, Physiker, Mythe* is commonly pronounced as French [y] is pronounced, save that the basis of articulation is not quite so high. The [y] of native German words, on the other hand, is frequently produced with a notable lowering of the level of the tongue, its general position being about that found for German [e]. The resulting increase in the size of the resonance cavity is offset by a very close rounding of the lips, that is, by a very small aperture, and the quality of the [y] thus produced is clearly that of the vowel type [i], not [e].

The high front unrounded lax, or open, vowel [ɪ] is the sound of the stressed vowel of German *Fisch, bitten,* or of English *fish, bitter.* This vowel is not a part of the normal French vowel system. The lips, when not quite neutral in the pronunciation of this vowel, are spread slightly. The velum is raised less vigorously than for [i], and hence not quite so high, though the occlusion of the nasopharynx is complete. The laryngeal articulation is lax, or open, rather than tense, or close, so that the quantity of air emitted is greater than in the case of [i]. The articulation of the tongue has the same general form as that for [i], save that it is, both in North German and in English, often farther from the arch of the palate than it is for the close vowel [e] of German *beten* or of English *hay.* On the other hand, the level of the tongue is frequently somewhat higher than that found for [e]. These variations are compensated for by changes in lip aperture, and perhaps also in laryngeal articulation, in ways not yet adequately described.

The high front rounded lax, or open, vowel [ʏ] is the sound of the stressed vowel in German *Hütte, Glück.* This vowel is not a part of the normal French vowel system or of the English vowel system. It is the relaxed counterpart of German [y] in native words. The level of the tongue blade is approximately that of the [ɛ] of *hätte*, but the lip rounding and the laryngeal articulation give the vowel the quality of an [i] vowel, rather than that of [e].

4.08　*Vowels of the Type* [e]: *Mid Front Vowels*

In the category of the mid front vowels we must recognize at least two unrounded vowels, [e] and [ɛ], and two rounded vowels, [ø] and [œ].

The mid front unrounded close, or tense, vowel [e] is the sound of the stressed vowels in French *été, fée*, German *beten*, or English *hate*. The lips, when they participate in the articulation of this vowel at all, are spread and the lip aperture is likely to be only slightly larger for [e] than it is for [i]. The velum closes the opening into the nasopharynx, but is not quite so high or so tense as for [i]. French [e] and German [e] are pure vowels, the former usually slightly higher and farther front than the latter. The shape of the tongue is in every particular similar to that for [i] save that the space between the tongue and the palate is somewhat greater throughout. The degree of fronting is less. English [e], notably in the standard speech of southern Britain, is pretty generally diphthongized, even before voiceless consonants, as in *bait, make*. The diphthongal form of [e] is usually [ei], that is, the vowel starts as a relatively close [e] and ends as an [i]. A relaxed form of the diphthongal vowel may be written [ɛe] to indicate that the initial portion is rather like [ɛ] in *bet* than like [e] in *fate*, and that the end portion is then correspondingly lower than in [ei], being more nearly [e] than [i].

The mid front rounded close, or tense, vowel [ø] is the sound of the stressed vowel of French *peu, deux*, or of German *Öl, Söhne*. It is not a part of the normal English vowel system. The lips are likely to be strongly rounded both in German and in French, although protrusion of the lips is often very slight or quite missing. The velum is raised as for [e]. The same difference exists between French [ø] and German [ø] as is found to distinguish French [y] from German [y]. The French basis of articulation is generally higher and more tense than the German. The tongue position for French [ø] is approximately that taken for French [e], while for German [ø] the general elevation of the tongue is notably lower than that for German [e], being very nearly the level usually found for English [ɛ], as in *bet*.

The mid front unrounded open, or lax, vowel [ɛ] is the sound of the stressed vowel in French *père, tête, tette*, German *Träne, Rätsel, Herz, Nächte*, English *met, said, head*. In French the distinctive difference between *bête:bette, faîte, fête:faites, la greffe:le greffe, maître, mètre:mettre, reine: renne, scène:senne, tête:tette, treize:très* is the quantitative difference alone and not a difference of quality. So also in standard German the distinctive difference between *träfe:treffe, Träne:trenne, Zähre:zerre, Täler:Teller* is purely quantitative, but the number of words showing this opposition is not large. In English the vowel [ɛ] is rarely long. The lips are either neutral or slightly spread for this vowel. The velum is raised, closing off the nasopharynx, with about the same elevation and energy as that found for [ɪ]. The shape of the tongue is in all essential features the same as that found for [ɪ], but the level of its upper surface is somewhat lower throughout. The mouth cavity is thus larger for [ɛ] than for [ɪ], the pharyngeal cavity smaller.

The mid front rounded open, or lax, vowel [œ] is the sound of the stressed vowel in French *peur, beurre, veuve, peuple, boeuf, jeune,* and in German *möchte, plötzlich, Götter.* This vowel is not a part of the normal English vowel system. French has both a long and a short [œ] but this quantitative difference appears not to be used distinctively. German has only short [œ]. The lips are slightly rounded for [œ], the velum is raised as for [ɛ], and the tongue position is essentially that of [ɛ]. Germans, for example, have to be warned to round the lips, lest *möchte* sound like *Mächte,* or *können* like *kennen.*[59]

4.09   *Vowels of the Type* [a]: *Low Front Vowels*

In the category of the low front vowels we have to recognize at least three unrounded vowels, which we may transcribe narrowly as [æ], [a+] and [a].

The vowel [a] is the sound of the stressed vowel in Italian *acqua.* For it, as for the other vowels of this type, the lips are usually neutral but may be slightly spread. The velum is raised to shut off the naso-pharynx and the level of its elevation is about that found for [ɛ]. The tongue has the same general shape as that observed for [ɛ], but it is lowered in the mouth cavity until its dorsum is almost, if not quite flat. The apical region of the blade of the tongue is thus considerably farther from the hard palate than for [ɛ], but the arch of the dorsum under the velum is appreciably closer to the velum at the fauces than it is for the vowel [ɛ]. The element of fronting is at its minimum. The base of the tongue fits snugly against the epiglottis, without pushing this back into the clear, tube-like resonator. Any further lowering of the level of the tongue in the mouth, however, will force the base of the tongue back toward the posterior wall of the pharynx, producing a constriction which divides the pharyngeal resonator into two parts, one of which becomes part of the front resonance cavity, which then includes the mouth and approximately the upper third of the pharynx. The pharyngeal cavity below this constriction is considerably smaller than the pharyngeal resonator for [a], but the effect of the narrow channel above it about offsets the decrease of volume, so that the pitch of the low formant produced here is not greatly changed. The pitch of the upper formant is notably lowered by the addition of the upper part of the pharynx to the mouth cavity to make its resonator. The vowel which results from this retraction of the tongue from the [a] position is the low back vowel [ɑ]. The formants given by Paget for the vowel [a+] are 1,084 and 1,932 c.p.s. and those for [ɑ] are 1,024 and 1,290 c.p.s. for the French of Mlle. Coustenoble.[60]

The vowel [a+] is the somewhat fronted or palatalized form of [a] which is found in French *patte, madame,* and to some extent in various regional forms of English as a substitute for [æ] in such words as *fast, chance, bath.* Standard Southern English and some American speech uses [ɑ] in words of this kind.[61]

The vowel [æ] is a still more strongly fronted [a] vowel, which approaches the general position and character of [ɛ]. This is the usual sound of the vowel in English *cab, catch, bad* in American and in most British speech. Northern and Midland English speakers tend to substitute some form of [a+] for [æ]. Cockney substitutions of [ɛ] for [æ] are frequent in London and not unknown in America. In Pennsylvania and the southeastern states a raised, and often lengthened variety of [æ] is the normal vowel of words like *bad, bath.* The sound of this closer [æ] approaches the sound of [ɛ:] or [e] heard in other regions but remains distinct from the sounds of these vowels in its own locale.[62] The sound [æ] is not a part of the normal vowel systems of French or of German.

Unless the difference between [a+] and [a] is used to mark a difference in meaning in the dialect to be transcribed the symbol [a] may be used for either sound. The difference between [æ] and [a+] in English is not a distinctive difference and in a broad transcription one may use either [æ] or [a] throughout for the vowel sounds of this category. There is a stylistic or a regional difference in the use of [æ] and of [a] in words like *half, bath, ask, aunt,* which may make the use of a narrow transcription with both symbols desirable.[63]

4.10　*Vowels of the Type* [ɑ]: *Low Back Vowels*

In the category of the low back vowels we have to recognize at least one unrounded vowel [ɑ] and one rounded vowel [ɒ].

The unrounded low back vowel [ɑ] is the sound of the stressed vowel in French *pâte, pas, trois.* The vowel of American English *father, calm, not,* and the usual vowel of German *Abt, Gras,* is a slightly advanced [ɑ+]. The Southern British vowel [ɑ] is very much like the French [ɑ]. The lips are usually neutral, but when they participate at all in the articulation of this vowel they are spread. The opening of the mouth is relatively wide. The velum normally is lifted to close the nasopharynx, but often this closure is lax and in some instances it is not even approximated, the velum remaining inert. The upper surface of the tongue is flat in the mouth, as for [ɑ], but the dorsum is much lower under the velum because the whole body of the tongue is drawn back and downward, so that a narrow channel is formed between the base of the tongue and the back wall of the pharynx. The lowest form of [ɑ] is made when this channel is formed as far down in the pharynx as the tongue can readily be drawn. The slightly advanced forms of [ɑ+] result from a slight generally forward and upward movement of this tongue articulation. When this advancement reaches the place where no narrowing of the pharynx is caused there is then no retraction of the tongue and the vowel is no longer the low back vowel but the low front vowel [a]. It is possible to distinguish at least four unrounded vowels in these two low categories, namely [ɑ], [ɑ+], [a], [a+], but no one language is likely to employ more than two of these four sounds distinctively.

The rounded low back vowel [ɒ] is the usual sound of the stressed vowel in British *not, long, sorry*. It has very nearly the articulation of [ɑ] except that the lips are slightly rounded. That is, the area of the lip opening is reduced somewhat. This vowel is not a part of the normal vowel systems of French or German. In American speech the vowels of many of the words of this class are frequently pronounced with [ɑ+] rather than [ɒ], though in some parts of the South and in New England [ɒ] may be heard in such words as *holiday, hot, watch, quality, swallow, what, pod, god*. In American English, however, the vowel [ɒ] is quite generally used as the accented vowel of words like *awful, wall, ought, water*. This vowel is articulated with a lower tongue level than that usual for American [ɑ+] of *father*, because the tongue is more strongly drawn back to the position of [ɑ] as in French *bois*. The mouth resonator is therefore about as large as it can be made and its pitch is still further reduced by whatever lip rounding may take place. The less the lips are rounded, the larger this front cavity needs to be, and hence the stronger the retraction of the tongue must be. Since many Americans use very little lip rounding for the vowel of *awful, loss, author*, the tongue is very strongly retracted when they produce this [ɒ]. The British vowel of these words is not [ɒ] but [ɔ] and belongs in the category of the [o] type vowels.[64]

4.11   *Vowels of the Type* [o]: *Mid Back Vowels*

In the category of the mid back vowels we must recognize at least two rounded vowels [o] and [ɔ] and two unrounded vowels [ɣ] and [ʌ].

The mid back rounded close, or tense, vowel [o] is the sound of the stressed vowel of French *saule, nos*, or of German *Sohn, ohne*. The velum is raised more vigorously than for [ɑ], closing the nasopharynx. The lips are rounded considerably, either with or without protrusion. The tongue has the same general configuration as for [ɑ], in that it is strongly retracted

at its base toward the back wall of the pharynx, but since it is raised somewhat as a whole toward the velum, its dorsum becomes more convex and
less flat from side to side. The blade of the tongue may lie low in the fore
part of the mouth, or it may be drawn back somewhat as the curve of the
dorsum towards the velum may require. The resonance chamber in front
of the pharyngeal constriction is usually a little larger for [o] than for
American [ɑ+], but the difference is not great. The element of lip rounding
added to the increased size of the resonator results in a relatively low
pitched upper formant for [o]. If the lip rounding is reduced the size of the
cavity is increased The constriction between the base of the tongue and
the back wall of the pharynx is close and the length of this narrow passage
is greater than it is for [ɑ]. The volume of the pharyngeal resonator is also
increased by the lowering of the larynx, which is characteristic of the vowels
of this back series. As a result, the low formant for [o] is considerably
lower than that for [ɑ].

The same effect of the basis of articulation may be observed in the mid
back vowels as in the mid front vowels: French has more actively rounded
lips, a more strongly retracted tongue, but probably as a rule a slightly
higher general tongue position than is usual for German. The English [o]
vowel is subject to diphthongal variations of the same sort as those observed
for [e]. When the vowel begins with a relatively tense [o] as in *soap*, it
is likely to end in a still higher vowel, and we may transcribe it [ou], but
if it starts with a more open sound, such as the vowel of *ought*, we may
write it [ɔo].

The mid back rounded open, or lax, vowel [ɔ] is the sound of the stressed
vowel of French *sol*, *noce*, or of German *Sonne*, *ob*. It is also the sound heard
in southern British pronunciations of *lawn*, *saw*, where American English
usually has [ɒ]. The velum is raised, closing the nasopharynx. The lips
are slightly rounded, usually without notable protrusion. The tongue has
the same general shape as for [o], but the level of the dorsum is slightly
lower below the velum and hence the surface may be less convex or more
flat from side to side. In many ways this sound is "intermediate" between
[ɑ] and [o], and Germans are warned not to substitute [ɑ] for [ɔ] in words
like *Gott*.[65] Here again the general basis of French articulation is higher
and there is less tendency to make such a substitution. English, on the
other hand, apart from Southern British "long [ɔ:],"[66] has substituted
either [ɒ] or [ɑ] in words etymologically entitled to [ɔ] such as *not*, *solid*,
top, or *dog*, *moss*, *short*, *form*, *thought*.

The mid back unrounded tense, or close, vowel [ɣ] is not part of the
normal vowel systems of French, German, or English. It is a phoneme
of Marathe (of Kolhapur),[67] of Tiwa (Taos, N.M.),[68] and of Kashmiri.[69]
It occurs in the Chinese of Pekin, where it interchanges with [ʌ], and ap-

pears after [ʃ], [dʒ], or [tʃh].⁷⁰ Essentially, this vowel has the articulatory characteristics of [o], except that the lips are neutral or slightly spread.

The mid back unrounded lax, or open, vowel [ʌ] is the sound of the stressed vowel in English *but, mother, front,* as pronounced in Southern British English. It has the same general tongue position as that for [ɔ] but lacks the lip rounding. Indeed, the lips are usually quite definitely spread for the British vowel [ʌ]. This vowel is not a part of the normal French or German vowel systems. In American English the stressed vowel of words like *hurry, borough, flourish, courage,* is likely to be that of the words *bird, first, fir,* that is, either [ɝ] or [ɜː], rather than [ʌ] as it is in Britain. Indeed, the stressed vowel of *come, up, money, ton* is for many Americans almost identical as to articulation and quality with the unstressed vowel of *companion, above, Monona, tonight.* In these cases this vowel may better be classed with the central vowels of the type [ə]. Other American speakers have a somewhat closer and more advanced [ʌ] than that usually heard in standard Southern British pronunciation.⁷¹

4.12 *Vowels of the Type* [u]: *High Back Vowels*

In the category of the high back vowels we must recognize at least two rounded vowels, [u] and [ʊ], and one unrounded vowel [ɯ].

The high back rounded tense, or close, vowel [u] is the sound of the stressed vowel of French *bout, bourg, four,* or of German *gut, Buch.* The velum is raised vigorously, closing the nasopharynx. The lips are rounded considerably, with or without protrusion, and this rounding is usually closer than that for [o]. The tongue has the same general shape as for [o] but the entire organ is slightly closer to the velum and hence the arc formed by the dorsum and the blade is likely to be sharper and the tongue tip consequently drawn back behind the lower teeth. The narrow channel between the base of the tongue and the back wall of the pharynx which is characteristic of the entire back series of vowels is formed slightly higher up for [u] than for any other of these sounds. It is of about the same size, both in diameter and in length, as the channel formed for [o], but the pharyngeal cavity is notably larger because of the slight elevation of the body of the tongue just mentioned and the quite considerable lowering of the larynx for [u]. The lower formant for [u] is the lowest of those of the vowels of the back series. The upper formant is likewise the lowest of those of the back series except for that of American [ɒː]. Since the mouth cavity for [u] is necessarily smaller as the tongue is raised toward the velum some degree of lip rounding is almost indispensable to the production of a satisfactory [u] vowel. The unrounded forms of this vowel type have rather the sound of [o] than of [u].

Here as in the case of [o], the basis of articulation makes its influence felt. French [u] is notably more intensively rounded, more strongly retracted and probably somewhat higher as to tongue position than is the usual German [u]. English [u] like English [o], [i], and [e], is frequently diphthongal rather than pure. It may begin with a sound like that of the vowel of *pull* and end with a sound like that of the vowel of *pool*. In that case we may write it [ʊu]. If the vowel begins with a sound like the [u] of *pool*, we may write the diphthongal vowel [uw] to indicate that it becomes increasingly tense, or close.

The high back rounded lax, or open, vowel [ʊ] is the sound of the stressed vowel of German *Mutter, Spruch*, or of English *pull, book, bush*. This vowel is not a part of the normal French vowel system.

The vowel [ʊ] bears the same relation to [u] as [ɪ] bears to [i] in the high front category. It is lax, rather than tense, as to air stream and general muscular tone. It is made with the same kind of articulatory movement as [u] but is less completely achieved. Neither its lower nor its upper formant is quite so low as the corresponding formants for [u]. The lip rounding is apt to be less close than for [u]. If this lip rounding is too much neglected the vowel may sound like [ɔ] and Germans have to be warned against this fault.[72] In some American pronunciations a similar laxity results in a vowel very much like British [ʌ]. For example *book* sounds something like *buck*, *foot* becomes [fʌt], and *good* becomes [gʌd]. That is to say, this lax [ʊ] vowel is often very nearly an [o] type, rather than an [u] type vowel. The change has become established in words like *blood, flood*.

The high back unrounded tense, or close, vowel [ɯ] is not a part of the normal vowel systems of French, English, or German. It is a part of the vowel system of Shan (Hsi Paw, Upper Burma),[73] of Turkish (Istanbul),[74] and of Korean (Seoul).[75] The articulation of this vowel is approximately identical with that of [u] except that the lip rounding is omitted. It is higher than [ɣ], with which it contrasts in Shan.

Theoretically, one might find a high back unrounded lax, or open, vowel corresponding to [ʊ] as [ɯ] corresponds to [u]. Such a vowel may be written [ɯ̞]. Doubtless some pronunciations of *book*, with an unrounded vowel, may be described as [ɯ̞] rather than as [ɯ], when the relaxation attending the loss of rounding does not also cause lowering of the general level of the tongue to that of [ɔ]. Illustrations of this vowel from languages in which the difference is distinctive have eluded me.

4.13   *Vowels of the Type* [ə]: *Central Vowels*

In the category of the central vowels we must recognize at least the accented vowel [ɜ] and the unaccented, schwa vowel [ə]. The essential characteristics of the articulation of the vowels of this category are **(1)** comparatively low, flat position of the dorsum and blade of the tongue, and (2) a moderate retraction of the body of the tongue of the same kind as that observed for [ɑ] but less extensive, leaving a considerably wider passage between the pharyngeal and the mouth cavities. Whatever arc may be assumed by the dorsum of the tongue is in its middle portion, that is, neither at the blade nor at the back under the velum. For this reason, these sounds are sometimes called Mittelzungenvokale,[76] and we call them central vowels. The amount of elevation given the body of the tongue may vary considerably without changing the character of the vowel distinctively.

The central unrounded vowel [ɜ] is the sound of the stressed vowel pronounced by those speakers of English who "drop the r" in words like *fur*, *earth*, *bird*. The vowel may be heard in Southern Britain, in New England and in some regions of the Southern United States. It varies considerably in quality from a quite low and open variety which verges on [ɑ] to a higher, somewhat more strongly retracted variety, verging on [ʌ]. A rounded variety of [ɜ] is produced by some speakers who use the higher variety of [ɜ] with lip rounding. The symbol [θ] is often written for this sound. The vowel [ɜ] is not a part of the normal vowel systems of French or of German. It is used in Tamil (Jaffna, Ceylon),[77] in Esquimaux (northwest Greenland),[78] in Tiwa (Taos, N. M.),[79] and in Thai.[80]

Those American speakers of English who do not "drop their r" in words like *fur* or *bird*, and whose usual [r] is a retroflex, rather than an apical [r], usually produce in such words a retroflex [ɝ]. The articulation of the retroflex consonant has become contemporaneous in whole or in large part with the articulation of the vowel, and the vowel is then sometimes said to have an "r-color." This coarticulation of consonant and vowel is not restricted to [ɜ] with retroflex [r], but occurs with other types of untrilled [r] as well, and with other vowels, notably with [ɑ] or [ɔ]. The essential feature of retroflex [ɝ] is that the tongue, while it assumes the normal position for [ɜ] also curls its apex back so that the under side thereof lies parallel to the line of the upper teeth, and the alveolar and prepalatal region. This retroflex vowel may be written [ɝ], although there has been much controversy over the use of this symbol.[81]

The central unrounded unstressed schwa vowel [ə] is the sound of the unstressed vowel of English *tuba*, *sofa*, *about*, of standard German *alle*, *beliebt*, *findet*, or of French "e" in *besoin*, *debout*, *leçon*. The vowel is articulated as a lax [ɜ] vowel, and like that sound, it may vary considerably in position without losing its essential character. In English almost all unstressed vowels tend to become [ə], though certainly not all of them arrive at that end as yet. Many speakers preserve something of the quality of the stressed vowel in the unstressed syllables of words like *affliction, adult, ballistic, baptismal, effect, engulf, enfold, explode,* or use an unstressed [ɪ] rather than [ə] in words like *deceit, define, erase, employ, heroic, added, credit.* The vowel [ə] is as nearly an unarticulated vowel sound as is to be found in human speech, and it seems to be used by most languages in some, at least, of their unstressed syllables.

Just as there is a retroflex [ʒ] so there is a retroflex [ɚ] in unstressed syllables containing a retroflex [r]. This sound occurs in the speech of those Americans who articulate a retroflex [r] more or less simultaneously with the neutral vowel [ə] in weak syllables, such as the unstressed syllables of *perceive, better, traitor.* There has been a long controversy over the transcription of this sound and the International Phonetic Association has refused to recognize the symbol [ɚ] commonly used in America.[82] The sound may be transcribed [ər] or [r], if the symbol [ɚ] is found objectionable.

4.14 *Centralized Vowels*

Vowels of the two high categories, that is, vowels of the type [i] and of the type [u] are sometimes centralized in the sense that although they remain high vowels, the whole articulatory position is moved horizontally so that the maximum elevation of the tongue is mediopalatal rather than prepalatal, as it is for a normal [i], or velar, as it is for a normal [u]. Sometimes this centralization is incident to other factors of articulation, and then the centralized vowels are conditioned variants of the more usual front or back vowels. In some languages, however, the usual form of one or another of the vowel phonemes is that of a centralized vowel. We need to recognize an unrounded and a rounded centralized vowel, and it is helpful in addition to say whether the vowel is a centralized front vowel or a centralized back vowel. The boundary between the latter two categories is very unstable and the International Phonetic Association does not recognize the difference.

As an illustration of the rounded centralized vowel the stressed vowel of Swedish *hus* is usually cited. This appears to be a centralized front vowel, for its acoustic effect varies from that of a sound like [y] to that of a sound like [ø]. It does not sound at all like [u]. To produce it, one may put the tongue and the lips in the position to produce a normal [y], and then retract the entire articulation slightly so that it becomes mediopalatal. It will then also be a trifle lower than [y]. Norwegian *u,* on the other hand, while centralized, is still a back vowel and does not resemble [y] or [ø].[83] As the alphabet of the International Phonetic Association is now constituted, this Norwegian *u* may be transcribed [u+] while Swedish *u* is rendered by either [ʉ] or [ü]. Some centralization of the back vowel [u] is produced by many speakers of English words like *Louisville, Tuesday, peculiar, purity,* when the stressed vowel begins with the onset [j] or [ç]. This becomes evident when one compares the vowels of the pairs *Tuesday : tool, peculiar : cool, purity : poor.*

The most convenient illustration of an unrounded centralized vowel is probably the Russian ьι or "jery," which is usually transliterated as *y.* The accepted I.P.A. symbols for this vowel are either [i] or [ï]. Either of these symbols is likely to be misleading,[84] so far as this Russian vowel is concerned, for it is not at all an [i] vowel, but rather a centralized back vowel, and hence more like [ɯ] with which it interchanges.[85]

4.15 *Diphthongal Vowels, Diphthongs*

Any good acoustic record of speech reveals that at least the first three or four cycles and the last three or four cycles of the vowel sounds show constant and radical changes, which may be called respectively the building-up and the dying-out phases of the sound. Quite apart from these two features, some syllabic sounds show notable initial or final segments in which the wave forms are distinctly different from those of the principal, or relatively stable, section of the sound. Such syllabic sounds are diphthongal vowels or diphthongs. We have observed the English diphthongal vowels [ij], [ei], [uw], [ou], characteristic of which are the facts that both elements of the sound belong to the same general category, that is, both are either front or back, that the course of the development of the vowel is from less to more tense or close, and that the first element is more prominent acoustically and usually longer than the second. The second or subordinate element of such diphthongal vowels is sometimes spoken of as a glide vowel,[86] rather than a full vowel.

The English diphthongs [aɪ] in *buy* and [ɑʊ] in *bough*, while they are normally front vowel type or back vowel type respectively, require the transition in sound from the quality of the low vowel to that of the high lax, or open, vowel in that type, and therefore the appropriate tongue movement from the position of the low vowel to that of the high vowel. The range of this movement is thus considerably greater than that characteristic of the diphthongal vowels. In American English, at any rate, the transition from low to high vowel quality takes place relatively quickly, and the low vowel element is usually the more prominent sound, though it often is shorter than the second element. In the English diphthong [ɔɛ] or [ɔɪ] in *boy*, the transition of sound and the movement of articulation is from that of a back vowel type to that of a front vowel type, and does not involve a notable change in the general level of tongue position, since both components are usually mid vowels. Here too the first element is acoustically the more prominent, though generally briefer, element. On the basis of the "direction" of the development of the acoustic energy and, in these cases perhaps also, of the development of physiological energy, the diphthongal vowels [ij], [ei], [uw], [ou], and the diphthongs [aɪ], [aʊ], and [ɔɛ] have been called falling diphthongs, since the energy appears to fall off or diminish as the sound shifts to its second component. A better name for such compound sounds would be diminishing diphthongs.

The English stressed syllabic sound of *beauty, cure, Europe, mule*, is the high back rounded vowel [u], often diphthongal [uw], preceded by an on-glide, which is most nearly identified with the consonant [j] of *your, Yule, yes*. We may transcribe it then [ju] or [juw] and call it a diphthong or a triphthong, as the case may be. By contrast with the other English diphthongal syllabics, [ju] may be called an increasing diphthong.[87]

In British English, when final *r* is lost, another kind of diminishing diphthong has been developed, the second and less prominent element of which is the central vowel [ə]. Thus, *fear, there, far, for, pore, poor, pur* are pronounced [fɪə], [ðɛə], [faə], [fɔə], [poə], [pʊə], [pəə]. These have been called centering diphthongs.[88] Most American speakers pronounce in such cases the analogous centering diphthongs [ɪɚ], [ɛɚ], [aɚ], [ɔɚ], [oɚ], [ʊɚ]. Theoretically, any vowel may combine with [ə], or [ɚ] to yield a centering diphthong. In English some happen to be less frequent than others. Thus, [iɚ] and [eɚ] occur, but much less often than [ɪɚ], [ɛɚ], while [uɚ] appears to be very rare.

When combined with diphthongs such as [aɪ] or [aʊ] this central [ɚ] results in a centering triphthong, as in *fire* [faɪɚ], *hour* [aʊɚ]. The difference between the triphthongal [aɪɚ] and a dissyllabic [aɪ-ə] or between [aʊɚ] and [aʊ-ɚ] is slight and depends upon the relative energy expended upon the last component [ɚ]. If this last component receives any notable stress at all, the triphthong breaks down into two syllables: cf. *hire : higher* [haɪɚ], *flour : flower* [flaʊɚ], or [haɪə], [flaʊə].[89] Since any vowel may, in theory be linked with any other vowel to form either an increasing or a diminishing diphthong the number and variety of diphthongs might be very large: it is, as a matter of fact, relatively small. Front diphthongs normally move from a lower to a higher articulation, e.g. [yj], [øj], [ej], [ɛj], [ɛe], [ae], [øy]. Back diphthongs may move either up or down, e.g [ɔu], [ou], [ao], [aɔ], [aɯ], [ɒu], or [uɤ], [ɯɤ]. Back-front combinations include [ai], [ɔi], [ui], [ʊi], [ɯa], [ua], [ɯe], [ae], [ɤa], and front-back combinations include [iu], [eo], [io], [ia], [iʌ], [iɤ], [ɛʌ], [au], [ɛu], [iɒ], [yu], [øo]. There are "inverted" centering diphthongs such as [əi], [əɛ], [əu], [ɜi], and even nasalized diphthongs like [ĩɛ̃], [ʌ̃ĩ], [õĩ], [ãũ], [ũĩ]. These lists are not intended to be exhaustive, but rather representative of the kinds of combinations one may meet.

Sweet defined a diphthong as "the combination of a full vowel with a glide vowel before or after it."[90] Our inclusion of forms with [j], such as [ju], [ij] [ej], raises the question of the adequacy of this definition or the propriety of our procedure. If the initial element of English *union* is [ju] or [jʊ] rather than [ĭu], may it be called a diphthong? The answer to questions of this kind must be given for each language in which they arise, and not for all languages from any general premise. The point to be determined is whether [ɪu] is a syllabic element subject to the same general conditions of combinations with nonsyllabics as governs the utilization of other comparable vowels of the language. For English [ju] we find that it may be initial, as in *use, unit,* or interconsonantal, as in *beauty, cute, duty, futile, huge, lute, mute, nutritious* and so on, or it may be final, as in *cue, dew, few, hew,* and others. We may compare [ju] initially with [jɛ], *yes,* [ji], *yield,* [jo], *yoke,* or we may compare *use* with *ooze,* and thus apparently isolate a consonantal element [j] from the sound [ju]. But the interconsonantal use of [ju] reveals its phonemic nature. The consonant clusters [bj], [kj], [dj], [fj], [hj] are not found in English before any vowel other than our problematical [u]. Therefore a contrast between *beauty* and *booty, cute* and *coot, mute* and *moot* is not a contrast founded on the opposition bj : b, kj : k, mj : m, but rather on the opposition [ju] : [u]. This kind of analysis soon shows that [ju] is utilized in English as a syllabic phoneme and not as a group of consonant [j] plus [u]. Hence we must classify English [ju] as a syllabic, and since it is clearly composed of two phases or elements, we may call it a diphthong. We revise our definition then, and say: a diphthong is a syllabic element, which begins with one sound and shifts to another, and we understand this to exclude consideration of those brief building-up and dying-out stages which characterize every speech sound. In a similar way, we define a triphthong as a syllabic element which begins with one sound and shifts through a second to a third sound within the same syllable.

4.16 *Nasal Vowels*

Some languages use as distinctive syllabic phonemes vowel sounds characterized by nasality, or nasal twang. The most convenient illustrations may be taken from French, where [ɛ̃], [ã], [ɔ̃], and [œ̃] are the typical nasal vowels.[91] Of these [œ̃] is the least frequent, and there is something of a tendency to substitute [ɛ̃] for it. Examples are: *vin* [vɛ̃], *vent* [vã], *vont* [vɔ̃] *pin* [pɛ̃], *pan* [pã], *pont* [pɔ̃], *un* [œ̃].

Acoustically, the distinguishing feature of these nasal vowels is the addition of at least two frequency components to the vowel spectrum,[92] one of which is a high-pitched tone ranging from 2,169 c.p.s. to 3,906 c.p.s. and the other a lower tone of some 400 to 450 c.p.s. This lower tone appears to be due to selective transmission of one of the cord tone partials through the nasal fossae. The high component is believed[93] to be produced by standing vibrations set up in the small space behind the velum and below the posterior nares. Since the nasal cavities are coupled to the pharynx and mouth cavities when nasal vowels are produced, the characteristic resonances of the latter are changed somewhat, usually toward a lower pitch. These nasal vowels are produced by adding the vigorous lowering of the velum, accompanied by some constriction of the palatopharyngeal arch, to the usual movements of the articulation peculiar to the analogous oral vowel. The mere lowering of the velum is not enough to produce the nasality characteristic of these French nasal vowels. The passing of a part of the breath stream through the nose as a result of an inert, or laxly lowered velum may cause the low component frequencies characteristic of the nasal cavities to be selectively passed and hence to be more clearly audible than when the velum is raised and these partials are not thus favored, but the quality difference produced by this lax lowering of the velum is not a change to nasality, but a "richening" or "mellowing" of the vowel sound. Nasality is produced only by a more vigorous lowering of the velum plus the constriction of the posterior pillars of the fauces. There are degrees of this vigor, to be sure, and the French nasal vowels are much more vigorously nasalized than are the nasal vowels of Danish, German or Portuguese dialects.

Any voiced speech sound may be nasalized, or spoken with nasal twang. In some parts of Vermont and New Hampshire, for example, the entire stream of speech sounds appears to be marked by a nasal twang. This then becomes a part of the general basis of articulation rather than a characteristic used to mark one or several sounds as distinct from those otherwise like them. On the other hand, nasalization may become a feature of conditioned variants of usually pure oral vowels. For example, in many dialects of central and southern Germany vowels before nasal consonants [m], [n] are nasalized, while the same vowels in other contexts are not nasalized. In some cases, when conditions are favorable, the nasalization of vowels before [m] or [n] has been followed by the assimilation of the nasal consonant with the nasal vowel to make a single sound, so that *Sohn* may be first [zõːn], then [zõː]. Later, since there is no longer a consonant [n] to induce the nasalization in this word, the nasality may be lost, and [zõː] may become [zoː]. Or, the nasality of [zõː] may induce analogous word forms to assume nasality even where no nasal consonant was ever directly involved. Thus if *Sohn* is pronounced [zõː], *Floh* may come to be pronounced [flõ:] if the habit of nasalization spreads. Something of this sort marked the local speech of Frankfurt a.M. and led Goethe to write:

> Es war einmal ein König,
> Der hatt' einen großen Floh;
> Den liebt' er gar nicht wenig,
> Als wie seinen eigenen Sohn.
>
> (*Faust*, 2211–14)

Various stages of this kind of interplay between phonetic and analogic influences may be encountered.

4.17   *The Syllabic Consonants*

Any sound which occurs medially in a group or cluster of sounds in such a way that it is preceded and followed by a sound of lesser acoustic prominence than itself is likely to be heard as a syllabic element. Initially, or finally, a pause may replace one of these sounds of lesser acoustic prominence. Each language has its own habits with respect to these differences. As a general rule the syllabic elements of most languages are vowels, but various consonants may be syllabic if they occur in the required environment. This may be illustrated by the groups [brd], [glt], [rbn], [rdʒ], [str] [skl], each of which shows a syllabic consonant performing the function normally performed by a vowel. In English the nasal consonants [m] and [n], the liquid consonants [l] and [r] frequently serve as syllabic elements. Examples are the unstressed syllables of *bottom* [bɑtm], *rhythm* [rɪðm], *button* [bʌtn], *bottle* [bɑtl], *butter* [bʌtr]. The case of [r] is obscured by the fact that this consonant in unstressed syllables is frequently so completely coarticulated with the schwa or neutral vowel [ə] that it is difficult to say whether [ɚ] or syllabic [r] is being pronounced. In regions where final [r] and [r] before a consonant is lost, the syllabic element is clearly [ə] in such words as *butter* [bʌtə], and *overture* ['ovətʃə]. In the stressed syllable of *pretty* the syllabic element is sometimes [r] or [ɝ], either of which may be whispered rather than voiced in this word.

Syllabic [r] is prominently utilized in many languages, e.g., Sanskrit, Czech, Bulgarian, Lendu.[94] Syllabic [l], [m], [n], are regular features of Sanskrit. Lendu and Czech use a syllabic [z], and we should have to consider [s] syllabic in the stage interjection *Pst!*

One evident difference between these syllabic consonants and the vowels is that the former may occur either in the function of a syllabic or in the function of a nonsyllabic, whereas the vowels can only occur as syllabics. English [j] and [w] appear to be peculiar. They do not become syllabic in the sense that [r], [l], [m], [n] become syllabic, but they do participate in the syllabic function of the diphthongal vowels [ij], [uw], [ju], while in other contexts they serve as nonsyllabic elements, e.g., *yes*, [jɛs], *will* [wɪl]. When either [j] or [w] comes to stand in a situation which would make it syllabic, as [r] or [l] are made syllabic, it becomes a vowel, [i] or [u]. A central [r] is related to the vowel [ə], or a retroflex [r] to [ɝ] very much as [j] is related to [i] or [w] to [u], but it serves no good purpose on that account to call [j], [w], and [r] semivowels.[95] If we define the syllabic as the element of major sonority in its syllable, or the carrier of the emitted breath pulse of the syllable, we shall have to exclude [j] and [w] from the group called syllabics. When they might become the element of major sonority in the syllable they are replaced by [i] or [u]. It is linguistic analysis, rather than peculiarity of acoustic or dynamic qualities, which justifies our including [j] and [w] as parts of the diphthongal syllabic sounds.

CHAPTER VI

THE NONSYLLABIC SOUNDS

5.01 *Definition*

The nonsyllabic sounds of any language are those sounds which precede or follow the syllabic sounds of its syllables. Gennemically, these sounds have less sonority than the syllabics; genetically, they result from movements which serve to release or to arrest the flow of the breath required for the production of the syllable. Thus in the English words *cape, safe, rave* the syllabic movement is released by the nonsyllabics [k], [s], and [r], and it is arrested by the nonsyllabics [p], [f], and [v]. To define nonsyllabics as the releasing and arresting elements of syllables is to define them according to a function.

Most of the speech sounds which are usually nonsyllabic can upon occasion become syllabic, that is, they may become the element of major sonority in their syllable, or the carrier of the breath pulse of that syllable. Some of these nonsyllabics, as we have seen in the cases of [l], [r], [m], [n], perform this function frequently. On the other hand, the sounds which we have called vowels rarely come to serve as nonsyllabic elements.

Sounds which are usually nonsyllabic in function are generally called consonants. Logically, what is not a consonant should be a sonant, and this is the opposition meant by the French terms *sonantes* : *consonantes*. This opposition of terms corresponds precisely to the opposition *syllabic* : *nonsyllabic*, and it is an opposition defined by function. The opposition given by the French terms *voyelles* : *consonnes* or by the English terms *vowel* : *consonant* is different, since these terms designate kinds of sounds, and the definition of this implied difference in kind is a very difficult matter.[1]

5.02 *The Consonants, Considered Gennemically*

The nonsyllabic speech sounds commonly called consonants are considerably less prominent acoustically than the vowels which occur with them. Each appears, however, to have its own characteristic acoustic structure. On the basis of the observed acoustic peculiarities of the consonants one may divide them into at least three groups, (1) consonants, the acoustic characteristics of which become distinctive only during the transitional periods between the consonant and adjacent sounds: (2) consonants which have resonance characteristics analogous to those of the vowels, and (3) consonants with high frequency characteristics. Examples of the first

116

group are the stops [p], [t], [k], [b], [d], [g]. Examples of the second group
are the open consonants we have already met as syllabics, [m], [n], [l],
and [ŋ]. These sounds have a distinctive low resonance between 200 and
400 c.p.s., a middle resonance around 600 c.p.s., and a high resonance ranging from 900 to 3,000 c.p.s. Examples of the third group are the sounds
[f], [v], [j], [ç], [ʃ], [ʒ], [s], [z]. These sounds have a high frequency component ranging from 2,000 to 8,000 c.p.s.

In general it must be said that the gennemic study of consonant sounds
has been prosecuted with much less vigor than that of the vowels, and as a
result it is not possible to offer a satisfactory detailed classification of
consonants on the basis of their acoustic characteristics. The consonant
sounds appear to be subject to wide variations, and some of them, such as
[s] or [z], are exceedingly complex hissing sounds with a large number of
high pitched components. We need extensive studies of the consonant
sounds, particularly to determine the ranges of their variability and thence
more precisely the minimum characteristic components of each type. Evident omissions from the lists just given are due to the absence of comparable acoustic analyses for quite a few non-English sounds.

5.03   *The Consonants, Considered Genetically*

STOPS, OPEN CONSONANTS

Consonantal sounds are produced by the complete or partial closure of
the channel by which the breath flows from the larynx to the lips. The
movements of the tongue, velum, and lips by which these closures are
effected are much too slow to produce audible vibrations by themselves.
The sound of the consonant is produced by the vibrations of the breath
stream as this is (a) confined by closures produced by the articulatory movements, (b) released by the movements which open these closures, or (c)
obstructed but not stopped by the narrowing of the channel at one or more
points. In each of these three cases the audible vibrations of the breath
stream, when there are no vibrations of the vocal bands, are due to the
impact of the stream of air from the larynx upon the surfaces of the channel
through which it flows as this channel is formed and modified by the movements of the tongue, velum, or lips. Two factors, at least, appear to determine the quality of the resulting sound: (1) the location of the obstruction
which causes the vibrations to be set up, and hence the size and openings
of the potential resonators behind and in front of the obstruction; (2) the
velocity of the breath stream which strikes the obstructing surfaces or
agitates the resonators. A still further distinctive difference results from
the nature of the closure effected. Sounds made with complete closure of
the breath channel produce an acoustic effect different from that of sounds

made with a partial closure of this channel, even when the location of the obstruction and the nature of the potential resonators are the same in the two cases. Sounds made with complete closure have an impulsive effect not present in sounds made with partial closure of this channel. Our basic classification of the consonants is therefore the division of these sounds into two major groups, (1) the stops, for the production of which the closure of the breath channel is complete, and (2) the open consonants, for which the closure is partial.

THE STOP CONSONANTS

5.11 *The Occlusion*

Since the breath channel is completely closed when a stop consonant is produced, there will inevitably be a period or a phase of such an articulation during which air will be completely enclosed somewhere between the lungs and the lips. The lowest point at which a complete closure can be made is at the glottis. The next lowest point is the lowest point at which the back of the tongue can make a complete closure against anything behind or above it. Usually this is at the back portion of the velum. From this point forward the tongue can produce complete closure of the oral channel by stops made against the velum, the palate, or the teeth; beyond the teeth, the lips may produce a complete stop. Evidently, however, the complete enclosure of air behind such stops depends, except for the glottal stop, upon the complete cutting off of the nasal passages by the raising of the velum against the back wall of the pharynx.

If the consonant is produced by stoppage of the breath channel at one point only, as is usually the case in the English stops [p], [t], [k], the air is imprisoned between the lungs and the point of the stoppage in the mouth, or in the case of the glottal stop, between the lungs and the vocal bands. Such stops are simple rather than compound stops. The air they imprison may be compressed if the volume of the thorax is diminished while the closure is maintained, or rarefied if the volume of the thorax is increased. When the stop is then released, air will flow, either out of the chamber in which it has been compressed, or into the chamber in which the air has been rarefied. It is convenient therefore, to distinguish between pressure stops and suction stops. Pressure stops are marked by the flow of air out of the cavity, suction stops by the flow of air into the cavity when its occlusion is released.

It is possible, and not at all unusual, for stop consonants to have a complete closure of the air channel at two, or even at three points simultaneously. Stops of this sort are compound stops. For example, the glottis may be closed at the same time that any of the tongue or lip closures is made.

Less frequently, a velar closure may be made simultaneously with a lip closure, or with an apical tongue stop. It is evident that the action of the rib-cage cannot under such circumstances influence the pressure of the air enclosed between the two occlusions of these compound stops. In French, for instance, the consonants [p], [t], [k], are frequently articulated with simultaneous glottal stop.[2] The air thus imprisoned between the two occlusions is subjected to a slight compression, not by the movement of the thorax, but by the raising of the hyoid bone and the larynx, thus re-ducing the length and the diameter of the cavity between the glottis and the lingual or labial stop. Such stop consonants are called ejective stops, or glottalized pressure stops. They may be written [p'], [t'], [k']. If the com-pound stop, let us say of an alveolar [t] and the glottal stop, be made when the larynx and tongue are raised, the air between the two closures may be rarefied by the depression of the larynx and the hyoid bone. If the front closure is released while this air is rarefied, outside air will rush into the cavity, and the stop has been made a glottalized suction stop. Sounds of this nature occur in Zulu and in some of the Asiatic languages.[3]

It is possible to articulate a compound stop of which the posterior of the two closures is between the tongue and the velum, while the anterior closure is either labial or between tongue tip and teeth, alveolar ridge, or palate. Such compound stops may be called velaric stops. The production of a velaric pressure stop is most unusual: the production of velaric suction stops is a conspicuous feature of the Hottentot dialects, and indeed these Hottentot stops are all lingual, not labial. The compound occlusion for the velaric suction stops is essentially a complete, more or less elliptical contact of the back, the tip, and the margins of the tongue with the velum and palate. Rarefaction is accomplished by drawing the center of the blade of the tongue downward while the circle of contact is maintained by back, tip, and rim of the tongue. This stop may then be released in front, on the teeth (hence a dental), or on the alveolar ridge (an alveolar), or on one side (a unilateral) or on both sides (a bilateral). These are the sounds most properly called clicks.[4] It is not unusual for these velaric suction stops to be accompanied by the simultaneous closure of the glottis. On the other hand it is possible for the velaric stops to be accompanied by a nasal tone, since the velum may be lowered enough behind them to permit the flow of the breath stream through the larynx while the oral occlusions are main-tained.

Just as there is of necessity one phase of a stop consonant during which the breath channel is completely closed, so there is also of necessity an antecedent phase during which this closure is effected and a subsequent phase during which it is released. The three phases may be called the contact, the hold, and the release.[5] The contact and hold phases are usually easy to observe, the release may be obscured, notably for instance, when the stop is the final element of the breath group. In the phrase, *and then he went to sleep*, the final [p] of *sleep* is often not released by a labial "explosion," but by the lowering of the velum for the resumption of normal breathing, the lips having simply remained closed. Such a release is usually not audible. The precise nature of the movements made to effect the contact of a stop consonant are determined (a) by the position or positions at which the stop is produced, and (b) by the positions from which the articulating organs have to move to get there. Any sound produced during these movements is inevitably a constantly changing sound: the contact phase or the onset of stop consonants is therefore sometimes called the on-glide of the consonant. Usually the audible sound produced by this onset is a modification of the preceding speech sound, whether vowel or consonant, but in any event, the sound of the onset results from the brusque interruption of the breath stream. Hence the contact phase of an initial [p] is inaudible, since there is no breath stream to interrupt. The hold phase of such sounds as [p], [t], [k], is quite inaudible, since during this hold the air around the speaker is not disturbed by any speech movement made by him.

5.12   *The Release*

The precise nature of the movements made to release a stop consonant depends also (a) upon the positions of the organs during the hold, and (b) the positions to which they next move. But there is, in the case of the release, the further factor of the dynamic nature of these movements. If they are impulsive, or sudden, the rush of the air out of (pressure stops) or into (suction stops) the stopped cavity may be vigorous and puff-like. In the case of the pressure stops this puff may readily become the distinctive mark of the stop. Stops which have it are called aspirated stops: stops which lack it are called unaspirated stops. Evidently the degree of energy displayed by these puffs depends upon the degree of compression or rarefaction achieved during the occlusion. On the basis of such differences in energy we describe some stops as strong or fortis, others as weak or lenis. When necessary, strongly aspirated stops may be written by adding [h] to the symbol, thus [ph], [th], while weakly aspirated stops may be written [p'], [t'], [k']. In many languages the aspirated [ph], [th], [kh], are functionally distinct from the unaspirated stops [p], [t], [k].

But the release of the stop may be slow, rather than sudden, and in this case the rush of air out of or into the stopped cavity will produce a fricative noise as it impinges upon the surfaces of the slowly increasing opening of the occlusion. Stops which are released in this way are called affricates. They are in effect the stop plus, i.e., released through, the homorganic fricative. In this way [p] may become [pɸ], or [t] may become [tθ], and [k] become [kx].

The release of the compound stops is complicated by the necessity of releasing both occlusions. In the case of the glottalized stops the first release of the tongue or lip articulation, whether impulsive or affricative, is followed by the release of the glottal occlusion. This is sometimes quite as audible as the simple glottal stop. In the case of the velaric stops the energy of the velar release depends somewhat upon the behavior of the thorax and the larynx below it. If air pressure is built up behind the velar closure, its release will produce a strong velar impulsive consonant. If no pressure has been built up behind it, its release may be weak or even inaudible. Such velaric stops may be glottalized, and in this case the velar release is likely to be inaudible and the glottal release heard; or the velar release may be the release of an [h] sound, or the entire compound velaric occlusion may be accompanied by a nasal tone, in which event the velar release is the release of a nasal vowel.

5.13　Voiceless or Voiced

Consonants of the type [p], [t], [k], are produced without voice vibrations from the larynx. They are therefore properly called voiceless consonants.[6] Paired with them in many languages are similarly articulated consonants of the type [b], [d], [g], which are produced with accompanying voice vibrations from the larynx. These are properly called voiced consonants.[7] The pairing in significant or phonologic oppositions of voiceless to voiced consonants is not confined to the stops. We find in English not only *peat* : *beat*, *team* : *deem*, *cap* : *gap*, but *ice* : *eyes* [s] : [z], *fife* : *five* [f] : [v], *ether* : *either* [θ] : [ð], *glacier* : *glazier* [ʃ] : [ʒ]. The production of voiced open consonants involves the addition of the glottal vibrations to whatever sound is produced by the impact of the breath stream upon the surfaces of the constriction characteristic of the particular closure of the breath channel required for the consonant concerned. The production of voiced stops is a more complicated procedure.

The primary requirement for the normal production of voice is that air under pressure in the thorax be alternately released and confined by the elastic action of the vocal bands when brought together along their median edges. When there is an open channel above the larynx through which the resulting puffs of air may escape, this kind of voicing requires only that the pressure of the air below the vocal bands be sufficiently greater than that of the air above them to force the edges of the bands periodically to part. When the channel above the glottis is stopped the puffs of air released when the vocal bands are parted increase the pressue of the air above the glottis and very soon there will be no difference between the pressure below and that above the vocal bands and hence no possibility of voice. It is evident that the way out of this difficulty is not to increase the subglottal air pressure, because to do so would force more air faster into the occluded cavity above and thus the more quickly equalize the two pressures. Certain observations of what actually happens in the articulation of voiced stops suggest an explanation of the speaker's solution of this problem. Paget found[8] that "the essential difference between the so-called unvoiced consonants . . . and the voiced series . . . is one of resonance, and that the latter series are produced either by the acoustic effects of direct access to the trachea (in the case of a whispered sound), or by[9] the effects of the resonance of a cavity formed between the true and false vocal cords." He cites further his observations with the pharyngoscope of Professor G. O. Russell to the effect that "in the case of b and v the false vocal cords rose up and formed a cavity of comparatively small aperture above the vocal cords." Hudgins and Stetson found[10] that "the fundamental differentiation of surd and sonant occlusives is the result of vertical movements of the larynx-hyoid unit. The larynx begins to move downward at the closing of the sonant occlusive; it may even start slightly in advance of the closure. It continues to move downward throughout the occlusion .... During the surd occlusion, on the other hand, the larynx-hyoid unit does not move downward .... The entire musculature of the pharyngeal region, as well as the infralaryngeal muscles, is tense during the surd occlusion."

There is no doubt that the normal English [b], [d], [g], are marked by the vibration of the vocal bands during part of their total length, and it is also clear that French [b], [d], [g], differ from their English counterparts by having a considerably greater part of their total length voiced. But it is equally clear that one can whisper these "voiced" sounds without thereby causing them to sound like the voiceless sounds of the same organic formation.[11] The characteristic articulation of the simple voiced stops involves (a) a reduction in the rate of flow of air from below the glottis into the occluded chamber above and (b) an increase in the size of this chamber. The reduction of the rate of flow results from the somewhat less frequent puffs of air, i.e., the lower pitch of the voicing of voiced stops, and from the reduction of the energy of the muscular pulse which drives the air from the lungs. Voiced stops are usually lenis rather than fortis. Lower pitch and lesser energy are interrelated phenomena, of course, but the formation of the small hood over the vocal bands, by bringing the ventricular bands together until they impede but do not stop the puffs of air from the glottis, aids the reduction by building up a back pressure in the limited space above the cords from which the air flows more slowly into the larger space above. All this would avail little or nothing, however, if the size of the occluded chamber were not at the same time increased. So long as the increase in the volume of this chamber occurs at a rate (in cubic centimeters per second) as great as or greater than the rate of air-flow from the larynx, the vocal bands can continue to vibrate. This rate of expansion is apparently not difficult to attain, for even glottalized suction stops can be voiced.[12] That means that the larynx can be lowered during voicing rapidly enough to create and to maintain negative pressure in the occluded chamber above the vocal bands. The voicing of simple stops like those of English or German requires much less rapid or vigorous laryngeal depression than is required for these suction stops.

5.14   *Intermittent Stops*

There are many consonantal sounds which are characterized by the rapid making and breaking of a simple occlusion at some point in the breath channel. The stoppage of the breath is complete but very brief, and as a rule a series of two or three such stoppages occurs during the articulation of a single consonant of this kind. The usual rate of these intermittent occlusions is between twenty and twenty-five taps per second.[13] At least one of these trills has been reduced to a single tap, and might therefore have been included with the simple stops. However, everything else about it resembles rather the intermittent than the simple stops.

A trill is produced in very much the same way in which the vocal bands are made to vibrate for voice production, but much more slowly. A momentary closure pens in the air of the lungs; this then becomes compressed and lifts the obstruction out of its path, thereby allowing the pressure to be reduced to the point where the weight or elasticity of the obstructing body restores the momentary closure. The muscular tensions of the organs brought into contact to stop the air channel must be neatly adjusted so that the obstruction is easily displaced while still retaining sufficient elasticity to restore the stop promptly when the puff of air has escaped. Trills can be and are frequently produced by various articulations, and we have glottal trills, uvular trills, lingual trills, and labial trills, of which more presently.

5.15   *Criteria of Description*

We may summarize the foregoing analysis of the manner in which stops are made by saying that in order to describe any stop consonant one must indicate certain distinctions. (a) One must state whether it is voiceless or voiced. If voiced, it may be desirable to say how much and what part of the total length of the stop has voicing.[14] If voiceless, it is desirable to say whether it is fortis or lenis. (b) One must indicate whether its release is

impulsive (i.e., sudden) or affricative, and if impulsive, whether it is aspirated or unaspirated. (c) One must say whether it is a simple, an intermittent, or a compound stop, and if compound, whether it is glottalized or
velaric. (d) And finally, one must indicate whether it is a pressure or a
suction stop. Thus English [p] is a voiceless, fortis, impulsive, aspirated,
simple, pressure stop. The [b̥] pronounced by many speakers in the word
lobster is a voiceless, lenis, impulsive, unaspirated, simple, pressure stop.
But English [t], like English [p], is also a voiceless, fortis, impulsive, aspirated, simple, pressure stop and it is therefore clear that in addition to
these criteria of manner there are further distinctive features which mark

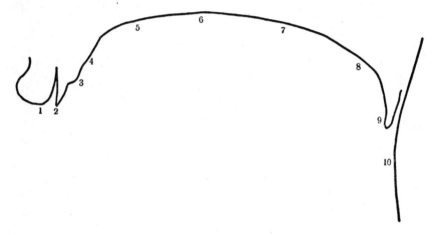

Plate 24. POINTS OF ARTICULATION

1—Labial. 2—Dental. 3—Gingival. 4—Alveolar. 5—Prepalatal. 6—Palatal. 7—Mediopalatal. 8—Velar. 9—Uvular. 10—Pharyngeal.

the articulation of these stops. These are best described in terms of the
place at which the articulation takes place.

Stoppage of the breath channel can be effected in the larynx and at
various points in the oral pharynx and mouth cavity. Compound stops
involve two or more such points and may generally best be described in
terms of the point of their release. The moving parts which produce the
occlusions are the vocal bands, the tongue, or the lips. Stops therefore may
be classed as laryngeal (or glottal) stops, and as oral (or lingual), or labial
stops. The range of incidence, or the range within which the moving organs
may produce an occlusion for the laryngeal stop is zero, that for the labial
stop is slight, but the lingual stops may be made at any point on the roof
of the mouth from the back edge of the velum to the inner surfaces of the
incisors. It is convenient for the purposes of description to assign names to

a number of regions in this area and the well-known names
ten terms indicated on the drawing (Plate 24) are usually
careful description of the stops, but they may be further qualified it this
seems necessary.

THE SIMPLE STOPS

5.21   *The Laryngeal Stop* [ʔ]

The simple occlusion and release of the edges of the vocal bands is used
as a speech sound in many languages and appears in many others as a
feature of articulation without functional significance. This sound is always
a voiceless, usually a fortis, impulsive, unaspirated, pressure stop. It is
called the glottal stop, or in French coup de glotte and is written [ʔ]. It
is characteristic of the vowel beginning of stressed initial vowels in standard
German. In French it is adventitious, but it may be heard before or after
vowels in interjections. In Italian it is quite unusual. In English it appears
sometimes between vowels in words like *extra-ordinary, tri-umphant*, or as
a device for marking morphemes in phrases such as *an ice man, a nice man*.
In the dialects of Scotland, Yorkshire, and Lancashire, and in London
Cockney, the laryngeal stop appears before or after consonants, and as a
substitute for [t] in words like *little* and *water*. In Danish, where the glottal
stop may occur either between a vowel and a following consonant, or after
a consonant, the sound is functionally distinctive and has its own name,
the stød.[15] In Arabic the sound is functional. It will be met again when we
consider the glottalized compound stops.

5.22   *Velar Stops* [k], [g̥], [g], [kx], [q], [ɢ]

Almost every language uses functionally one or more simple stops made
by raising the back of the tongue to make contact with the soft palate or
velum. Typical of the voiceless, velar, fortis, impulsive, aspirated, simple,
pressure stops is the [k] of English *cool*, German *Kugel*. In contexts which
render the other terms superfluous this may be called the voiceless velar
stop. Many dialects of German use another voiceless velar stop functionally
distinct from this [k]. We may describe this sound as a voiceless, lenis,
impulsive, unaspirated, simple pressure stop, and write it [g̥]. This stop is
normal also, but not functionally distinctive, in standard German for the
consonant written *g* in words like *folglich, Wagnis*, or often in *Krug* and
words like it. Here and elsewhere no attempt at completeness of illustration
is made; the stop [g̥] occurs in many other languages.

The voiced, velar, impulsive, unaspirated, simple, pressure stop may
be observed in the [g] of English *goon, goal*, German *gut*, French *gourmé*.
This is the usual voiced velar stop.[16]

The voiceless, velar, fortis, affricative, simple, pressure stop is a functional speech sound in Hottentot.[17] We may write it (kx). The sound is not infrequent in German dialects[18] and is one of the stages in which the reflex of Germanic [k] is found under Grimm's Law in Alemannian and Bavarian.

A voiceless, velar, simple, suction stop can be produced and would be written ['k]. I can cite no cases. A voiced, velar, simple suction stop ['g] probably does not occur.

By retracting the articulation of a voiceless velar [k] or a voiced velar [g] as much as possible, one whose native tongue is English, or some other, related Germanic language, can produce the postvelar simple pressure stops sometimes heard in the Semitic languages.[19] The voiceless postvelar stop may be written [q] and the voiced postvelar stop [G]. These sounds have shown a strong tendency in the various Semitic dialects to be replaced by the glottal stop [ʔ], or by the simple velar stop [g], if indeed they have not been shifted to open consonants of one type or another.

5.23   *Mediopalatal Stops* [c], [ɟ], [ɟ], [cx]

The stop consonants of the mediopalatal category are closely analogous to those of the velar category. Indeed, in most languages they are conditioned variants of the velar stops rather than functionally distinct sounds. The region called mediopalatal centers around the junction of the hard palate with the velum, which is about two-thirds of the way along the vault of the mouth from incisors to uvula. In one sense, therefore, both velar and mediopalatal stops are back rather than front stops. The entire distance from the edge of the upper central incisors along the arch of the palate to the tip of the uvula, when the velum is raised to the position of the vowel [ɑ], is something like 85 to 90 mm. The length of the velum from uvula to hard palate then is from 28 to 30 mm. Since the usual velar and mediopalatal stops (of English, for example) are made with about the same part of the dorsum of the tongue in contact with the roof of the mouth, when the point of contact is advanced even as little as 5 mm. there is a notable difference in the mouth cavity ahead of the occlusion. The whole mass of the body and blade of the tongue is advanced and the cavity is thereby largely filled up. The pitch of the puff of air released from a mediopalatal stop is notably higher than that from a velar stop.

As an example of the voiceless, fortis, impulsive, aspirated, simple, mediopalatal, pressure stop we may take the [k] of English *keel*. The difference between this stop and the [k] of English *cool*, or between the stops of German *Kiel* and *Kohle* is immediately apparent when the two words are pronounced successively. If one then pronounces in succession the English words *keel, kale, coal, cool* it becomes clear that no two of these

[k] sounds are precisely alike. If we assign the stops of *keel* and *kale* to the mediopalatal category and those of *coal* and *cool* to the velar category, we are but dividing a series arbitrarily into two parts. Linguistically, the [k] of English *keel* is identical with the [k] of *cool*; phonetically, we may find it useful to observe the difference, particularly when we come to apply phonetic observations either to the practical task of teaching articulations or to the scientific task of explaining certain historical developments in the phonology of various languages. In a broad transcription we may properly neglect the difference and write [k] for the voiceless mediopalatal as well as for the voiceless velar stop. If we desire to indicate the difference observed, we may write [c] for the mediopalatal stop of *keel, kale*.

As an example of the voiceless, lenis, impulsive, unaspirated, simple, mediopalatal, pressure stop we may cite the sound written *g* in German genü*g*sam, Fei*g*ling, or heard in many American pronunciations of medial *k* in words like *baker, tobacco*.[20] In broad transcription this stop may be written [g̥]; in narrow transcription it would appear as [ɟ̥].

As an example of the voiced, impulsive, unaspirated, simple, mediopalatal, pressure stop we may cite the [g] of English *geese*. The difference between the mediopalatal and velar [g] becomes apparent when *goose* and *geese* are pronounced in sequence. What has been said of this difference in the case of the voiceless stops [k], [c], may be applied, *mutatis mutandis*, to the voiced stops. We may, in broad transcription, write [g] for both voiced stops; if we wish to distinguish the mediopalatal stop, we may write it [ɟ].

A conditioned variant of velar [kx]—the voiceless, fortis, affricative, simple, pressure stop—is the mediopalatal [cx] indicated for Hottentot.[21] It is observed that the fricative release [x] tends to lose its identity when thus "fronted" to the mediopalatal position and to become rather an aspiration, so that the affrictive [cx] tends to be replaced by the aspirate [ch].

5.24 *Palatal Stops* [c], [ɟ], [t], [d̪], [tʃ], [dʒ]

For some speakers the simple stop consonants of the types [k] and [g] are prevelar rather than velar, and the advanced forms of them are then articulated still farther forward than the mediopalatal forms just described. The point of contact between the dorsum of the tongue and the palate is definitely ahead of the junction of hard palate with the velum and wholly on the arc of the former. These are then palatal but not prepalatal stops, but they are usually written with the same symbols we have used for the mediopalatals. Apart from their more forward articulation they are like the mediopalatal stops in every particular.

There is another kind of stop, the contact for which is made between the very tip—and indeed usually the under surface of the tip—of the tongue and the hard palate approximately where its vault is highest. Insofar as the tongue is flexed backward to make this contact, the name retroflex seems appropriate for this group of sounds. They have also been called cacuminal, and with even less propriety, cerebral. The voiceless, retroflex, palatal, impulsive, simple, pressure stop is common in the Dravidian languages and it is frequently heard in the English pronunciations of natives of India. It may be written [t]. The voiced congener of this sound is written [d]. Both sounds can be found in Kashmiri,[22] in the Marathe of the Kolhapur district,[23] in Tamil of Ceylon,[24] in the Bantu district of Herero[25] and in other languages in these regions. The lingual series of mutes in Sanskrit had this retroflex palatal occlusion.[26]

English has both a voiceless and a voiced, affricative, simple, pressure stop in the palatal region. Indeed, these sounds may often be prepalatal. They are the consonants of words like *itch*, and *edge*. It is worth while to point out that the affricate in *itch*, *hitch*, *batch*, *hatch*, *stretch*, *wretch* results historically from the palatalization of an earlier geminated [k], while the affricate in *edge*, *hedge*, *bridge*, results from the palatalization of a geminated [g]. The advanced articulation due to the palatalization sounded to English ears more like the stops of the [t] and [d] types than like mediopalatal [k] and [g], and so they have come to be written conventionally *tch* and *dge*, and indeed by many phoneticians as [tʃ], and [dʒ]. What these sounds are historically has nothing to do with how they should be described now; they are quite clearly in English palatal affricates. They may be transcribed either [tʃ] and [dʒ], as is the approved practice of the International Phonetic Association, or [č] and [ǰ]. They should not be transcribed [c] and [ɟ]. Russian has both voiceless and voiced palatal affricates, though Trofimov and Jones call them palatoalveolar affricates.[27] Italian has the affricates perhaps even farther forward in *pace*, *luce*, *dolce*, *celeste*, *vicine*, *acerba*, and the like, with [tʃ], and *regina*, *soggiorna*, *gentile*, *faggi*, and the like, with [dʒ].

It is evident that the palatal stops, whether affricative or impulsive, represent approaches to the boundary of a kind of stop: everything we have considered from postvelar [q] and [ɢ] to palatal [c] and [ɟ], except the retroflex stops, can be regarded as a kind of [k] or [g] sound. In the same sense, every stop we shall find articulated from the palatal region forward to the lips may be regarded as some kind of a [t] or [d] sound. When we observe that the retroflex sounds in the palatal regions are not classed as [k] or [g] sounds, but as [t] or [d] sounds, and when we see the shift of classification in the case of the geminated Germanic stops which became English [tʃ] and [dʒ] beside palatal [c] and [ɟ] sounds articulated in the same region, we infer that the difference results rather from the behavior of the tongue than from the precise point at which it makes its occlusion. The lingual oral stops fall into two major classes, then, according as they are made with the dorsum of the tongue or with its apex. Consonants of the types [k] and [g] are dorsal stops which have a range of incidence from postvelar to palatal: consonants of the types [t] and [d] are apical stops which have a range of incidence from palatal to interdental, as we shall see.

5.25 *Alveolar, Gingival, Dental Stops* [t], [d̪], [d], [ts], [dz]

If the tip or the fore part of the blade of the tongue be raised to produce a simple stop against the alveolar ridge and this stop then be released with some aspiration, the result, if voiceless, will be the sound of English [t]. If the same type of articulation is shifted forward so that the contact is with the gums, rather than the alveolae, the sound will be that of the gingival German or Danish [t]. If the point of contact be shifted still farther forward until it is on the inner surfaces of the upper incisors, the result is a Spanish dental [t]. The same articulation with lenis rather than fortis energy and no aspiration will give the standard Russian [t]. The differences alveolar, gingival, or dental, while important for the careful description of these sounds and essential for the correct reproduction of any of them, are not sufficient to change the type of stop consonants made in these areas. It is customary to speak of stops like [t] or [d] as dental stops, and there is no objection to this practice if the term dental be taken to include all three of the regions named.

The voiceless, impulsive, simple, dental, pressure stop is the stop of the type [t]. English [t] is usually fortis, aspirated, and alveolar. German [t] is likely to be fortis, aspirated, and gingival. Russian [t] is lenis, unaspirated, and dental.

The sound represented by written *d* in words like German *niedlich, mündlich*, is a voiceless, gingival, lenis, impulsive, unaspirated, simple pressure stop, which may be written [d̪]. Jespersen observed[28] this stop in American pronunciations of words like *water, better*. Other writers[29] now observe in such words a sound to which they refer as "voiced t." There is no doubt that the sound in question is lenis rather than fortis, and unaspirated rather than aspirated, as Jespersen observed. But there is also no doubt that, as many speakers now utter it, the voicing persists throughout the occlusion. What I have been able to find out about this situation may be summarized thus:[30] (a) The sound referred to as "voiced t" does not occur in the speech of all Americans, and (b) it does not regularly occur in the same words in the speech of all those who do use it. (c) This stop is a sound of extremely short duration, being rarely more than 0.03 seconds long, or from one-third to one-half as long as a normal voiceless

[t]. (d) The voiced dental stop [d], when intervocalic or postconsonantal, is reduced by these same speakers to a very short sound usually identical in length with the "voiced t" in analogous contexts, e.g., in *latter : ladder, shutter : shudder.* (e) Speakers who regularly pronounce voiceless [t] produce a voiced [d] in analogous contexts which is about one half as long as their [t], though not so short as the dental stops of those who use "voiced t." (f) These intervocalic and postconsonantal dental stops are uniformly shorter than the comparable labial stops, but it is noteworthy that the voiceless labial stop [p] in such contexts is usually 1.6 times as long as the voiced stop [b], which averages a little less than 0.06 seconds in duration. The situation in American speech has all the earmarks of a sound change in progress. It suggests a weakening rather than a strengthening of the articulation of these stops, and if this continues, the next stage of the process may well be that of an open dental consonant in place of one or of both dental stops, unless, as happened in one of my subjects, the laryngeal stop replaces [t] in some of these words. (Hunc fortasse post me ramum serra dissecabunt.)

The voiced, impulsive, simple, dental, pressure stop is the stop of the type [d]. The differences as to the precise point of articulation which have been noted for [t] apply equally to [d]. English [d] is lenis, unaspirated, and alveolar. Russian [d] is lenis, unaspirated, and dental. The chief difference between the two sounds is not, however, the small difference as to the point of articulation; it is rather the difference as to the degree and place of voicing. Initial English [d] is likely to be unvoiced for some 0.4 of its duration, only the final 0.6 being fully voiced. Russian [d] is likely to be "completely" voiced throughout its duration. Even though this "completeness" is more nearly 0.9 than 1.0, it is notably longer than either English or German speakers can manage to voice the stop without effort and close attention to this aspect of its production. In English an intervocalic [d] is apt to be more continuously voiced than either an initial or a final [d]. The latter has a tendency to lose its voicing towards the end, and again it is something like 0.6 voiced, with the final 0.4 voiceless.

The voiceless, dental, affricative, simple, pressure stop is the sound [t] plus the homorganic fricative, or more precisely, the sound [t] released through the fricative produced on the opening margins of its occlusion. The affricate, like the impulsive stop, may be either alveolar, gingival, or dental. It may be written [ts] and is found in numerous languages. In German it is conventionally written *z* or *tz* and is historically a development of Germanic [t] in *zu, Zeit,* or of geminated Germanic [t] in *Hitze, heizen.* The affricate [ts] is rare in English, though it may be said to occur in borrowed words like *tsetse, tsar, Tsing-Tau.* The Russian uses [ts] widely, and there it is not dental, as is the Russian impulsively released [t], but alveolar, unaspirated, and lenis rather than fortis. Italian uses the affricate [ts] extensively in words like *Venezia, avanza, canzonetta, dolcezza, amazzano*. There it is dental rather than alveolar.

The [ts] which occurs frequently in English words like *Betsy, Patsy, eats, nuts, Pittsburg*, is not recognized as an affricate by writers on English phonetics. There are valid linguistic reasons for regarding these combinations in English as two, rather than as one speech sound, and although the acoustic and neuromuscular characteristics of the affricate [ts] are well-nigh indistinguishable from those assumed at times by the combination [ts], the phonetician should follow linguistic rather than mere acoustic analysis in this and all similar cases. It is interesting to observe that when English borrowed German *ätzen*, perhaps by way of Dutch *etsen*, with the affricate [ts] from a geminated [t], this affricate was not heard as [ts] by English speakers, but rather was heard as their own affricate [tʃ], and the word came to be associated with words like *itch, pitch, stitch, batch, hatch, patch, stretch, wretch*, which owe their affricate to the palatalization of a geminated [k]. The same thing happened when Dutch *schets* developed into English *sketch*. Indeed, even native words with geminated [t], like *fetch*, which should have developed [ts], shifted to the affricate [tʃ] from geminated [k]. The difference between the affricate [ts] and the combination [ts] may appear to be subtle or nonexistent, but it is nevertheless linguistically real and important.

The voiced, affricative, simple, pressure stop [dz] may be alveolar, gingival, or dental. The sound is found in a limited number of Italian words such as *zona, Zefiro, orizzonte, bizzarro*, and also in words like *bronzi, senza*, though here the voiceless affricate [ts] also appears. Russian uses [dz] medially, but not initially or finally.[31] The situation in English is analogous to that observed for [ts]. The combination [dz] occurs in words like *adze, bids, heads*, but the true affricate is missing.

There is another type of affricative release found with [t] and [d] in some of the Slavic languages, notably in Polish and Slovak.[32] Here instead of the fricative [s] or [z], there has developed the palatalized form of these sounds, written [ɕ] and [ʑ], so that the affricate is then [tɕ], and [dʑ], as in Polish *kość, dziad*. The release of the stop is into a prepalatal or alveolar constriction between a flat surface of the blade of the tongue, not far back from the apex, and the hard palate. This constriction may or may not be a long one, but the aperture through which the breath stream flows must be a flat slit, not a round hole, and there must be no cupping of the dorsum of the tongue behind the constriction and no rounding of the lips in front of it.

5.26 *Labial Stops* [p], [b̥], [b], [pΦ], [bβ], [pf], [bv]

A full occlusion of the breath channel may be effected by the closure of the lower lip against the upper lip. Usually this closure is made chiefly by contact of the median and inner surfaces of the two lips, but more vigorous contraction of the muscles of the labial sphincter group can bring the outer edges of the lips into the closure. Stops produced by the two lips alone are called bilabial stops. A slightly different type of closure has been evolved in a number of languages. The median edge of the lower lip is brought into contact with the bottom edges of the upper incisors and the outer edge of the lower lip is then rolled up until it effects a complete closure against the middle and inner surfaces of the upper lip. Such a closure is properly called a dentilabial, or a labiodental stop. The International Phonetic Association does not provide a special set of symbols for these dentilabial stops, although the voiceless one used to be written with the Greek π. The symbol Greek β, however, is not available for the voiced dentilabial stop, since it is conventionally used for the bilabial fricative. If special symbols are required they may be selected and defined when used.

The voiceless, fortis, impulsive, aspirated, simple, bilabial, pressure stop [p] may be observed in English words like *pit, pack, pun*. Russian [p] is unaspirated, but otherwise very much like English [p].

The voiceless, lenis, impulsive, unaspirated, simple, bilabial, pressure stop [ḅ] occurs in standard German for a written *b* in words like *unglaublich, Knäblein, Betrübnis*. Jespersen observed[33] this sound in English pronunciations of words like *lobster*, and in American pronunciations of words like *copper, upper*.

The voiced, impulsive, unaspirated, simple, bilabial, pressure stop [b] may be observed in English words like *bit, back, bun*. Russian [b] differs from English [b] as Russian [d] differs from English [d], in the duration of voicing.

The voiceless, affricative simple, bilabial, pressure stop may be observed as a substitute for the labiodental affricate [pf] in some German pronunciations of words like *Dampf, impfen*. A combination of bilabial [p] with the bilabial fricative can be observed in some English pronunciations of words like *triumph*, or *camphor*. Linguistic analysis indicates that these combinations, like English [ts], are not affricates in English, but groups of two speech sounds. The affricate, as well as the combination, may be written [pΦ]. I can offer no useful illustration of a voiced, bilabial, affricate, such as might be written [bβ].

The voiceless, fortis, affricative, simple, dentilabial, pressure stop is readily observable in standard German in words like *Pferd, empfangen, hüpfen*. This labial affricate does not seem to be widely used in other languages, though it appears in Logo, in the Sudan, along with the voiced dentilabial affricate [bv] as an occasional substitute for [f] and for [v] respectively.[34] In some Dutch pronunciations of words like *water, weder*, *wreed*, the initial sound is a voiced labiodental stop, though many speakers use the labiodental fricative [v] in such words.[35]

5.27   *Simple Stops with Palatalization* [p̣], [ḅ], [ṭ], [ḍ], [k̇], [g̣]

It is possible to bring the blade of the tongue into close contact with a considerable area of the arc of the hard palate near its forward slope and in the prepalatal region while at the same time effecting a more or less normal occlusion for the simple stop consonants. When this is done we call the result a palatalized stop consonant.[36]

In the case of the labials [p̣] or [ḅ], no adjustment of the normal stop is required. In the case of [ṭ] or [d] the apical stop is usually merely extended in area, there being then a long occlusion reaching from the dental or gingival region clear back to the prepalatal region. Sometimes, however the tip of the tongue, instead of being put into contact with the teeth, gums, or alveolar ridge above, is lowered until it actually touches the alveolar ridge of the lower teeth, while the dental occlusion above is then made by the blade, rather than by the apex of the tongue. When this happens the occlusion is very little different from that of the palatalized velars, except that it is farther forward and that the release is from the dental occlusion backward. For the velar stops [k̇] and [g̣] the primary occlusion is advanced to the mediopalatal region and then extended into the prepalatal area. This is another long occlusion.

When these palatalized consonants are released, the opening begins at the normal point of release for the stop, after which the prepalatal occlusion is "peeled off" quickly. In effect, the ordinary homorganic fricative of the usual affricate has been replaced by a prepalatal fricative of very brief duration. The difference between the palatalized stop and a combination of the stop followed by the palatal fricative is that in the latter case the two articulations are less completely superimposed one on the other and that the fricative is longer than the affricative release of the palatalized stop. Illustrations of the palatalized simple pressure stops may be drawn from Russian, where labials, dentals, and velars all are affected.[37]

5.28   *Simple Stops with Labialization* [k̫], [g̫]

It is possible to produce the simple laryngeal, velar, or dental stops with simultaneous partial closure of the lips in such fashion that the release of the stop is in the form of a labial fricative of increasing aperture. The result is a simple pressure stop with a very short labialized affricative release. The difference between such a simple pressure stop and a compound stop, whether a glottalized labial or a velaric labial, is slight but real. For the simple stop there is but one complete occlusion; for the compound stop the lips also make a complete closure. Illustrations of the labialized simple pressure stops can be found in some Russian pronunciations and in Karbardian, a North Georgian language of the Caucasus.[38] Russian has the labialized velars [k̫] and [g̫] before [o], Karbardian has aspirated labialized velar [q̫h] and mediopalatal [k̫h], also unaspirated [g̫], [g̫], and [ʔ], or the velar, postvelar, and laryngeal stops with labialization.

5.29   *Simple Stops with Velarization* [p̴], [b̴], [ƚ], [d̴]

During the labial occlusion of simple pressure stops the tongue is free to assume various positions, either in anticipation of subsequent speech sounds, or as an integral part of the labial occlusion. We have observed the palatalization of the labials. When the back of the tongue is raised to the position of the velar fricative during the labial stop the latter may thereby acquire a velarized release in place of its normal impulsive or homorganic affricative release. The difference between the velarized labial simple pressure stop and the velaric labial compound pressure stop is precisely the absence of a complete velar occlusion in the simple stop. Some Russian speakers use velarized voiceless [p̴] and voiced [b̴], notably before [o] or [i].[39] Velarized dental stops [ƚ] and [d̴], neither of them aspirated, are found in Egyptian Arabic. Evidently the velarization of the dental occlusion will bring practically the whole of the upper surface of the tongue into contact with the roof of the mouth, with some retraction of the most forward dental articulation, perhaps, as the back of the tongue is raised to the velar region. These Arabic stops are the so-called emphatic consonants Ṭa and Ḍad.[40]

THE INTERMITTENT STOPS

5.31   *The Laryngeal Trill*

The glottal trill, sometimes called "Intermittent Voice," or Knarrstimme, is produced by the periodic occlusion of the breath stream by the vocal bands, which appear to interrupt the much more rapid vibrations of voicing. The mechanism of this trill has not been described convincingly, but the trilling appears to result from more than normal relaxation of the vocal bands while they are still held in the position to stop the flow of air if not blown apart by the pressure below. By a very nice adjustment the period of their occlusion can be reduced to 25 or 30 vibrations per second. Instead of producing clear or steady voicing at this low pitch, however, the cords "speak" with voice vibrations of a much higher period momentarily when thus blown apart, but quickly subside again to their position of lax closure, from which they are then once more blown by the breath which accumulates behind the occlusion. As a form of voice production this glottal trill may be substituted for clear voice, either habitually by the very lazy, or by corpulent people, or occasionally by others when momentarily lazy, facetious, or annoyed. As a nonsyllabic sound this glottal trill is sometimes superimposed upon a vowel sound more or less completely when the syllable calls for a vowel plus "r." I can cite no language in which it is a regular and distinctive speech sound, and I suspect that frequently what is called a glottal trill is rather a glottal fricative, in the sense that the occlusions are too irregular in time to merit the name of a trill.⁴¹

5.32   *The Uvular Trill* [ʀ]

The uvula can be so placed in the medial depression of the raised dorsum of the tongue that a gentle air pressure from below will cause it intermittently to rise and fall in this channel, and thus intermittently to stop the breath stream. The point of the uvula lies forward in the groove of the tongue and the edges of the velum at the glossopharyngeal arch usually make contact with the top surface of the dorsum of the tongue, thereby forcing the breath to pass through the groove in the median line of the tongue. This kind of trill has become quite common in Europe, notably in urban speech in France and Germany. It is called "uvular r" and written [ʀ]. Usually uvular [ʀ] is voiced, but it may be voiceless. Usually it is rolled, or trilled, but occasionally it is reduced to a single tap. In that case it may be said to be a flapped, rather than a trilled [ʀ].

5.33   *The Dental, Gingival, Alveolar Trill, or Tap* [r], [ɾ], [ŗ], [ɽ]

The apex of the tongue is usually supple enough to execute a good trill when properly poised near the alveolae, the gums, or the front upper teeth. Many languages use this kind of a lingual trilled *r*. It is the standard *r* of the German stage. It is commonly used in Russian and Italian, and in the French of the provinces. The usual rolled [r] has perhaps two to four occlusions, Scotch [r] is likely to be more exuberantly trilled. The normal [r] of the Eastern Sudan is a strongly rolled alveolar trill.⁴²

The dental (gingival, or alveolar) trill [r] is particularly susceptible of reduction to a single tap. In Spanish the single tap, or flapped [ɾ], contrasts distinctively with rolled [r], e.g., in *pero : perro, cero : cerro*.⁴³ A similar flapped [ɾ] is normal in Tagalog in the Philippines.⁴⁴ Hottentot *r* is usually a single tap.⁴⁵ British speakers of English often use a single tap [ɾ] intervocalically, in words like *very, bury*, or as the linking *r* (cf. Section 7.056).

The dental trill, or rolled [r], is regularly palatalized in Russian before a front vowel. Evidently the palatalization of a trill cannot be accomplished in quite the same way as that of a simple stop, since a long complete occlusion involves a larger mass of the tongue than can readily be made to vibrate. The r-mouillé of Russian is a very rapid apical trill against the alveolar ridge, above the front incisors. That is to say, the mass of the tongue which vibrates is even less than that for the normal rolled [r]. Behind this trilling apex, however, the blade of the tongue is raised much closer to the palate than for [r], and in such a way that the margins of the tongue make a closure with the gums and palate on either side of the moving apex for a very considerable distance back. The breath stream which activates the trilling tip of the tongue is thus forced through a comparatively long, narrow, central channel between the raised tongue and the palate.[46]

If a palatalized [ṙ] of this type stops its trill before the dorsum of the tongue is lowered from the position of palatalization, the release of the [ṙ] is likely to be followed by a fricative sound resembling [ʒ] as in *azure*, or when unvoiced, by [ʃ] as in *fish*. Polish has this affricative [ṙʒ] from Indo-European [r]. In Czech it has become the spirant [ʒ] or [ʃ].

The performance of a trill with the retroflex articulation of the tip and underside of the tip of the tongue against the palate above the alveolae in the prepalatal region is less difficult than might be supposed. In Herero, a Bantu language of South-West Africa, the r is usually a flapped retroflex [ɽ], but it may also be a rolled retroflex [ɽ].[47] In Tamil, the retroflex [ɽ] is a strong flap.[48]

5.34   *The Labial Trill* [ʙ]

A trill can be made with the two lips, as one frequently does when one says what is conventionally written "Brr!" German teamsters still use this trill, accompanied by a high pitched and very loud voice note, to induce their draft horses to stop. The name of this noise, the "Kutscher R" is reminiscent of another age. The sound may be written with the Greek letter *rho* [ʙ]. I know of no language in which it is a regular speech sound.

THE COMPOUND STOPS

5.4   *Glottalized Stops*[49]

If the breath stream is wholly occluded by the vocal bands while it is also stopped at any one of the positions possible for the tongue or lips, the result is a glottalized stop. The air confined between the glottis and the lingual or labial occlusion may be (a) compressed, (b) rarefied, or (c) merely confined.

5.41   *Glottalized Pressure Stops*

Air may be compressed in a glottalized stop by raising the larynx, the hyoid bone, and the base of the tongue toward the lower jaw, that is, upward and forward, after both stoppages have been securely made. The result is a glottalized pressure stop, sometimes called an ejective stop, and the approved graphic symbol is an apostrophe set after the symbol for the analogous simple stop, for instance [p'], [t'], [k']. The pressure stops of this category may be released impulsively, or affricatively, in the same manner as the simple stops. The energy of the release of a glottalized stop is dependent upon the degree of compression achieved by the raising of the larynx and this may vary from considerable force to very little indeed. Voiceless ejective stops are by no means unusual. Karbardian, in the Caucasus,[50] uses [p'], [t'], [k'] and a labialized [k']. Georgian has [p'], [t'], [k'] and the affricatively released glottalized [ts'] and [tʃ'], i.e. the dental and prepalatal affricates.[51] Taos, in New Mexico,[52] and Pomo, in California,[53] have the voiceless ejectives. Grammont[54] distinguishes between French [p] and the [p] of certain Germanic dialects by ascribing to the French stop in detail the ejective mechanism of a glottalized pressure stop. What he says of [p] is equally valid for [t] and [k]. There may be some doubt as to the universal validity of his description for French,[55] but that it fits the performance of considerable numbers of Frenchmen seems clear enough.

5.42 *Glottalized Suction Stops*

The occlusions made for the glottalized suction stops are the same as those observed for the glottalized pressure stops, but the hyoid bone and the larynx are high when the glottal occlusion is made and are then depressed with greater or less energy. This movement downward and back greatly increases the volume of the chamber between the two occlusions, and when the oral stop is released, the outer air will enter the cavity above the glottis. This air meets air from below the glottis when the closure there is released, and for this reason the behavior of the air from outside the anterior occlusion depends upon the time of the release of the glottal stop. If the air from below the glottis is admitted to the occluded cavity before the anterior stop is released, the effect is to produce outward pressure, or no pressure at all behind this stop, and then the release may be more or less identical with the normal simple pressure stop of the same oral articulation. If the glottal closure is released simultaneously with the oral stop, the result is likely to be inaudible. If the glottal closure is released later than the oral stop, air will enter the mouth from outside with a degree of energy directly related to the degree of rarefaction produced by the downward movement of the larynx. The subsequent glottal release may or may not be audible as a glottal stop [ʔ]. The usual symbol for these glottalized suction stops is an apostrophe before the symbol for the analogous oral stop, thus ['p], ['t], ['k], or with voicing ['b], ['d]. Voicing of the glottalized suction stop can be accomplished only if the rate at which air from the lungs is admitted to the occluded cavity above the glottis by the voice vibration is lower than the rate of rarefaction due to the depression of the hyoid bone and the larynx. Such voiced glottalized suction stops exist in Zulu-Xhosa,[56] and in the Moru-Madi group of the Sudan.[57]

5.5 Velaric Stops

If, when the breath stream has been stopped by the lips or by the apex, or fore-part of the tongue, the dorsum of the tongue is also raised until a full contact is made in the velar or prevelar region, there may be a small cavity between the front and back occlusions of the tongue in which air is confined. This air can be compressed by drawing the dorsal occlusion forward a bit, and in this way a pressure stop might be produced. It is easily possible to produce a suction cup with the lingual occlusions described by drawing the central parts of the upper surface of the tongue downward while the margins and the forward and velar occlusions remain sealed against the roof of the mouth. The degree of rarefaction produced in this way can be considerable, and when the front occlusion or one of the marginal occlusions is impulsively released, the result is a loud popping sound quite properly called a "click."

5.51 Velaric Pressure Stops

In the Moru-Madi languages of the Eastern Sudan,[58] and in the Bantu languages on the upper Congo[59] the stops of double articulation which are written *kp*, *gb*, are probably to be regarded as velaric pressure stops impulsively released, so that the sound resembles simple [p] or [b] when heard.

5.52 Velaric Suction Stops

Velaric suction stops may be labial, dental, gingival, alveolar, prepalatal, palatal, or inverted or retroflex. Such stops may be released at the front of the stoppage or at the side, in which event they are lateral clicks. The languages in which these velaric suction stops are used at all, generally use more than one variety of them. Clicks, or velaric suction stops are characteristic of the Hottentot languages, and are found also in Bushman dialects, and to some extent in southeastern Bantu.[60]

The International Phonetic Association provides only three symbols for the clicks, which is far from enough to write all of the various kinds of occlusions and releases which actually occur. The symbol [ʖ] is written for an affricatively released lateral velaric suction stop which sounds much like the "clucking" once used by drivers to urge their horses to bestir themselves. This is an affricate, hence not a "popping" but a "scraping" sound; but it is vigorous. The symbol [ɕ] is used for an alveolar, impulsively released, velaric suction stop, which may or may not be retroflex in its apical articulation. The symbol [ʔ] is used for the dental, affricatively released, velaric suction stop. This sounds something like the noise made when suction is applied by the tongue to remove small particles of food from between the incisors. More detailed transcription is in use by specialists in languages which use the clicks widely.

THE OPEN CONSONANTS

6.1 General Features of Open Consonants

The second major class of nonsyllabic sounds is that of the open consonants. The characteristic feature of these sounds, as distinguished from the stop consonants, is the fact that in their production the breath stream is not completely blocked; air is not completely enclosed and then released, it is made to flow either out of the lungs through the pharynx and mouth or nose, or into the mouth from outside the lips. The breath stream may flow through the open consonant articulation under pressure from the lungs, or under negative pressure, or suction, produced by thoracic or laryngeal movements. Open consonants may therefore be classified as expiratory or inspiratory. Most languages use only expiratory open consonants, some languages use one or two inspiratory open consonants.

Pressure in the lungs to drive the breath stream outward through the open consonant articulation is produced by the contraction of the thorax, by the weight and elasticity of its walls after the taking in of breath, plus whatever muscular contractions may occur in the production of the syllable pulse. Negative pressure, or suction, to draw air inward through the open consonant articulation is produced by mechanisms analogous either to that of the simple suction stops or to that of the glottalized suction stops; that is, by increasing the size of the thorax, thus drawing air inward into the lungs, or by the closure of the glottis and the subsequent depression of the larynx and hyoid bone. The two mechanisms produce what may be called (a) simple inspiratory open consonants, or (b) glottalized inspiratory open consonants.

In order to be heard, the breath stream of the open consonants must be set into characteristic movements which in turn produce vibratory excitation of the air at audible frequencies. This is achieved by causing the breath stream to impinge against or to be deflected by an obstruction placed in the path of its free flow. The acoustic qualities of the resulting vibratory disturbances will depend upon the size of the cavities in which the air vibrates and the nature of their openings, and upon the speed of the air stream which activates the air of these cavities. In a general sense, any sound produced in this way is produced by friction of one sort or another. The friction may be that of air against some surface or surfaces, or of air against air, as is the case when a thin stream of air is released from a small jet or nozzle. For this reason, many of the open consonants are usually called fricative sounds. In a few cases the friction is so difficult to describe that these sounds have been called nonfricative, or frictionless continuants. For a quite different reason the nasal consonants are not usually thought of as fricative consonants.

Open consonants may be voiceless or voiced in the sense that the flowing breath stream may be impeded by the periodic vibrations of the vocal bands or caused to vibrate periodically as it passes in puffs between the edges of the opening and closing vocal bands. Voicing the breath stream causes it to flow in rapid pulses rather than continuously, and, if the difference of pressure below and above the larynx be the same in each case, to flow more slowly than the unvoiced breath stream. For this reason, and perhaps also in some cases because it takes a faster air stream to make the consonant audible, voiceless open consonants are often, but not always, fortis, while voiced open consonants are more likely to be lenis. There is no necessity for the depression of the larynx to produce voicing for expiratory open consonants. The voicing of inspiratory open consonants is produced very much as that of the glottalized suction stops is managed.

When an open consonant is voiced it may approach in its gennemic aspects the sound of the vowels, provided the fricative noises produced are relatively slight. Insofar as such sounds derive their distinctive character from the selective transmission of the voice tone through characteristic resonance chambers, they are likely to be acoustically much less complex than the voiceless fricative noises such as [ʃ] or [s]. Indeed, there are consonantal sounds and vowel sounds the differences between which are rather differences of degree than of kind, so far as acoustic analysis reveals. Examples are the French nasal vowel [ã] and the nasal consonant [ŋ], or the English consonant [r] of *red* as pronounced in the American Midwest, and the vowel [ɜ] of such a word as *bird*.

Just as there are three phases of the normal articulation of a stop consonant, so there are three phases—the onset, the hold, and the release—of the articulation of an open consonant. The middle phase involves in the latter case rather the production of a controlled opening than the production of an occlusion, but this is nevertheless just as definite a position as that assumed for a stop. The middle phase of open consonants, like that of stops, may be of very brief duration. It is also possible for the third phase, the release, of open consonants to assume an acoustic prominence, a duration, and a movement pattern more characteristic of the sound than either its first or its second phases. The latter, of course, occur each time the sound is made, but it is the third phase which appears more prominent. This is true notably of English [w] and [j] and only slightly less evidently so of some forms of American [r].

6.11 *Classification*

It is convenient to divide the larger class of open consonants into at least three subordinate classes, on the basis of the manner in which the sounds are produced. In turn each of these classes may be further subdivided by classifying the sounds of each according to the place at which the characteristic articulation is produced.

Consonants produced by the occlusion of the oral passage while the breath stream is allowed to flow freely through the nose are nasal consonants. Consonants produced by the occlusion of the central region of the oral passage while the breath stream is made to flow over the sides of the tongue, through the teeth and thence forward to the lips are lateral consonants. The other open consonants may be grouped together as fricative consonants, unless one wishes to segregate from the others of this group the fricative "r" sounds and those few which are particularly marked by the relative prominence of their third or final phase.

The regions of articulation defined for the stop consonants are sufficiently numerous to serve adequately the requirements for the description of the open consonants. Some of the open consonants, like some of the stops, are subject respectively to velarization, palatalization, and to labialization. Open consonants other than the nasals are likewise subject to nasalization. Indeed, from one point of view, the nasal consonants themselves may be viewed as essentially stop consonants with nasalization, and therewith the extremes of our classifications meet: no sounds are more unlike the vowels than the stops; no sounds are more like the vowels than the nasal consonants and the liquids, [l] and [r].

6.2 *The Nasal Consonants*

It is typical of the nasal consonants that they have a resonance chamber in the mouth, although the breath stream is not allowed to flow through this chamber to escape at the lips; it is forced rather to flow through the nasopharynx and the nasal cavities to escape at the nose. The major acoustic differences between the several types of nasal consonants are due to differences in the character of the oral resonator. This has its lowest range of frequencies for [m] and its highest range for [ŋ], with an intermediate range for [n].[61] We classify the nasal consonants therefore according to the observable peculiarities of their oral articulation. Since the oral articulations of the nasals are quite similar to those of the simple stops made in the

same regions, the nasal consonants may acquire distinctive forms by virtue
of the nature of the release of their oral occlusion. They may be released
with aspiration, so that we find nasal aspirates like [mh], [nh], [ŋh], or the
release may be affricative, so that we find affricates such as [m̥Φ], [mβ], or
[m̥f], [ɱv], as in the Bantu languages.[62]

6.21   *The Bilabial Nasal* [m]

The articulation of [m] usually comprises (1) a bilabial closure similar
to that made for [b], (2) the lowering of the velum, which is moderately
rather than vigorously drawn down, and (3) voicing of the breath stream.
The position of the tongue does not play a distinctive role in the production
of English, French, or German [m].

A labiodental [ɱ] may be produced rather than bilabial [m] in some
German pronunciations of *fünf schimpfen*, *Strümpfe*, and the like, in which
a labiodental [f] is involved. Some English speakers make a labiodental
[ɱ] in words like *triumvirate, camphor*. The sound is frequent in Spanish,
in words like *enfermo, un favor*.

The bilabial, or labiodental, nasal is not infrequently voiceless, notably
in French, in words like *prisme*. This sound may be written [m̥].

Since the oral articulation of [m] is very similar to that of [b], [m] is
susceptible to palatalization. The tongue in this event is raised to make a
long contact between its blade and the hard palate in the prepalatal region.
The sound may be written [ṁ]. Also, it is possible to velarize [m] by raising
the dorsum of the tongue to make contact in the velar or mediopalatal
region, as for [g]. Velarized [m] may be written [m̴].[63] Either palatalization
or velarization can produce a notable difference in the quality of the [m]
sound while the labial stop is maintained. However, the release of the
labial occlusion is likely to make the feature of palatalization or velarization
even more prominent when these oral articulations are broken after the
labial release.

6.22   *The Dental Nasal* [n]

In the category of the dental nasal [n] are included alveolar, gingival,
and dental nasals. These are made by producing oral occlusions similar to
those described for [d], but with simultaneous moderate lowering of the
velum and voicing of the breath stream. This is the sound of written *n*
in English *thin*, French *inégalité*, German *dünn*. Like [m], the dental nasal
may be released with aspiration or as an affricate, and it may upon occasion
be voiceless.

6.23   *The Palatal Nasal* [ɲ], [ɳ].

The dental nasal is so frequently palatalized that it is then simply classed by itself as a prepalatal [ɲ]. The occlusion is between the blade of the tongue and the palate from the alveolar ridge backward over the prepalatal region. It is a long occlusion. This kind of [ɲ] is well known in French words like *agneau, vigne,* in Spanish *pequeño,* Italian *ogni.* Russian palatalized [ɲ] appears to differ from French palatal [ɲ] somewhat, because its articulation is dental rather than alveolar, and because its contact, while ample, is not so long towards the palatal region as the French *n*-mouillé.

The retroflex nasal [ɳ] or [ṇ] is made with the tongue articulation of the retroflex palatal [ḍ], plus the lowering of the velum and the voicing of the breath stream. Languages which use the retroflex palatal stops [ṭ] or [ḍ] (Sec. 5.24) are likely to use also the retroflex palatal nasal [ɳ].

6.24   *The Velar Nasal* [ŋ], [N]

Just as we find two varieties of [g], the velar and the mediopalatal *goose : geese,* so we have two varieties of the velar nasal in *sung : sing.* The oral occlusions differ for the two nasals as they do for the simple stops. The nasal of *sing* is notably different from the palatalized dental nasal [ɲ] of French *vigne,* particularly in its release, where the palatalization of [ɲ] becomes distinctively prominent. A graphic distinction between the nasal of *sung* and that of *sing* may be made, if desired, by the use of a diacritic to show an advanced [ŋ], thus: [ŋ] in *sung,* [ŋ+] in *sing.* When this articulation is carried still farther forward it loses its distinctive velar quality. People who speak words in which the velar [ŋ] has thus been fronted are commonly accused of "dropping their g's," in such forms as "comin', sittin'." They have substituted a prepalatal or alveolar [n] for [ŋ] but they have not palatalized the stop, in the sense in which we have used the term palatalized to mean produced with a long prepalatal occlusion.

A postvelar nasal, sometimes called a uvular nasal [N], is found here and there in less well-known languages. The Eskimo dialect of northwest Greenland has a series of postvelar sounds, the stop [q], the voiceless fricative [χ], the voiced fricative [ɣ], and the nasal [N].[65]

6.3   *The Lateral Consonants*

The articulatory feature which characterizes the lateral consonants is the production of an occlusion along the median line of the roof of the mouth in such a way as not completely to stop the flow of the breath stream but to force it to escape over the lateral margins of the tongue, through the teeth, and along the inside of the cheeks to the lips. Some lateral articulations permit the breath stream to escape on one side only, others permit it to flow over both lateral margins of the tongue: we have unilateral and bilateral open consonants. The unilateral articulation appears to be the usual form.

The sounds usually classed as lateral consonants are the various "L" sounds, but it must be observed that other lateral sounds occur. There are lateral [s] and [z] sounds, for example, in the Bantu languages.[66] These Bantu sounds are strongly retroflex articulations which force the breath to flow over the lateral margins of the tongue.

The position of the lips may or may not distinctively affect the sound of the laterals; that is to say, laterals may or may not be labialized. Since they involve various lingual occlusions, the laterals are variously subject to palatalization, velarization, or nasalization. The primary occlusions of the laterals may be dental, retroflex, palatal, or velar, and the breath stream may be voiceless or voiced. Glottalized pressure laterals [l'] occur, with closure of the vocal bands and vigorous elevation of the hyoid bone and larynx, and there are also inspiratory lateral sounds.

Since the occlusion along the median line of the palate involves a rather neat adjustment of the margins of the tongue, the laterals sometimes begin with a complete occlusion in the dental region, which is then followed immediately by the lateral fricative. This kind of lateral is sometimes written [tl] [dl], or more minutely [tɬ], [dɮ]. The laterals may also be released with aspiration.

6.31   *The Dental Lateral* [l]

The usual "L" sounds of English or German are alveolar or gingival laterals without labialization or nasalization. The apex of the tongue makes a medial occlusion in the same general region as that for [d], the sides of the tongue are relaxed so that the breath stream flows between the teeth near the first premolars. The usual German [l] has a clear [ɪ] quality, which results from the position of the convex upper surface of the blade of the tongue near the palatal or prepalatal region. English [l] frequently has more of the quality of [ʊ], particularly when [l] is syllabic. This in turn is due to the elevation of the back of the dorsum of the tongue in the prevelar or mediopalatal region. This back elevation produces a concave upper surface of the tongue behind the alveolar occlusion. One might say, therefore, that this type of English [l], as in *title*, *bottle*, is slightly velarized. It has become customary to speak of [l] with [ɪ] quality and convex tongue surface as a "light" [l], and of [l] with [ʊ] quality and concave tongue surface as "dark" [l]. The latter variety may be written [ɫ], and this symbol is likely to be met in works dealing with Russian sounds, since Russian has an [l] sound in words like *lampa, palka*, which is more strongly velarized than English [l] sounds.

The dental, alveolar, or gingival [l] sounds may be voiceless, and French offers ready examples of a voiceless "light" or clear [l] in words like *peuple*. English, French, German, and Italian [l] are produced with such weak friction that this can only be heard clearly when the sounds are voiceless. Indeed, the International Phonetic Association classes this [l] as a lateral nonfricative consonant. It is true that by comparison with the lateral *ll* of Welsh or the *hl* of Icelandic the English [l] sounds may appear to be frictionless, but the difference is one of degree, not one of kind. Welsh *ll* is a strongly fricative dental lateral, usually voiceless, and when initial, strongly aspirated. This strong fricative sound is reflected in the conventional English spelling *Floyd* for Welsh *Lloyd*. The aspirated strongly fricative lateral may be written [ɬh]. Medial and final Welsh *ll* is sometimes, at least, preceded by a complete dental stop immediately released into the lateral articulation [tl]. This type of articulation may be called a stopped lateral. Icelandic *hl* initially is weaker than Welsh *ll* and is not aspirated; medially and finally Icelandic *hl* is released by a stop [t], or [d] when voiced.[67] Sandawa, a Hottentot dialect, uses the stopped laterals voiceless [tɬ] and voiced [dʮ] in addition to the voiceless, strongly fricative lateral [ɬ] and the usual alveolar [l]. Of these "L" sounds in Sandawa, the voiceless [tɬ] appears to be the only one that is velarized.[68] Karbardian, in the Caucasus, uses a glottalized, ejective, lateral fricative [l'], the simple fricative [ɬ], and a so-called nonfricative [l].[69] The mechanism of the ejective lateral is analogous to that of the ejective stops; the air is driven through the articulation by the elevation of the hyoid bone and the larynx. The lateral openings of the these ejective fricatives are likely to be comparatively small.

The well-known tendency of Chinese, Japanese, Turkish, Tartar, and Caucasian speakers to fail always to distinguish between English [l] and English fricative [r] has its foundation in their native use of a lateral consonant which begins with a sound resembling a fricative [r] and passes to a more normal alveolar [l] sound.[70] This complex sound is written *rl*.

6.32   The Palatal Lateral [ʎ], [ɭ]

Two types of [l] are produced with a medial stop in the prepalatal region. One is the retroflex [ɭ] which is found in languages which use retroflex [ʈ] and [ɖ], such as Marathi[71] and Tamil.[72] The other is a palatalized [l], usually written [ʎ], which is produced with a long contact from the alveolar ridge well into the palatal region. Convenient illustrations of this palatalized [ʎ] can be had from Italian words like *figlio* and *luglio*, which also show a variation from prepalatal [ʎ] after [i] to a palatal [ʎ] after [u]. This [ʎ] is heard in Swiss pronunciations of French and in the Midi of France, although in Paris it is usually replaced by [j] in words like *fille, bouillon*. The Russian palatal [ʎ], like Russian [t̬] does not have quite the long prepalatal contact of Italian [ʎ], but is made with a broad alveolar-apical occlusion and the elevation of the blade of the tongue to the position for [j].[73]

6.4   *The Fricative or Spirant Consonants*

The use of the term fricative, or the term spirant, as a class name for those open consonants which are not nasal and not lateral consonants is defensible only on the grounds of convenience. All open consonants are spirants or fricatives, in the sense that they are produced by an unstopped breath stream. Genetically, however, there is no positive distinguishing characteristic by which these nonnasal, nonlateral open consonants may be identified as belonging to a single class. They are just not nasals and not laterals. Gennemically, they might be divided into two or perhaps into three groups; certainly the "hissing sounds" or "Zischlaute" might be thus set apart from the others. But the practical utility of such an attempt is slight, and the scientific value of a gennemic classification is questionable in the light of our presently available data. Hence these sounds will be treated here as a single, negatively marked class, and within this class we shall consider in turn the r-sounds, the laryngeal, the pharyngeal, the velar, the palatal, the dental, the labiodental, and the labial spirants or fricatives.

6.41   *The* r-*Sounds*

In addition to the intermittent stops which we have described as lingual trills, uvular trills, lingual taps, or uvular taps, [r], [ɾ], [ʀ], there are in various languages a number of open r-sounds of the fricative type, some of which indeed have so far lost their friction as to become very much like vowels. If we ask whether such a sound as the [ɹ] of English *Rome*, as this is pronounced in midwest American, should be classified with the sound of [ʀ] as produced by a native of Berlin in the word *Rom*, or either of these with the [r] of an Italian's *Roma*, we can find an affirmative answer only in linguistic considerations which transcend the phonetic criteria of the genetics or the gennemics of these sounds. It is clear, to be sure, that the initial consonant of English *rich*, German *reich*, and all of their cognate forms in other Germanic languages, is historically the same sound as the initial consonant of Celtic *ri*, Latin *rex*, Sanskrit *raja*, and that the [r]

of the Italian's *re*, the [ʀ] of the Berliner's *reich*, and the [ɹ] of the Chica-
goan's *rich* are historically the same sound. To speak strictly, however, the
phonetician must reject this fact as impertinent to his problem of classification. Phonetically [r], and [ʀ], and [ɹ] are very different sounds. But the
phoneticians may perhaps in this instance defer to the uses of linguistic
history to the extent, at least, of grouping together as r-sounds some of the
very disparate end results of the phonetic changes which have befallen
the Indo-European consonant [r], if they make abundantly clear the fact
that this group is an extraphonetic category set up to direct attention to
one of the more perplexing speech sounds in the human inventory.[74] We
observe, therefore, that the r-sounds comprise (a) intermittent stops,
whether rolled or flapped, and (b) fricative open consonants. These sounds
may be produced by trills of the lips or of the apex of the tongue in the
dental region, either flat or retroflex; or by the uvula in the groove of the
dorsum of the tongue; or by fricative noises between the tongue tip and
the dental, alveolar, or palatal region, either flat or retroflex; or between the
central region of the dorsum of the tongue and the arch of the palate; or
between the edges of the velum and the dorsum of the tongue. Indeed,
even friction between the base of the tongue and the back wall of the
pharynx is sometimes called a "pharyngeal r."

6.411   *The Dental Fricative* [ɹ]

A strictly dental articulation of [ɹ] is probably more rare than the
gingival or alveolar articulations commonly found in English as spoken in
parts of Great Britain. To produce the [ɹ] usually heard in the initial
position in Southern British pronunciations of words like *red* or *street*, the
whole body of the tongue is raised considerably, the tip of the tongue blade
is curved upward to point at the alveolar region behind the upper incisors,
and the lateral margins of the front part of the tongue blade make contact
around the sides of the teeth ridge, so that a comparatively narrow central
channel over the tip of the tongue is formed. This is very much the same
general articulatory position as that required for the rolled dental [r]
except that the front margin of the tongue is usually less elastic and somewhat thicker than when the trill is to be produced. The amount of friction
produced at the point of articulation, or by the constriction produced there,
depends upon the area of the opening through which the breath stream is
forced and the speed at which this breath stream flows. This varies considerably from one language to another and from one phonetic environment
to another in the same language. The mid-dorsal elevation of the tongue
and the throat cavity produced thereby is about the same as that required
for the central vowel [ə].

6.412   *The Retroflex* [ɽ]

Very much the same kind of constriction as that required for [r] is frequently produced between the under side of the apex of the tongue and the post alveolar or prepalatal region. This gives a retroflex [ɽ], which is often, though not always, found in languages which use retroflex [t], [d], and [n]. This articulation is frequent in the languages of India, notably in those under Dravidian influence, and the retroflex [ɽ] is the normal initial *r* of many American speakers of English. Some speakers use both [ɹ] and [ɽ] in such a phrase as, "it never rains."

6.413   *The Mediopalatal* [ɹ]

In Midwest American pronunciations of English there is an open *r* sound, which is formed by raising the middle region of the dorsum of the tongue towards the mediopalatal junction between hard palate and velum until the margins of the tongue make contact with the gums near the molar teeth. The tip of the tongue usually remains low, near and behind the front lower incisors.[75] This may be called a central *r*, if the term mediopalatal *r* seems too unwieldy. Many speakers for whom this is not the usual initial *r* use it in words like *crutch*, *great*, or *crate*. The amount of friction produced by such an articulation as this is usually very slight, since the elevation of the body of the tongue is not often great enough to produce a really narrow channel for the breath stream in the mediopalatal region. Often the elevation is very little more than that normal for the vowel [ɜ]. This kind of *r* may be produced with simultaneous retroflection of the apex of the tongue; indeed, it appears likely that central *r* has evolved from dental and retroflex *r* by the loss of the apical constrictions, in part compensated for by slightly greater mid-dorsal tension and elevation. There is no special symbol for central *r*.

6.414   *The Velar* [ʁ]

If the uvula, instead of curling forward in the median depression of the dorsum of the tongue provided for it in the articulation of [ʀ], lies in this groove with its tip pointing towards the pharynx, the breath stream cannot easily lift it. In this event, instead of a rolled uvular [ʀ], a fricative noise is produced as the air is driven between the top of the tongue and the edges of the velum near the median depression. This kind of sound replaces uvular [ʀ] in some Parisian speech.[76] It is a well-known sound in other languages, in some of which it is not an r-sound, but a variant of the velar or postvelar stops [k] or [q].[77] In French this dorsal fricative [ʁ] is sometimes called the R-grasseyé, or thickly spoken R, and this term is frequently found in descriptions of this and other postvelar constrictive sounds.

6.415   *Labialized* [ʀ̞]

The mediopalatal [ɹ] and the uvular rolled [ʀ], as well as the dorsal, velar [ʁ], are are frequently labialized. Indeed, the labialization sometimes becomes so prominent that one might say that the labiovelar [w] has been substituted for *r* by those who speak of the *"weal weasons for the Fwanko-Pwussian war."* This labialized [ʀ̞] is not confined to the speech of infants and radio comedians, but occurs in the pronunciation of individual speakers of high intelligence and refinement, both in Britain and in America.

6.416   *Fricative or Frictionless*

It is clear that the open *r* sounds may be fricative sounds in the proper sense of this term, if the area of the constriction is sufficiently small and the speed of the breath stream is sufficiently great to produce audible noise because of its obstruction. When either of these factors is inadequate to produce frictional noises that can be heard, the articulation of the consonant *r* becomes essentially identical in kind with that of a vowel and the acoustic components of the *r* sound are then predominantly frequencies of the same order as those characteristic of the selective transmission and reinforcement of partials observable in vowel sounds, and not frequencies of the higher range characteristic of hissing sounds. Fricative *r* may become frictionless *r*, either because the constrictive obstruction in the path of the breath stream is reduced, or because the speed of the breath stream is reduced. Usually any reduction of one factor is accompanied by a reduction of the other. Tendencies toward reduction either of articulation or of energy are commonly realized in different ways under different syllabic conditions, or in different motor contexts. The *r* sounds of English, for example, have behaved differently in different motor contexts. Initial *r*, or the *r* which serves to release the syllable movement, as in *rat, street*, is comparatively strongly articulated; *r* before a consonant, or final *r*, being in either case a part of the arresting mechanism of the syllable, has a tendency to be lost, or to be replaced by a vowel sound. That is to say, English *r* before a consonant or when final is reduced, both as to its constrictive obstruction of the breath stream and as to the speed of the breath stream through the articulation. The reduction takes different forms according to the type of articulation which is reduced. In Southern British speech this *r* simply disappears from words like *far, farm, fur, first*, but is replaced by [ə] in words like *fear, fair, fire, floor, boor*, or in *fierce, fairs, fires, floors, boors*. In the same circumstances midwest American speech has either a reduced central *r* or a retroflex vocalic sound, sometimes called an r-colored vowel, which results essentially from the superimposition of a retroflex apical articulation upon a mid-dorsal articulation of [ə] or [ɜ] or even of [ɑ]. Thus we have [fɑʳ], [fɑʳm], but [fɜ], [fɜst], and [fiɚ], [fɛɚ], [faɪɚ], [flɔɚ], and [buɚ]. One may write an exponential r [ʳ], or the r-hook with the vowel symbol [ɜ] to indicate the superimposition of either central or retroflex r upon the vowel articulation. Thus the symbol [ɚ] means the central vowel [ə] with either kind of r-coloring. These reduced forms of r appear to be the end forms of a long process of reduction. There is little doubt that rolled [r], dental flapped [ɾ], and the dental fricative [ɹ] are three variants of a single speech sound, and it appears probable that the central and retroflex varieties of open [ɹ] are by-forms resulting from the wide range of variation possible with this open sound because of its loss of distinctive fricative components. The problem of the relationship of the uvular or dorsal forms of r to these lingual forms is a historical rather than a phonetic problem. In any case, the uvular [ʀ] and its variants in the Indo-European languages are substitutes for, rather than developments of the lingual r sounds.[78]

6.42   The Laryngeal Open Consonants [h], [ɦ], [ḫ̣]

Fricative noise can be produced by an obstruction put in the way of the flowing breath stream by the vocal bands, or by the ventricular bands above them, or by both sets of bands operating in conjunction one with the other. An example of the voiceless laryngeal fricative is the ḥâ of Syrian Arabic.[79] The fricative noise in this case is said to be produced by closing the intermembranous glottis and leaving the intercartilaginous glottis slightly open, so that the breath stream is constricted as it is forced through the narrow opening. Dutch h is said to be a moderately strong laryngeal fricative, with the friction produced by the margins of the vocal bands.[80] Arabic 'ain, written phonetically [ɦ], is the voiced congener of ḥâ, with somewhat stronger constriction of the laryngeal muscles, so that fricative noises are added to the voice vibrations of the vocal bands. The voiced fricative in Dutch is described as the result of voicing plus the opening of the intercartilaginous glottis, where slight frictional noise is produced.

The usual h sounds of English and German, to take the most accessible examples of a very wide spread phenomenon, can hardly be said to be glottal or laryngeal fricatives at all, since no audible sound is produced by the air as it passes through the larynx. If one whispers the words *here, hare, hole, hoot,* or *hier, hehr, hohl, Hut,* the ear does not usually observe any transition from the initial consonant to the vowel; the two sounds are fused in a single voiceless vowel in each word. Since the movement of the tongue plays no part in the production of the laryngeal fricative, the tongue may be brought into the position required for the vowel next to be produced while the fricative is still being sounded. Such anticipation of the articulation of one sound while the other is being uttered may come eventually to be a complete coarticulation of the two sounds. But when the tongue assumes the vowel position, the breath stream flowing through the fricative constriction in the larynx will cause the vowel resonators to sound, just as they do when the vowel is being whispered, and this sound is much more prominent than the glottal friction. When the latter ceases to be heard it ceases to be reproduced, and we have the situation as it commonly is in present-day English and German. What once was a voiceless glottal fricative [h] is replaced by a voiceless vowel preceding the voiced vowel. This is revealed when one tries to whisper the [h] alone, as this is suggested by the words *here, hair, hole, hoot.* There are as many varieties of English [h] as there are syllabics before which it may stand. This is equally true of German.[81] When such an initial [h] is pronounced before a normal voiced vowel, let us say in English *heel*, the voicing for the vowel must be started by bringing the vocal bands together while the breath is flowing freely through the larynx to produce the [h]. This results in a vowel onset, or vowel attack, distinctly different from that which one hears when the breath stream starts to flow just as the vocal bands assume the position for vowel voicing, as in *eel*, or that heard when the breath stream is released by the glottal stop before the vowel, as in standard German *Iris.* Vowels may be started in any one of these three ways, and we shall speak of the stopped attack when the vowel is released with a glottal stop, of the even attack when the onset of the breath stream is simultaneous with the closing of the glottis for voice, or of the breathed attack when the breath stream starts slightly before the vocal bands are brought together. Phonetically, then, a reduced [h], bereft of its laryngeal friction, may come to be indistinguishable from the breathed vowel attack. This raises the question of the proper classification of the [h] sounds of languages like English or German, and the right answer to this question must come from a linguistic analysis of the particular language concerned. It is unlikely that we shall need more than one category for all of the many phonetically different [h] sounds of any language like English, for these sounds are each a conditioned variant either of a mode of vowel release, or of an open consonant [h] with no laryngeal friction. The propriety of classing such an open consonant as a laryngeal consonant may be questioned and some would call this kind of [h] a breathed open consonant rather than an articulated open consonant. Since in English and in German increased emphasis of utterance frequently leads to the production of audible laryngeal friction for [h], it is not unreasonable to regard the normal frictionless [h] as a reduced form of the laryngeal fricative. Also the phonological oppositions involved in such a series of words as *feel* : *veal* : *seal* : *zeal* : *reel* : *kneel* : *heel* : *eel* rest upon a distinctive difference between *eel* and each of the other words. The difference between *eel* and *heel* is a minimum difference between a marked and an unmarked form, and it is probably necessary to look upon *eel* as the unmarked member. It seems impossible to show that the vowel phoneme of *heel* is [hi], and that this is a variant of [i] in *eel*, since both forms occur initially with distinctive functions and therefore cannot be "sames." It is contrary to the general structure of English to set up a series of compound vowel phonemes [hi], [he], [haɪ], etc., which can only be used initially and can therefore have no consonant before them. Linguistic analysis indicates, then, that initial *h* in English is consonantal in function and that it is not a part of the several vowel phonemes.

Intervocalic *h* in English is sometimes voiced. When this happens, it results from the failure completely to open the membranous glottis for [h] between vowels. Usually the tension on the bands is somewhat reduced and the quality of the voicing changes to what E. A. Meyer called "die lufterfüllte Stimme."[82] This sort of voicing is not infrequent in words like *behind, beheld, behave, perhaps*. The usual symbol for this voiced *h* is [ɦ]. On the whole, the sounds which in various languages are written *h* resemble more or less closely the usual English or German [h] or [ɦ] sounds and have little or no audible friction.

The simple breathed [h] of English is readily susceptible to labialization. The sound produced is approximately that heard when one gently blows out a candle. In English speech it is likely to occur before labial sounds, notably before [w] in words like *when, which*, particularly when these are spoken with some emphasis. The usual symbol for rounded, or labialized [h] is [ḫ].

6.43   *The Pharyngeal Open Consonants* [ħ] and [ʕ]

By drawing the body of the tongue back toward the posterior wall of the pharynx with very considerable force, one can produce a constriction of the pharynx slightly below and behind the extreme edge of the velum. No stop consonant is produced by such a constriction, but distinctive pharyngeal fricatives are thus produced. Examples are afforded by Egyptian Arabic, which uses both a voiceless [ħ] and a voiced [ʕ] extensively.[83] The two sounds are also found in Somali, and have been well described by Stephen Jones, who says they are produced with raised larynx and the laryngeal part of the pharynx contracted.[84] Jones also observed very vigorous vibrations of the ventricular bands while [ʕ] was being produced and the tracheal air column was so strongly agitated that a very deep "undertone" was heard, while the vibrations produced a tactile sensation in the speaker which he localized as "in his belly," but which resulted probably from the movements of the bronchi as these absorbed the energy of the vibrating air column within the trachea.

Consonants which require such extreme constriction as [ħ] and [ʕ[are often spoken of as emphatic consonants. Such sounds are characteristic of the Semitic and the Hamitic languages. Indeed, the laryngeal fricatives Ḥâ and Ain are originally emphatic forms beside a simple [h], while Ḥâ and Gain are originally emphatic pharyngeal consonants [ħ] and [ʕ]. Sometimes these sounds are called Presslaute, and the type of squeezed voicing which results for [ʕ] is referred to as Pressstimme. There is a tendency in the various Semitic dialects to reduce these emphatic consonants in one way or another.

6.44   *The Velar Fricatives* [x], [ɣ], [χ], [ʁ]

A constriction between the velum and the back portion of the dorsum of the tongue can be made at any point from the junction of the velum with the hard palate to the uvula and back edge of the velum. Both voiceless and voiced fricatives are regularly produced by these velar constrictions. The usual requirements of analysis are served by recognizing the velar fricatives [x] and [ɣ], and their postvelar analogues [χ] and [ʁ].

The velar fricative [x] is most familiarly known from German pronunciations of written *ch* in words like *noch*, or *Aachen*. The constriction is in the same velar region as that touched by the tongue when producing [k] as in *Kuh*. The opening through which the breath stream is forced is vertically flat but horizontally broad; that is, it is a slit rather than a groove. The voiced velar fricative [ɣ] is produced in the same general way, with the addition of voicing. German speakers substitute [ɣ] for the uvular [ʀ] when they fail to contract the upper surface of the tongue to produce the necessary medial groove in which the uvula may vibrate. French speakers may substitute [x] for voiceless [ʀ] in a word like *quatre*, or [ɣ] for [ʀ] in words like *égaré*, or *égarement*. To be sure, the fricatives substituted for the voiceless or the voiced uvular trill may be rather the postvelar [χ] and [ʁ] than the velar [x] and [ɣ]. All four of these forms may be heard from speakers of the same area. The postvelar fricatives are also frequently substituted for the pharyngeal fricatives [ħ] and [ʕ] in Semitic dialects, and, to choose more or less random examples, Armenian,[85] Kabardian,[86] and Eskimo[87] use the postvelar fricatives [χ] and [ʁ].

6.45   *The Palatal Open Consonants* [ç] and [j]

The palatal open consonants [ç] and [j] bear the same relationship to the mediopalatal stops [c] and [ɟ] as the velar open consonants [x] and [ɣ] bear to the velar stops [k] and [g]. They, too, are articulated with the dorsum of the tongue flat rather than grooved, and the breath stream is forced through a broad, shallow slit, rather than through a groove or round hole. As in the case of the velar spirants, the place of articulation of these palatal open consonants may vary over a considerable area of the palate between the mediopalatal and the prepalatal regions.

The voiceless palatal open consonant [ç] is the sound of written *ch* in German *ich*, *Milch*, or of written *g* in the suffix *-ig*, as in *fleissig*. Approximately the same sound is often produced in English for the written *h* of *hue*, or for the aspiration between *p* and *u* in *pure*. The sound [ç] is not phonemically distinct from [x] in German and it has no independent place in the English consonant system. In French it sometimes appears as the voiceless variant of [j] for a written *i* in words like *Pierre*, *pied*, although the usual sound is voiced [j] rather than voiceless [ç]. The sound [ç] is also heard for a written *s* in some American Spanish speech in words like *listo*.[88]

The voiced palatal open consonant [j] is perhaps more widely used than [ç]. It is the initial consonant of German *Jahr*, *ja*, *jung*. It may be heard in the English words *yield*, *year*. It is sometimes substituted for mouillé *l* in French words like *fille*, *oeil*. Many phoneticians regard the usual [j] of English in words like *yoke*, *yell*, *yam* rather as a glide vowel than as a consonant. Others speak of this [j] as a semivowel. Both groups put particular emphasis upon the "gliding" or "moving," which characterizes the English prevocalic [j]. A typical statement is that of Daniel Jones: "In forming a normal *j* the organs of speech start at or near the position of the vowel *i* and immediately proceed in the direction of some other vowel."[89] Or, we may cite Kenyon: "Thus it is seen that *j* is a glide sound made by the modulation of the voice as the tongue moves continuously from the position for *i* to that for another vowel."[90] No one seems to inquire how the tongue manages always to start "from the position for *i*" or how it gets there. Clearly, the articulation of [j], like that of any other speech sound, has three phases: (1) the constriction, (2) the hold, and (3) the release. The second phase may be so short as to be in effect nonexistent, but the third phase is impossible without the first. In the case of English or of Russian [j], the audible portion of the sound is its release, since the second phase is normally so short as to be inaudible. In other words, a constriction is formed for [j], as for any true fricative, when the tongue blade is raised towards the prepalatal region, so that its flat upper surface produces a broad but shallow channel for the breath stream under the vault of the palate. This constriction is likely to be less tense, or the tongue less high for English [j] before [ɑ] than for [j] before [i]. Indeed, if the latter is to be heard, there must be some consonantal friction while [j] is held, because the release involves little or no movement of the tongue to reach the position for [i].

If there is no friction, *yeast* becomes *east*. The tongue position which is characteristic of the fricative [j] in such cases is about the same as that required for the vowel [i], but slightly higher, or closer to the palate. The actual distances involved in a comparison of this sort are of the order of one or at most two millimeters, and it may well be the mode of voicing rather than the degree of tongue elevation that distinguishes [j] from [i]. It must be conceded, however, that we really know nothing about the pharyngeal resonators involved in the production of [j]. In the case of [j] before [ɑ] or [u], a considerable movement of the tongue takes place in the third phase, or release, of [j]. Since voicing continues throughout the movement and since the resonance chambers activated by the voicing change continuously, the resulting shifting tone complex has become characteristic of the sound. As a result, the constriction may be reduced somewhat when the truly fricative position, the hold, of this consonant is omitted, because it is not necessary to raise the tongue quite so high to produce the characteristic shifting of tones during its release.

A postconsonantal [j] when final, as in Russian *sem′* [semj], is of necessity released, and as the constriction is loosened the consonant glides into a neutral [ə]. The alternative is to stop the breath stream before the constriction is released. This is analogous to the situation met in English when the vowel [i:] is final. This sound in English is usually diphthongal [ij], and when released, an [ə], either voiced or whispered, is likely to be heard as the sound stops. This may be observed in the pronunciation of *sea*, when final in the phrase. The same kind of thing occurs in the New Englander's substitute for "Yes" or "Yea," which might be transcribed as [e·ij ə], or even [e·ija].

6.46　*The Prepalatal Open Consonants* [ç] *and* [ʑ]

If the same general type of tongue articulation as that described for [ç] be advanced somewhat, so that friction is produced by the breath stream as it flows through a narrow slit between the fore part of the blade of the tongue and the prepalatal region just above the alveolar ridge, and if the lips be spread actively by drawing back their corners, the sound produced will be the "soft *s*" of Russian or Polish, or the sound of written *sj* in Danish. Often this sound is described as a palatalized *s* or a mouillé *s*, and it is indeed sometimes made with a long articulation in which the constriction may extend from the upper edge of the alveolae backward past the prepalatal region. It is, in any event, essential that the articulation be of the flat, slit type, that there be no spoonlike cupping of the tongue blade behind it and no lip-rounding before it, and that the anterior limit of the constriction be near the top of the alveolar ridge. The voiced fricative [ʑ] is like [ɕ] except for the addition of the glottal note. Both sounds occur in the Polish word *wodzić*, meaning "to lead."

6.47   *The Dental Open Consonants* [ʃ], [ʒ], [s], [z], [ʂ], [ʐ], [θ], [ð]

There are numerous variables and compensatory adjustments possible in the formation of the several dental, alveolar, or gingival open consonants and there are therefore discrepancies in the various written accounts of how they are produced.[91] The sounds are essentially of three types, the [ʃ] sounds, the [s] sounds, and the [θ] sounds, each with its voiced counterpart, respectively, [ʒ], [z], [ð].

6.471   *Sounds of the Type* [ʃ], [ʒ]

The sound written *sh* in English *she, shy, fresh*, or the sound of German *sch* in *Schule, schön, frisch*, or of French *ch* in *chat, achèté*, are not identical, but they are each of the type [ʃ]. For the usual English [ʃ] sound a narrow slit-shaped constriction is formed between the very front of the upper surface of the tongue and the roof of the mouth at the top of the alveolar ridge. In some cases the constriction is between the margin of the apex of the tongue and the alveolar or supra-alveolar region. Indeed, there are forms of [ʃ] in English which might even be called retroflex, since the constriction involves not only the margin but the underside of the apex of the tongue. The blade of the tongue behind any of these constrictions is cupped, or made concave, and the margins of the tongue make contact with the sides of the palate and teeth only from the first premolars backward. The lips may be inert, spread, or protruded. Generally in American speech they appear to be inactive, or only slightly protruded, but their position is unimportant for this kind of [ʃ], provided only that the aperture be kept large. For the usual German or French [ʃ] sounds the constriction is made between the flat upper surface of the blade of the tongue and the alveolar or supra-alveolar region, while the tip of the tongue is low, sometimes even behind the lower teeth. There is no concavity of the dorsum of the tongue behind this constriction but there must be a more or less active rounding of the lips. In German this rounding is accompanied by active protrusion of the lips. In French the protrusion is less conspicuous. The exact point of the constriction is relatively unimportant for the sound [ʃ], except that it may not be against the upper teeth themselves, for in that event an [s] sound results, but the [ʃ] may be gingival, alveolar, or as the International Phonetic Association describes it, palatoalveolar. A good deal of the friction of this variety of [ʃ] is produced by the swirl of the breath stream against the inside surfaces of the lower teeth. Speakers who have lost their lower teeth have difficulty in producing a satisfactory [ʃ] sound.

The voiced congener of [ʃ] is [ʒ], which is heard in English pronunciations of a written *s* in *measure*, or of *z* in *azure*. It is considerably more frequent in French than in English and occurs as the sound written *j* in words like *jour*, or *g* in words like *genie*, *gilet*. The sound occurs in German only in borrowed words like *Jalousie*, *Genie*. It is the sound heard as the fricative portion of the affricate [dʒ], for instance, in English *judge*.

6.472   *Sounds of the Type* [s], [z]

The acoustic analysis of [s] and [z] sounds shows them to have a principal characteristic of very high frequency, of the order of 6,000 to 7,800 cycles per second.[92] This is notably higher than any component prominent in the other consonantal sounds. It results apparently from standing vibrations in a very small resonance chamber which is vigorously blown. This may well be the region around the front aperture of the [s] constriction. This constriction is produced in the alveolar or gingival region by raising the apex of the tongue and the blade just behind it, so that a very small round opening is left over a ditch or groove along the medial line of the tip of the tongue. The breath stream is forced through this narrow groove with relatively high velocity and the emission of this air is analogous to that of air under pressure from a small nozzle. Very complex high-pitched sounds are produced as the breath strikes the air around this opening. Other noises are produced by the impact of the breath upon the gums or the alveolar ridge. The lips are usually spread somewhat, in order to avoid damping the high-pitched partials which are characteristic of these sounds.

The exact point of articulation, or the precise point at which the jet of air is released may vary over a considerable range. Indeed, it is possible to produce a labiolingual [s] or [z] by forming the required small groove under the margin of the lower lip. On the other hand, if the [s] or [z] articulation is made against the back surfaces of the upper teeth the result is likely to be a lisped [s] or [z] since it is impossible to confine the breath stream between the teeth and the tongue sufficiently to produce the high frequencies required for a normal [s] or [z] sound.

Voiceless [s] is observable in nearly every language. English uses it in words like *hiss, missing, sister, race*. German has it in *lassen, schiessen, das*. French uses [s] initially as in *sol*, finally as in *plus*, and medially as in *naissance, esclave*. The sound [z] is the voiced congener of [s]. English has it for written *s* in *days, headsman*, or *z* in *daze, hazard*. German uses [z] initially as in *sein, sicher* and intervocalically as in *Wesen*. French has it in words like *zèle, usure*, or *treize*.

It is possible to produce an [s] or a [z] sound with a retroflex articulation of the tongue tip, so that a small aperture is produced between the rather narrow under surface of the margin of the tongue and the supra-alveolar region. The farther back this constriction is made, the more the sound approaches in timbre the sound of the type [ʃ]. Marathe, in Kolhapur, uses a retroflex [ʂ].[93] Pekinese speakers substitute [ʂ] for [ʃ] and [ʐ] for [ʒ] to some extent. Jespersen observes something very much like a retroflex [s] in Norwegian and Swedish, when the combination *rs* has been reduced by the loss of *r*.[94]

Speakers of the Bantu languages use an [s] and a [z] sound with added labiodental friction, which they produce by making the usual [s] or [z] fricative in the alveolar region and simultaneously bringing the lower lip into contact with the edges of the upper teeth.[95]

The Semitic and the Hamitic languages have what may be called emphatic forms of [s] and [z]. These sounds in Syrian Arabic are Ṣâd and Ẓâ. They are distinguished by a considerably stronger muscular effort of constriction than is given to simple [s] and [z], and by a generally larger area and somewhat retracted position of contact between the tongue and the roof of the mouth. These sounds in Syrian Arabic, for example, are described as palatal rather than as dental,[96] but it is perhaps more accurate to say that the dental articulation has been retracted to the alveolar and prepalatal ranges and more space is actually covered by the contact made. There is also a notably stronger breath stream for the emphatic consonants. When voiced, the emphatic consonants have a timbre somewhat different from that of the nonemphatic consonants, because they involve a more forcible constriction of the vocal bands and of the laryngeal muscles generally. These emphatic palatals, or dentals, tend to lower the resonances of vowels used with them, so that [æ] becomes [ɔ], [ɪ] becomes [ɜ] and [ʊ] becomes [ɔ] in some regions.

6.473   *Sounds of the Type* [θ], [ð]

The sounds [θ] and [ð] which may be heard in English pronunciations of written *th* in *thin* and in *this* respectively, are, like [s] and [z], produced by friction of the breath stream at the apex of the tongue. They differ from [s] and [z] in that the form of the constriction produced is that of the narrow slit and not that of the groove. It may be desirable on occasion to distinguish between dental and interdental [θ] and [ð].

The usual English [θ] and [ð] are produced by bringing the tip of the tongue lightly into contact with the inner surfaces of the upper teeth, possibly even with the lower gingival region, and forcing the breath stream to flow over the flat surface of the tongue tip either between tongue and gums or between the front teeth, or both. Such [θ] and [ð] sounds may be called dental spirants of the type [θ].

In Spanish words like *cerca, escudo, cocido*, the sounds [θ] and [ð] are usually interdental in the sense that the tip of the tongue touches lightly the lower edges of the upper teeth while the underside of the tongue rests upon the top edges of the lower incisors. The difference between the kind of [θ] and [ð] sounds produced by contact of the tongue with the edges of the upper teeth and the labiodental spirants [f] and [v] is very slight, as Jespersen pointed out,[97] and as one may observe from substitutions such as, "*I had only free (three); gimme (give me) anover (another) one.*"

6.48   *The Labiodental Open Consonants* [f], [v]

The constriction required for the labiodental spirants [f] and [v] is produced by bringing the inner edge of the lower lip into light contact with the edges of the upper teeth. The upper lip is inactive and the breath stream is driven out between the upper teeth, or around the outer faces of the incisors when these are so close together that some of the breath is forced out in the region of the canine and premolar teeth. Overvigorous driving of the breath stream frequently produces slow vibration of the inner surfaces of the upper lip near the canine teeth. It is possible to produce acceptable substitutes for [f] and [v] by bringing the lower teeth into light contact with the upper lip, and there are individual speakers of English and other languages who do this. Since the bilabial spirants are more easily produced by most speakers, this variant articulation of the lower teeth against the upper lip is unlikely to become a general feature of any language. Some variation in the exact region of contact between lower lip and upper incisors may be observed, in that in some cases the middle or even the outer edge of the lower lip is involved. The more energetically the labiodental spirant is produced, the more likely it is that the contact will be with the central or outside margin of the lower lip.

Examples of voiceless [f] occur in English *phase, fan, affect, laugh,* French *façade, philtre, affaire, naïf,* German *Vater, Fisch, schaffen, half.* The voiced congener of [f] is [v]. In general, the distinctive difference between the two sounds is the voicing of [v]. However, one frequently finds that [v] is less closely constricted than [f], and that the breath stream flows more slowly. In other words, [v] is frequently lenis while [f] is often fortis. Examples of [v] are in English *vase, van, avert, halve,* or in French *vaste, wagon, ouvert, trouve,* or German *Wasser, Vakanz, Valuta, Devisen.*

Since the position of the tongue is normally of no importance to the formation of these labiodental fricatives, they are subject to velarization and to palatalization, which may become apparent if the constriction at the lips is released while the tongue is raised. Palatalized [f] and [v] occur in Russian.

6.49   The Bilabial Open Consonants [Φ], [β], [w], [ɥ]

With or without protrusion, the two lips can be brought together in such a way that only a small, more or less circular opening is left through which the breath stream may flow. When not protruded, the lips may be so brought together that a horizontally long but vertically narrow passage-way between them is left for the flowing breath stream. This is the lip constriction characteristic of [Φ] and [β]. The constriction for [w] or [ɥ] is of the circular, or hole, type.

6.491   The Bilabial Slit Fricatives [Φ], [β]

The voiceless bilabial fricative [Φ] is considerably less readily found in the speech of Europeans than is the voiced fricative [β]. The Japanese use [Φ], as do speakers of the Athabaskan dialect Loucheux.[98] This bilabial [Φ] sound also often appears as the fricative portion of the affricatively released [p] of English words like camphor, Humphrey.

The voiced bilabial fricative [β] is the normal sound of written b in Spanish words like Cuba, doble, alba. It occurs in German quite frequently for written w or u in words like zwei, Schwester, quälen. It is spoken in a number of German dialects instead of the standard voiced stop [b] between vowels in words like aber, leben. The Dutch w of water, kwartje, bewonen, is often pronounced [β].

The tongue position is in general unimportant for the production of [Φ] and [β]. Therefore these sounds are subject to velarization or to palatalization. Usually, however, it is the hole type bilabial fricatives rather than the slit type which are so modified, although the Dutch of some of the coastal towns of Holland use a velarized slit-type voiced [β] for written w.[99]

6.492   The Bilabial Hole Fricatives [w], [ɥ]

The initial sound of French oui, oiseau is a bilabial fricative [w] of the hole rather than of the slit type, as indeed is the same sound in French bois, foyer. However, this [w] is velarized, for the dorsum of the tongue is raised toward the velum and the tip of the tongue is low behind the incisors, as when the vowel [u] is pronounced.[100] The fricative noises produced by the articulation of [w] are slight, but such as they are, they come rather from the labial than from the velar constriction.

English [w] in words like wind, willow, watch, is articulated in essentially the same manner as that just described for French [w]. Differences of degree of voicing, of degree of velar elevation, and of degree of lip constriction may be discerned. In French the lips are likely to be vigorously protruded and the aperture is small and tense. In English the protrusion of the lips is likely to be negligible and the aperture lax. Both French and English [w] are sometimes replaced by a voiceless *w* which may be written [ʍ]. French shows this [ʍ] in occasional pronunciations of words like *toi, foi.* English speakers sometimes use [ʍ] for the written *wh* of words like *which, wheel.*

A palatalized bilabial fricative [ɥ] is found in French in words such as *nuit, lui, cuisine.* Sometimes this [ɥ] is more or less wholly unvoiced in words like *cuisine* or *puis.* The lip position is the circular, protruded constriction for [w], but the blade of the tongue is raised toward the palatal region, roughly in the same way as for the rounded front vowel [y.]

English [w] is regarded by many as a labiovelar semivowel, or as a vowel glide sound. The same description may be given for the coastal variety of [w] in Dutch, except that the lip articulation there is of the slit type. The case of [w] is analogous to that of [j], and it is probably correct to say that the distinctive acoustic features of this sound, as it is pronounced in English *wee,* or *too,* are due rather to the shifting modifications of the voice note during the release of the constriction than to any friction produced by the articulation. The relative prominence of the release of this consonant has made that phase of its production the characteristic one. Here too, when the change of tongue and lip position required to pass from the constriction for [w] to the vowel after it is slight, as in *woo,* the fricative elements of the sound are more likely to be heard. When the changes are great, as in *watch,* or *we,* the transitional sounds of the release of [w] acquire greater prominence. Fundamentally, however, the articulation of English [w] requires a bilabial constriction accompanied by velarization. When vigorously pronounced, or when whispered, the fricative sounds which can be heard are produced at the lips. English [w], then, is a bilabial sound with velarization which may or may not be marked by audible fricative noises. It would appear to be idle to speculate as to whether the movements of the tongue or the movements of the lips characterize the changing timbre of the third or releasing phase of this open consonant.

English words with initial *wh,* such as *whale, what, wheel, whey, which, while, whir, whit, white,* are widely pronounced in southern Britain with initial [w]. A voiceless [ʍ] is used in these words in Scotland, Ireland, and northern England, beside a variant [hʍ], which is voiceless, and which begins with an *h* sound, sometimes [h], sometimes [h̰] or [x]. The same three versions of written *wh* are current in America, though it is as yet a minority of our speakers who make no distinction between the pronunciations of *whale:wail, wheel:weal, whey:way, which:witch, while:wile, whir:were, whit:wit, white:wight.*

Many American speakers produce this voiceless *wh* sound as a strong

voiceless bilabial slit fricative with velarization, which one might equally
well describe as an [x] sound with labialization, [ẍ̬]. This differs from [ɯ̥]
chiefly in the degree of friction produced, [ɯ̥] being weaker than [ẍ̬]. Other
speakers actually produce an *h*-sound, either [h] or [x], before the lip
constriction reaches its maximum, thereby justifying the transcription
indicated by [hɯ̥]. Finally, there may be speakers who pronounce [h] before
a voiced [w], or [hw] in these words. In this "wh" sound, as in English [w],
the third phase, or the release, is usually the most prominent, even when
the spirant [x] is audible before the first phase is complete. The second
or holding phase is normally very brief, and the release is apt to be brisk.

CHAPTER VII

SPEECH SOUNDS IN CONTEXT

7.1 *Introductory Considerations*

In the preceding pages we have described speech sounds as these may be produced singly by speakers who have learned to isolate them from the stream of speech in which they constitute the significant features of utterances. The genetic or the gennemic features of a speech sound thus isolated do not always exactly coincide with the genetic or the gennemic features of the same speech sound in its usual motor or acoustic contexts and we have now to observe some of the discrepancies between our initial descriptions and the character of speech sounds in speech contexts.

If one observes the physical form given to the letter *o*, as this is usually written in the two words *bone* and *home*, or the form of the letter *m*, as this is written in the two words *same* and *some*, it is evident that the two *o*'s are not exactly alike and that the two *m*'s differ as to their initial strokes.   Evidently, there is in each case a neuromuscular adjustment due to the context in which the graphic movements occur, and this results in slightly different forms of the same movements. In somewhat the same way, the movements of the organs of speech suffer minor, or sometimes quite notable, neuromuscular adjustments due to differences in the motor contexts in which the speech movements occur. Such an adjustment may be observed in the onset of the vowel of *you* in the two utterances, *Wont you? Did you?* as compared with the onset of the same vowel in *You did?* In the latter case the behavior of the apex of the tongue is quite different from its behavior when it must leave the occlusion of [t] or [d] to take the vowel position, and there is apt to be an adventitious sound, [ʃ] or [ʒ], before the onset of the vowel of *you* in the phrases, *Wont you? Did you?* The adventitious sound results from a modification of the release of the dental stop coupled with a modification of the movement of the tongue for the initial [j] of the vowel onset of the pronoun *you*. No such adventitious sound develops between the dental stop and the vowel in the phrases, *Did I? Wont I?*, and the forms of the release observable here appear to be those which are usual for the two dental stops in most contexts.   Or, if one compares the articulatory form and the sound of initial [k] in the word *king* with the form and the sound of [k] in *cling* a difference in the position of the occlusion and a notable difference in the release of the two forms of [k] is readily observable.   It will be evident upon reflection that such modifications of movement and of sound due to

163

differences in motor context result from differences in the neuromuscular patterns of the individual speech sounds as these fuse in the configurations of speech forms. This is by no means to say that speech forms are mere aggregations of speech sounds, but rather that those speech sounds which analysis extracts from speech forms as "sames" have in their several motor contexts several neuromuscular patterns with variations which result from the nature of their neighbors in the configuration.

7.11 *Ballistic Movements*

Most consonant movements may be described, with Stetson,[1] as ballistic movements, each of which has a characteristic constriction or occlusion of the vocal channel as its normal goal. The organs of speech when thrown by the beat stroke of this ballistic movement into their characteristic positions of constriction or occlusion may be withdrawn therefrom by the contraction of muscles or muscle fibers opposed in their pull to the action of the fibers which produce the beat stroke. We describe the movement which results from this pull of the opposing muscles as the back stroke of the ballistic movement. The back stroke may be replaced by a relaxation of the muscles which have produced the beat stroke and the organs moved will then relapse into their positions of rest. Or the organs may be held in their position of occlusion or constriction by a controlled movement which requires the pull of two or more sets of opposed muscles working simultaneously. Each speech movement results from the activation of a complicated pattern of nervous impulses initiated in the higher nervous centers and the variations of movement which we observe in different motor contexts appear to result chiefly from the automatic blocking and mutual interference of nerve impulses in the ganglia and nerve fibers when the rate at which one pattern succeeds another becomes so high that the back stroke or the relaxation phase of one ballistic movement is overtaken by the beat stroke of a succeeding one. Since every performance changes the pattern either by reinforcing it or by altering it, the fusion of speech sounds into larger units has resulted in modified total patterns or configurations which are wholes in the stimulus-response function of speech. This is quite as true of the controlling auditory pattern of the speech form as of the motor pattern, and the interaction of these two nervous patterns is constant. For the practical phonetician the validity of his usual practice of dealing with the several speech sounds individually and the comparatively subordinate importance for him of these contextual variations is attested by the fact that a learner who produces the individual speech sounds with acceptable accuracy will tend, as his skill and speed of utterance increase, automatically to make those contextual adjustments that have become a part of the pattern of the normal speech form, although there are certain over-all or general habits of contextual modification peculiar to each language, and certain of our English habits of modification have to be restrained, for instance, when English speakers attempt to speak French.

7.12　Modifications in Context

In the nature of the case it is the onset and the release of the several speech sounds which are most readily modified by these contextual adjustments, although the central element of any speech sound may come to be affected if the modification of the transitional phases becomes drastic. The histories of many languages record such phonetic modifications as the abandonment of the central phase (the hold) of stop consonants, as in the case of the evolution of Latin [k] in *centum* to French [s] in *cent*, or of Indo-European [t], as in Latin *tres* to Germanic [θ] as in Gothic *þreis*, English *three*. Matters of this kind lie outside the scope of general phonetics and belong rather to the field of historical phonetics. Yet changes such as these often result, it is believed, from phenomena which were once similar to those modifications of speech movements which we must now observe in various motor contexts.

The phonetician may assume for the purposes of his study of the mutual interaction of speech sounds that the minimum phonetic context of these sounds is the simple form, or morpheme.[2] If he describes adequately the phonetic form of every morpheme in a given language and the sandhi phenomena which affect these simple forms when they are combined into the larger units of utterance, he will no doubt account for all of the contextual modifications to which the speech sounds of his language may be subject. In this study of general phonetics we shall consider general principles rather than exhaustive inventories of morphemes. We shall proceed most simply if we consider first how initial elements are begun, how final elements are concluded, how transitions are managed, and lastly, some of the adaptations due to fusion.

7.2　Initial Elements

The initial element of any utterance will be either a consonant, a group of consonants, or a vowel. The organs of articulation will, under normal circumstances, move from their positions of rest to the positions described as characteristic of the initial element. In this respect the onset of the initial element of any utterance will be identical with that of the same element produced alone, unless there are differences in energy and tempo of movement induced by emotional reaction to the meaning of the utterance.

How this onset is managed depends upon the synchronization achieved between the movements which force the breath stream through the vocal channel, the movements of the vocal bands, and the movements of the other articulatory organs, notably the tongue, the velum, and the lips.

7.21   *Vowel Beginnings*

Initial vowels may begin with the stopped beginning, the even beginning, or the breathed beginning. These terms refer to various forms of synchronization, or the lack of it, between the movements which induce the flow of breath and those which put the vocal bands in the vowel position required. The stopped beginning occurs when the vocal bands are brought together before the breath begins to flow outward from the larynx, and the beginning of vowel voice is then preceded by the building up of pressure under the closed glottis. This pressure is released with a more or less vigorous explosion [ʔ] immediately preceding the vowel sound. This type of beginning is usual for accented initial vowels in standard German. The even beginning of a vowel occurs when the movements which drive the breath stream are so synchronized with those which bring the vocal bands together that the onset of breath and the onset of vowel voice are simultaneous. This type of even vowel beginning should be cultivated by singers and public speakers; it is the usual type of vowel onset in French and in most English speech. Henry Sweet called it the clear vowel beginning. The breathed vowel beginning results when the breath stream is driven through the throat and mouth before the vocal bands have been brought closely enough together to begin their voice vibrations. When a vowel is thus produced it may be said to be pre-aspirated. It is likely that pre-aspirated vowels were once normal for French in words like *humain*, *hôtel*, *homme*, where now one finds the even vowel beginning; likewise French words from Greek words with initial rough breathing, like *hecto*, *hemo-*, *hipp-*, probably once had the breathed vowel beginning, though now they are usually produced with the even beginning. The English *h*, which we write in the initial position before a vowel in words like *hear*, *hand*, *hit*, when these are initial in an utterance, may be regarded as the symbol for the breathed vowel beginning, or it may be regarded as the symbol for an initial consonant. Phonetically, there is no basis for a choice between these two interpretations: linguistically, each has its own repercussion upon the general analysis of the facts of these utterances and hence upon the nature of the "system" of sounds which may be alleged for English. As has been said (p. 152), it appears more satisfactory linguistically to regard this kind of [h] as a consonant than to take it as a type of vowel onset.

There is a further possible factor of synchronization in vowel beginnings. This is the set of movements required of the tongue, the lips, and the velum for each vowel in conjunction with the laryngeal position and the breath flow. It is conceivable, though I cannot cite a clear case of it, that a vowel might begin, in any one of the three ways described, before the supralaryngeal movements peculiar to it had been made. Such a vowel might then well have as its initial phase the "unarticulated *uh* vowel" [ə]. Something very much like this vowel onset can be observed in over-lazy, inert articulations of English diphthongs in words like *I* or *out*, but the laryngeal position alone appears to give some definition to the initial vibrations produced. Raising the velum too soon would have no audible effect on an initial oral vowel; raising it too late might make the beginning of the vowel somewhat different from the remainder, though real nasality requires active lowering of the velum, not just its intertness, and the difference due to a delayed raising of the velum from its position of rest is not likely to be heard. In the same way, a too early rounding or too early spreading of the lips will not change the sound of the vowel onset, whereas a too late rounding might become audible as a sort of diphthongization of the vowel.

7.22 *Consonant Beginnings*

The same problems of synchronization present themselves in the case of initial consonants. These may have the even beginning; that is, the flow of breath through the constriction may begin just as the constriction is formed. They may have the stopped beginning, if the breath stream is first stopped by the closed glottis and released into the constriction by the explosion of that stop. Or they may have the breathed beginning, if the breath stream is caused to flow through the vocal channel before the oral articulation has been made.

English, German, and French initial open consonants usually have the even beginning. One may observe, however, that the Indo-European initial consonant groups *kl*, *kr*, and *kw* which developed into *hl*, *hr*, and *hw* in the Germanic languages, must have given us at some stage in the evolution of English and German, initial *l*, *r*, and *w* with the breathed onset. One might think of the initial consonant group of Old English *hlûde*, *hring*, or *hwanne* as pre-aspirated open consonants, or open consonants with breathed onset, for it is quite clear that this *h* was weakly pronounced and soon lost altogether, except in words like *who*, and perhaps for some of us who have a strong *h* before a weak *w*, in words like *when*, *wharf* (cf. p. 161).

The stopped beginning of initial open consonants is, with one exception, unusual in English. Many speakers of English, when they have taken in breath for speaking, or when in their speech they have reached the end of a phrasal unit, or speech measure, will pause momentarily before emitting more breath in further utterance. The air is stopped within the lungs and trachea by the closure of the vocal bands. When speech is begun again this closure is released, usually so unobtrusively that it is not observed. But sometimes, when the several movements are not well synchronized, the release is audible as a stopped beginning. This kind of stopped beginning of open consonants is then adventitious and not linguistically significant, but English does use this device upon occasion to point a difference otherwise poorly marked phonetically. For example, the phrase *an ice skate* may be clearly distinguished from the phrase *a nice skate* by using the stopped beginning for the diphthong [aɪ] of *ice* and by using the stopped beginning for the nasal open consonant [n] or *nice*, and either phrase may be unmistakably marked by this process without the utterance of the contrasting phrase. However, there are languages which use the stopped beginning of open consonants as a distinctive mark of semantic difference. An example is provided by Nootka, an American Indian language.[3]

Initial stop consonants may begin without the flow of breath prior to the occlusion and without a glottal stop below the oral articulation. One may, with a little license, call this the even beginning of stops. More justly one may speak of the breathed beginning of initial stops when the flow of the breath stream precedes the occlusion. Such pre-aspirated stops are semantically distinctive in the Fox Indian dialect.[4]

When the glottis is closed so that the flow of air is stopped before the oral occlusion of an initial stop consonant is accomplished, we might think of the result as a stop consonant with stopped beginning. Usually, however, this type of occlusion results in what we have called (pp. 136-37) glottalized pressure stops. English, which has no glottalized stops, does produce adventitiously stops with stopped beginning after pauses by the same process as that by which it produces initial open consonants with stopped beginnings.

7.3 *Final Elements*

The final element of a morpheme may be a vowel, a consonant, or a group of consonants. The organs of articulation, under normal circumstances, will move from their positions of articulation to those of rest at the end of a speech measure or phrase.

7.31 *Vowel Endings*

A final vowel may end with the oral release of the breath not required for the speech measure; it may end with a diminishing phase terminating with the end of the flow of breath; or it may end with closure of the vocal bands. Vowels, then, may have a breathed release, an even release, or a stopped release. The problem of synchronization among the several movements required to end a final vowel is basically that of adjusting the movements of laryngeal and oral articulation to the movements of the rib cage and diaphragm.[5] It appears probable that the breath flow of each syllable results from a single ballistic movement of the chest muscles. In any event, pressure to produce the flow of breath results in a ballistic pulse of the breath stream energy when it is released by the initial element of an utterance, and this pulse may either run its course until the energy is exhausted, be checked by some articulatory constriction or occlusion in the path of the air flow, or be arrested by some opposing movement of the rib-cage mechanism. Every speech articulation imposes more or less of a brake on the flow of the breath thus propelled, but more often than not the final articulation of the utterance is completed before the energy of the breath stream for that pulse is exhausted. Three things are then possible: (1) the breathed release, in which surplus breath is allowed to escape through the mouth or nose while the organs are moving to their positions of rest, (2) the even release, in which the breath flow and the articulation terminate simultaneously by virtue of a rib-cage arresting movement which checks the breath, or (3) the stopped release, in which the breath stream is arrested by the closure of the vocal bands while the articulatory positions are reduced and the air then allowed to escape either through the nasal cavities or through the mouth.

The breathed release of a vowel occurs when the vocal bands are opened while the oral articulation of the vowel is in its final phase, thereby releasing a puff of unvoiced breath through the changing oral cavities and apertures as these approach the final closure of the rest position. Vowels which end with the breathed release therefore often appear to be followed by a secondary sound which is produced by this puff of breath released through the closing oral channel. The Sanskrit *visarga* is probably this kind of breathed vowel release. Like the breathed vowel onset the breathed vowel release results from the imperfect synchronization of the several movements involved. When the organs of speech are at rest and the mouth is closed, the upper surface of the blade of the tongue is in contact with or very close to the palatal and prepalatal region of the roof of the mouth. For this reason the vowels [i] and [e] with breathed release are likely to appear to be followed by a more or less voiceless [j], which is the result of the flowing of the postvocalic puff of breath through the closing constriction between tongue and palate as the organs approach their positions of rest. The vowels [o] and [u] under analogous circumstances are likely to appear to be followed by a more or less voiceless [u] or [w] respectively, since the closing lip aperture affects the residual breath stream more notably than does the shifting tongue position. This is not the same phenomenon as the diphthongization of [i], [e], [o], and [u], to [ij], [ej], [ou], and [uw] commonly heard in English speech, for in these diphthongal vowels the second element is normally clearly voiced. That the two phenomena are similar, and that the breathed vowel release may lead to the diphthongization of final vowels is altogether probable. This, however, is not to say that these English diphthongal vowels did so originate. The answering of that question is the business of historical English phonology. Breathed vowel releases are observed in Dutch.[6] In English they produce no notable accessory sound, since the final vowels with which these accessory sounds might occur are normally diphthongized. However, when it is strong, the breathed release does change the end-phase of vowels from voiced to whispered vowels, so that *say* [sei] may sound like [seiç].

The even release of a final vowel requires that the cessation of the breath stream, the opening of the glottis, and the resolution of the oral articulation of the vowel shall be synchronized, and this probably requires that the ballistic beat stroke of the breath pulse be checked by a back stroke of the rib-cage muscles. This type of vowel release is said to be characteristic of careful pronunciation in Dutch and in French.[7] It appears to be unusual in English final vowels.

The stopped ending of final vowels involves the stoppage of the breath stream by the complete closure of the vocal bands before the oral articulation of the vowel is released. This stoppage must in turn be released, and there are two ways in which this is done. In English the asynchronism between the end of the breath pressure and the stoppage of the breath stream by the glottal occlusion is usually not great enough to produce notable subglottal pressure. The oral articulation is reduced to the rest position and the small amount of pent-up breath beneath the glottis is then released through the nasal cavities with little or no audible sound. When the breath stream is cut off by the stopped vowel ending while it still has considerable energy, the usual procedure is to reduce the oral articulation by a back stroke of the muscles to the neutral, rather than by relaxation to the rest position and to release the subglottal pressure audibly into this oral opening, which is then closed to the rest position. This kind of vowel ending is frequent everywhere in exclamatory utterances, such as *Ha! Hey!* Danish and Lettish make extensive use of the stopped vowel ending as a distinctive phonemic mark, and this is then called the stød, or stöd danois, Stoss or Stosston.

7.32 *Consonant Endings*

Open consonants when final in the phrase or speech measure may be finished with the even release. In that case the articulation is maintained until the energy of the breath pulse is so far reduced that the breath stream causes no audible sound. The open consonants serve in a sense as escape valves for the flow of breath and they fulfill this function best when they terminate with the simultaneous exhaustion of the breath pulse energy and the reduction of the articulatory constriction.

Asynchronism in the termination of final open consonants may result from the reduction of the oral constriction before the breath pulse has exhausted its energy. It may result, if the consonants are voiced, from the opening of the vocal bands before the resolution of the oral constriction. In the first case a different result ensues according as the oral constriction is reduced directly to the closure of the rest position or suffers first the reduction to the neutral vowel position before the closure is effected. If the oral constriction, or occlusion in the case of the nasal consonants, is resolved directly into the closure of the rest position before the breath pulse has spent itself, the residual breath will be emitted as a puff of greater or lesser energy through the nasal cavities. The English interjection which we write "Humph!" is a case in point. When open consonants with oral constriction, such as [ʒ] or [s], have the breathed release through the nasal cavities, the sound produced by this release is usually not observed unless it is strong enough to suggest a "snorting" utterance, and then it is likely that the release has been stopped rather than even, that is, that there has been a stoppage of air flow by the glottis. If the oral constriction is resolved first to the open position of the neutral vowel [ə] before the rest position is assumed and before the breath pulse has spent itself, the result will be a sound either of voiceless [ə̥] or of a murmured [ə] with diminishing energy. It is readily observed that in these circumstances a voiceless [ə̥] cannot be distinguished from [h], since the sound is simply breath escaping through the neutral oral position. When the vocal bands are not yet opened, the murmured [ə] which results in these circumstances is sometimes called an inorganic vowel. One may find it after the final sound of a phrase such as the English *"Tell that to the judge!"* However, the other type of asynchronism is not infrequent in the production of final voiced consonants. That is, the vocal bands may be opened while the consonant constriction is still in position, thereby increasing the pressure of the breath stream against the oral constriction. One may observe this in the final sound of the English phrase, *"He always cuts off their heads."* The release of such open consonants may then be either the even release or one form or the other of the breathed release just described. It is not likely to be the stopped release.

It is possible to check the breath pulse energy of final open consonants by completely closing the glottis while the constricting articulation is reduced. The pent-up breath is then generally allowed to escape through the nose, as in the case of vowels with the stopped release. This type of consonant release is rarely audible except in emotional utterances of the type one may describe as "snorting."

Lack of synchronization in the release of final nasals can lead to the addition of an oral stop to the complex, if the velum is raised to cut off the nasal pharynx before the oral occlusion of [m] or [ŋ] is broken. Thus [m] is often followed by an inorganic [b] when it is final, and [ŋ] acquires a final [k] to which it is not etymologically entitled. English words like *hymn, limb, trim,* when final may terminate in the inorganic stop [b], although we reject this as substandard speech. German words like *Empfindung, Gewinnung* frequently end in [-uŋk] in the speech of cultured native speakers. This too is not accepted as standard German, but it has a much better position socially than the same phenomenon in English, where in the substandard pronunciation of our urban speakers with foreign background we may hear [nʌθɪŋk], [sɪŋɪŋk], and even [kɪŋk] for *nothing, singing,* and *king.*

Finally, the arrest of open consonants may be accomplished by an oral occlusion not part of the normal mechanism. This happens notably to the articulation of final [s], which is often stopped by raising the tip of the tongue to form a complete oral stop. The result, whether this stop is exploded or not, is to add a final inorganic [t] to the form. Thus, English *once* becomes *oncet* [wʌnst], which we have hitherto refused to accept as good usage, whereas standard German *einst* goes back to exactly the same kind of consonant termination of a form *eines,* as both words are developments of the adverbial genitive singular forms of the numeral.

Stop consonants when final may be said to have the even release when their occlusion checks the energy of the breath pulse so that the articulating organs return to the rest position without the audible explosion of the stop. Since the air is released in such circumstances by the lowering of the velum, one might speak of the velar release, rather than of the even release of these occlusions. This type of release is very frequent in American English speech, and usually results in the impression that the final stop has been lost. Thus *west* is heard as *wes, lost* as *los.*

The breathed release of final stop consonants may take one of two forms. If the occlusion is broken suddenly, that is, if the stop is released impulsively, the puff of pent-up air will take the form of an aspiration or [h]-like release before the organs move to their rest positions. This type of release is frequently the final sound in forceful English utterances such as *"Stop that!"* If the resolution of the occlusion is slow, the breath stream may be forced out through a constriction made by the same organs as those which produced the stop, and the release is then not by aspiration, but takes the form of the homorganic fricative. Where this is an established form of consonant release the result is called an affricate and the release of the fricative portion of the sound becomes analogous to the release of the open consonants. Usually affricates have what may be called the even release, since the major energy of the breath pulse has been checked by the occlusion which precedes the fricative.

Stop consonants may have the stopped release when final in the phrase. The breath stream is stopped by the glottis as well as by the oral occlusion without the production of either pressure or suction stops. If the oral occlusion is broken first, the stopped release may ensue in two ways, as in the case of the stopped release of open consonants. If the oral stop is merely relaxed, the glottal release will be through the nasal cavity. If the oral occlusion is broken by a back stroke, the glottal release may result in a murmured or a whispered vowel [ə]. This happens frequently in French when something like [ə] is heard after a final stop, as in *petite*, or in *robe, malade, vague.*

7.4 Speech Units, Linguistic Forms

The morphemes of a language are the minimum phonetic-semantic forms of that language.[8] Utterances usually comprise a number of morphemes fused into configurations or linguistic forms. In various languages the beginning or the end, or both, of the morpheme and the word may be marked by various means. Some languages use these boundary markers very extensively, others much less so.[9] For example, the sound [j] in standard German, or the stopped-vowel attack in German or in Czech, mark the beginning of a morpheme. A discussion of these phenomena belongs in a phonological rather than in a phonetic analysis of the language concerned.

Utterances are divided physically into breath groups of forms, that is, into larger units between each two of which a breath is, or may be, taken in. To be intelligible, each breath group must also be phrased. That is, the constituent linguistic forms must be set off distinctly by minor interruptions of the flow of speech movements. Each such unit between two of which the speaker may pause considerably, or ad libitum, without destroying the distinctness of his utterance may be called a speech measure (Sprechtakt), a phrase-group or a sense group (groupe d'énonciation). The double vertical lines divide the following sentences into breath groups and the single vertical lines mark the divisions between speech measures.

It will at once be evident that these divisions are not all equally inevitable, or that other speakers might phrase the utterances differently, but some such division is indispensable to clarity. || The phenomena of onset | and of release | which have just been described || regularly occur | respectively | at the beginning | and at the end | of a speech measure. || Within the speech measure | we have various types | and degrees | of modification | of the several speech sounds || due to fusions | of the constituent phonetic units | into morphemes | and more complex | speech forms. || Transitional sounds | or adaptive changes | in speech sounds | which occur | at the boundaries | of lexical units, | or words, || are often spoken of | as sandhi phenomena. || They are | in no essential way | different from | transitional sounds | or adaptive changes | within a morpheme. ||

It will be clear that each speech measure or phrase unit may comprise a number of syllables, or to put the same thing another way, it will be clear that within each speech measure there may be a number of successive impulses of the breath-stream energy, each with its own release and arrest. This fact adds a dynamic factor to the mechanics of transition from one speech sound to another, and this in turn involves the factor of rate or tempo. One of the characteristics of English speech is that the fusion of its morphemes into complex speech forms involves a considerable acceleration of the utterance of some of the components of the configuration. Fully stressed morphemes are apt to have about the tempo of lexical pronunciation; less heavily stressed morphemes are likely to be pronounced more rapidly. Take first a simple illustration. Compare the release of the stop [p] in the two forms *step* and *pest* in lexical pronunciation. Then pronounce deliberately the phrase, "*Step on the pest!*" Now pronounce that phrase with normal vehemence and éclat. The final stop [p] of *step* in lexical pronunciation is likely to have the even or velar release; that is, the occlusion is merely relaxed and there is no back stroke of the muscles to move the lips apart. If there is a back stroke and an explosion, it is likely to be very weak with no notable aspiration of the stop. The initial [p] of *pest*, on the other hand, has the breathed release and is, as we say, rather strongly aspirated. These forms of the stop consonant may be retained in the deliberate utterance of the phrase indicated, but when the normal tempo and dynamic distributions are achieved, the final [p] of *step* is strongly aspirated and it is closely joined to the vowel of *on*. This vowel is no longer initial, as it is in the isolated morpheme *on*, but has become postconsonantal, after [p], as it is in the word *pond*, and the vowel with the nasal becomes part of the arrest of the second breath pulse. The final, arresting top [p] of *step* has shifted to the function of a releasing stop in the phrase.[10] The analogous shift of [t] in the phrase *at all* (to *a tall*) is a great nuisance to teachers of declamation. This sort of thing can have linguistic repercussions of importance when it leads to what is known as false syllable division and gives us words like *apron* instead of *napron* beside *napkin*, or provides us with the morpheme *-ness* instead of *-es* or *-is*, as in *baldness*.[11]

What has happened to the relationship between *step* and *on* in this utterance, "*Step on the pest!*" becomes clearer if one compares with it the utterance, "*They took this step on behalf of those who could not be present.*" The [p] of *step* in this context is an arresting consonant and is not aspirated; it does not release the breath pulse of the syllable *on*, which is either chest-released, or released by the vowel onset. The close nexus between [p] and [ɒ] of our first example is missing from the second because here the two sounds belong to two different speech measures, and the normal mark of this fact is a slight pause at the boundary between them. When such a pause is brief, the most noticeable evidence of it is likely to be this lack of nexus between the sounds which are contiguous at the boundary between the two measures. The phenomena of fusion occur within speech measures, not across the boundaries between them. Fusion is the unifying process by which the speech measure becomes a single configuration.

7.5 *Fusion*[24]

Within the speech measure a number of different kinds of phenomena of fusion may be observed. These may be classified under one or more of the following rubrics: (1) dynamic displacement, (2) doubling, (3) reduction, (4) omission, (5) glides, (6) linking, (7) adaptive changes. These various phenomena of fusion present grave difficulties to the linguistic analyst who approaches an unknown language without benefit of lexicon or written records. It is only by the recognition of the many possibilities of modification in context that the student of such languages can arrive ultimately, if he collects enough evidence, at the unity which underlies the variety in which the morphemes of the language appear.

7.51 *Dynamic Displacement*

We have seen in the sentence, "*Step on the pest,*" how the dynamics of the speech measure has caused the arresting consonant of the morpheme *step* to shift to the releasing function, with appropriate change in the character of its own release. This kind of shift is readily observed in English speech. The [t] of *at* in the phrase *at any rate* is very likely thus to be displaced. French speakers of English very frequently shift the [n] of the phrase *an aim* and say instead *a name*. A vowel which may serve as the releasing movement of its morpheme may become an internal vowel in the fused configuration of the speech form and thus lose its dynamic function. It then becomes subject to complete omission, if the tempo of the utterance increases sufficiently. The vowel [ɒ] of *on* has become an internal vowel in the phrase *step on the pest,* and may be reduced or omitted. A fully stressed vowel in the releasing position in its morpheme is less likely to be displaced and deprived of its function. In the speech measure, *the deliberate utterance,* the final [t] of *deliberate* remains an arresting stop and the initial [ʌ] of *utterance* retains its releasing function, frequently with the stopped vowel onset. The displacement of this [t] leads to the perception of a form [tʌtəns], which is unacceptable as a variant of the symbol [ʌtəns], and hence the dynamic displacement is resisted.

7.52   *Doubling*

When two morphemes are so juxtaposed in a speech measure that two identical speech sounds become contiguous, these two sounds may fuse to a single sound, which may be either a long sound or a double sound. For example, in the speech measure: *we have various types,* the final [v] of *have* and the initial [v] of *various* are not likely to be separately formed. Almost inevitably they fuse to a single labiodental constriction. The back stroke of the first and the beat stroke of the second [v] might be said to cancel each other. However, the syllable movement of *have* is arrested by this single constriction, and the syllable movement of *va-* in *various* is released by the same constriction. A single stop or constriction which serves both to arrest one syllable and to release the next is called a double stop or a double constriction. It does double duty, although it is not twice articulated. Careful measurements by Stetson[13] indicate that there is an arrest and a new chest pulse during the occlusion or constriction of these double consonants.

Double consonants due to fusion are susceptible to further change by reduction to single, long, consonants. This means usually that the arresting function of the double consonant has been abandoned. The releasing function appears to be less subject to disturbance by fusions. Double consonants appear frequently in phrases and in some lexical forms they result from the combining of a simple word with a prefix or suffix. We have, for example, a double *n* in *unknown,* or in *keenness,* a double *l* in *illegible,* or *tailless,* a double *m* in *immaterial,* a double *d* in *adduce.* We have both single and double *k* in forms of *book case.* Doubles due to fusion in context are very frequent in English. Some examples are the following: *who had died, he is loaded down, in a photographic kind of way, a war of national liberation, idealism may not be, I have no notion now, to keep peace, its debt to the past, he is forced to work, by that time, with the issues, thus separating them, that are related, war reporting.*

7.53 *Reduction*

The reduction of the adventitious double consonants due to fusion in speech measures or to compounding of simple forms with suffixes or prefixes is not infrequent. Increasing the speed of utterance is likely to reduce the double [v͡v] of *we have various types* to a single releasing [v] of *various*, and in the process another phenomenon of reduction appears clearly. The "unstressed" verb form *have* is reduced in the phrase by the suppression of its vowel [æ] to [ə], the initial [h] is rather omitted than reduced. As the reduction proceeds, one of two things may occur. Either the final [v] of *have* loses its arresting function and the double [v͡v] of *have various* is reduced to a single [v], the phrase being [wiəvɛrɪəs], or the double [v͡v] may be retained while the rest of *have* is lost, and the phrase becomes [wiv͡vɛrɪəs]. The double [d͡d] of the phrase *and degrees* is the more readily reduced to a single [d] as the arrest of the syllable *and* can be accomplished by the [n]. The reduction of [n͡n] in *unknown* to [n] is frequent in rapid speech and unusual in careful speech. The reduction of [l͡l] to [l] in *illegible* or *illegal* is probably more often heard than the double [l͡l].[14] Italian forms like *troppo*, *tutto*, *oppresso* are usually cited as illustrations of double consonants. As many Italians pronounce these words, the consonants written twice are indeed double consonants; that is, the single articulation serves both to arrest one syllable and to release the next. It is, however, not unusual to hear these words spoken by Italians with single long releasing consonants, the arresting function of the double having been taken over by the chest muscles, so that [trɔp͡po] becomes [trɔp:o].

The loss of the vowel of *not* is frequent in forms such as *wouldn't, hadn't, didn't*. In the form *can't* the reduction has been more drastic; a syllable has been omitted from the phrase *cannot*. The two [n]'s thus juxtaposed probably first were double [n͡n], but this has long since been replaced by a single [n] which, since the vowel of *not* was also lost, has become part of the syllable arrest. The form *didn't* frequently suffers a similar loss of syllable by the adaptive change of the cluster [dn] to [n͡n] which may in turn become a long [n:]. This is not often further reduced to short [n], as is the case in *can't*.

The fusion of two vowels which become contiguous in the speech measure, or by composition of affix with simple word, necessarily involves a reduction of the number of syllables of the form. Hence, if the meaning of the morpheme is not absorbed in that of the fused form, both vowels are likely to be preserved. This is the case in English forms such as *biannual, biennial, coauthor, coequal, diurnal*. The first syllables of these words are chest arrested and the second syllable either begins with an initial vowel onset, either even or stopped, or a glide sound is developed between the two vowels which may come to serve as the releasing movement of the second syllable. As these juxtaposed morphemes fuse more intimately in the speech form of the phrase or compound and the meanings of the individual components are overshadowed by a derived meaning of the whole, real fusion of the two contiguous vowels becomes more probable. An example is our treatment of *extraordinary*. Americans pronounce either [ɪkstrɔrdnɛrɪ] or [ɛkstrəɔrdnɛrɪ], probably more often the form with five syllables than the form with six.

Theoretically, in a language in which the same vowel can occur both finally and initially, one may find a doubling of the vowel in these contextual fusions. That is, the same vowel articulation may do double duty as the arrest of one syllable and the release of the next. Any shift in the function of either vowel will result in the loss of a syllable. Normally the arresting function will be given up and a single releasing vowel will result, but this can maintain itself only if the semantic features of the symbolism of the language demand it. Otherwise the vowel will tend to become internal and the consonant release of the preceding syllable will be transferred to the succeeding one. Thus the phrase *the eternal one* may become *th'eternal one* [ðitɜnlwʌn], and this in turn has yielded to Yankee ingenuity of analysis the article *the* and the adjective *tarnal*.

When two vowels which become contiguous are reduced to a single vowel, as is the case in [ɪkstrɔrdnɛrɪ], the process is called contraction. When the result is a diminishing diphthong (p. 111) as it was when Latin made *coepi* (I have begun) out of *co-epi*, the process is also called contraction, but when the result is an increasing diphthong, as it is when French makes [dɛm'jœr] out of *demi-heure*, or [ija] out of *il y a*, the contraction is sometimes called synaeresis or synezesis. The fusion of two words is less likely to become a fixed feature of the language and hence less likely to be recorded. Contractions of this sort did become fixed in Greek when τὰ ἄλλα became τἀλλα, or when the abstract noun καλοκἀγαθία (idea[1] human perfection) was evolved from the phrase καλὸς καὶ ἀγαθός. This kind of contraction of contiguous vowels is called crasis (mixture). Something akin to crasis may be seen in the reduction of the contiguous vowels in English phrases like *serve to arrest, the arresting function, to a single sound*. More often when reduction takes place in such phrases it has the form of an omission.

7.54 *Omission*

Fusion of morphemes in phrases frequently results in the complete omission of certain of the constituent elements. If the initial vowel of a morpheme is lost when it follows the final vowel of another, the grammarians speak of aphaeresis. When something is omitted from the interior of a morpheme, the phenomenon is called syncope, and when the final element of a morpheme is omitted, the term applied to the process is apocope.

Aphaeresis is more commonly met than its name. Examples are such English forms as *I'm* for *I am*, *I've* for *I have* [aɪəv], *you're* for *you are*, *the people round him* for *around him*. Shakespeare wrote: "*But might you do't, and do the world no wrong?*" and we still may hear this *do't* in youthful expostulations such as, "*I didn't do't*, or perhaps, "*I wont do't!*" The term aphaeresis is also applied to the loss of initial vowels in such forms as *'twont* for *it wont*, or *'mid* for *amid*, even though these omissions are not produced by the fusion of articulatory movements when they occur initially in the phrase. It is probable that such forms are indeed the result of fusions in other contexts just as *round* for *around* may be used initially. Whether these are two morphemes or two forms of the same morpheme is a question for morphology rather than for phonetics.

Syncope occurs frequently in the fusion of speech measures. Sometimes the syncopated form becomes established in usage and is then quite independent of the purely phonetic exigencies of the phrase. This is surely the case with English *whoe'er*, and *where'er* for *whoever* and *wherever*. The dissyllabic form of *several* is probably at least as frequent as the full form. Other syncopated forms remain outside the pale of good usage. English *civilization* frequently suffers syncope to [sɪvləzeʃn], *profitable* is sometimes reduced to three syllables by the syncope of the vowel [ɪ], *considerable* may be reduced from five syllables to four by the syncope of the sound or sounds represented by *-er-*, *believe* becomes a monosyllable by loss of the vowel after *b*. This shortening has an analogy in German, where modern *glauben* results from the syncope of the first vowel of an older *galouban*. English *before* sometimes is reduced to a monosyllable, which is written *'fore*, or sometimes the initial stop is omitted and we have two syllables [əfɔr]. Syncopated forms abound in *The Bigelow Papers*, where one finds *pop'lar*, *gov'ment*, *reg'lar*, *gin'rous*, *el'kent* (eloquent), *the'ry* (theory) *buff'lo*, *presdunt* (president), *librate* (liberate). Radio announcers are generous in providing us with illustrations of all manner of speech phenomena. This morning's syncope was *abanding* for *abandoning*. This kind of reduction is sometimes classed as dissimilation and called haplology.

Syncope explains many forms historically. Thus, for instance, we recognize in the so-called allegro forms of Latin *soldus*, *postus*, *caldus* the syncope of a vowel in *solidus*, *positus*, *calidus*, or we know that Germans say *es brannte* instead of *es brennte*, because they once reduced *ez brannita* to *ez brannta* by the syncope of [ɪ] and thereby prevented the umlaut of the short [a] to [ɛ]. When J. R. Lowell wrote, "*So'st no one couldn't pick it out*," his readers probably understood the syncope perfectly, but the time has come when an explanation of *st* is needed. This reduction of the phrase *so as*, or *so as that*, in any event involves the loss by aphaeresis of the vowel of *as*: the *t* either results from the syncope of [ðæ] from *that* or is an inorganic epithesis to a final *-s*.

The final element of a morpheme may be omitted by apocope. Thus the [v] of *of* is omitted in *out o' doors, Land O' Lakes, bill o' fare*,[15] or the final [d] of *and* is omitted with greater frequency than we perhaps realize. Lowell's line, *"That's fair an' square an' parpendicler,"* illustrates this syncope of [d] and provides an additional example of syncope in *parpendicler*. The final [d] of *hold* is often lost in forms such as *hold on, hold up*. Similarly *cold* becomes *col'*, *field* becomes *fiel'*. Final [t] is lost in the same way when *crust* becomes *crus'*, or *just* becomes *jes'*, and students write: *"The pair remained standing and look up at the dark fellow,"* or *"But they could not go pass him."*

When the final vowel is omitted before a following initial vowel the apocope is called elision. French *la* becomes *l'* by apocope in forms like *l'estrade, l'écriture*. So also *le* loses its vowel by apocope in *l'échelon, l'économe*, but does not lose it in *le onzième*. This kind of apocope has become so important in French that the grammars of that language deal with its occurrence extensively. But we have elision in English also in such phrases as *the eternal*. Shakespeare wrote:

> "There was a Brutus once that would have brooked
> Th' eternal devil to keep his state in Rome."

The apocope of this *-e* from *the* is not confined to verse, but meets the ear in everyday experience in groups such as *the easiest way, the other one*. One should observe that *devil* in the line just quoted was probably the monosyllable [di:l], to its author. Intervocalic [v] is syncopated and the two vowels contracted and assimilated to [i:], in much the same way as that in which *over* becomes [ɔ:r], or *ever* becomes [ɛ:r]. Modern Scotch spells this word *deil*.

7.55   *Glides and Intrusive Sounds*

Aphaeresis, syncope, and apocope represent a reduction of the number of sounds produced; glide sounds are additional, adventitious sounds produced in the transitions from one speech sound to the next in the configuration. It is evident that the sound-producing mechanism must shift its highly integrated movements from one set to another as speech sounds are produced in speech forms. This shifting is so prominent that in fluent speech there seems to be no fixation at all of the speech mechanism within the speech measure. Everything seems continually to change.

Yet, it is self-evident that unless the organic positions normal for the several speech sounds when they are produced alone are adequately[16] approximated the sounds in question will neither be produced nor heard. In that event they will appear to be lost by contraction or omission, or to suffer some adaptive change. Losses and changes of this sort are normal in all languages since linguistic signals can be drastically abbreviated and yet function adequately in most situations. But there is another possibility. If the articulatory positions required are adequately approximated and if the breath stream continues to be forced through the shifting channel above the larynx while the back strokes and the beat strokes of successive sounds are being executed, sounds which are not part of the patterns of the several components of the configuration may be added to the whole. These adventitious transitional sounds are glides and they may be linguistically important, since many glides have developed into regularly recurrent speech sounds and thus have become a part of the pattern.

Not every adventitious transitional sound is a glide, in this sense. Some are intrusive stop consonants, which do not result from the flow of breath through a shifting channel above the larynx but from a lack of synchronization in the consonant mechanism of one member of the configuration which produces the interruption of the flow of breath. These intrusive stops sometimes acquire a place in the pattern of words, as may be seen from the comparison of English *timber* with German *Zimmer*. In English the release of the labial occlusion has lagged behind the raising of the velum in the release of [m] so consistently that a nonetymological [b] has intruded itself into the word-form. The same explanation accounts for the [b] in *gun limber*, or in *humble*, from Latin *humilem*, although in this case our French friends inserted the stop, as they did in *encumber*, before we borrowed the words from them.

A simple classification of glide sounds will group (1) glides between a consonant and a following vowel, (2) glides between a vowel and a following consonant, (3) glides between two vowels, and (4) glides between two consonants. A cross-classification may distinguish between off-glides and on-glides. An off-glide is a transitional sound produced during the release or back stroke of a speech movement, and an on-glide is a transitional sound produced during the attack or beat stroke of a speech movement. It is often impossible to be sure whether a sound is an off-glide or an on-glide, that is, whether it is a modification of the release of one articulation or of the onset of the next. These terms were first given wide circulation by Henry Sweet[17] and it should be specifically observed that the meaning given them by Sweet and his followers is not that here intended. Sweet meant by on-glide and off-glide what we here mean by onset and release, respectively. I use the term glide only to refer to modifications of the normal onset and release of speech sounds which result in an adventitious sound peculiar to the fusion within the speech measure. Thus, the murmured vowel sometimes heard after the back stroke of [t] in French *petite* (cf. p. 173) is called an off-glide by many writers. This sound, however, is not conditioned by what follows, and is rather a phenomenon of consonant release than a modification of that release due to fusion in the speech measure.

7.551 *From Consonant to Vowel*

We have observed the change of the release of final [p] when this becomes a releasing rather than an arresting stop in the phrase, *step on the pest!* The aspiration it thus acquires, however, is a normal feature of the releasing stop and is therefore not a glide sound, in the sense of that term here intended. In the phrase, *all but universal* we may have the same kind of dynamic displacement of the [t] of *but*, but here a further modification is often observed, by virtue of which neither the release of [t] nor the onset of the vowel [ju] is identical with these phases of the two morphemes in other contexts. What often happens is that the release of [t] shifts from aspiration to affricate and the onset of [ju] becomes voiceless, so that [bʌt'jun] becomes [bə't∫un], with a very much reduced [ə] before the stop, while the release of the first syllable of *universal* is more or less identical with that of *chew*. Some careful speakers avoid this shift when the nexus is between lexical units but accept it when it is within a word, such as *nature*. Others reject the fusion even here and say *nate your*, thus preserving the even release of [t] and the voiced onset of [ju]. The analogous modification of the release of the stop in the phrases, *wont you? did you?* was observed at the outset of this chapter. Some phoneticians speak of the [∫] or [ʒ] which result in such fusions as glide sounds, but it is at least equally correct to regard [t∫] or [dʒ] as adaptive changes of [t] or [d] before a following [j]. In the same sense, the modification of the release of [p] before [ju] which makes the aspiration more or less identical with [ç] in words like *pure, impunity, puny* is also rather an adaptive change than an intrusive adventitious sound or glide.

On the other hand, when the release of [l] is so prolonged that *column* sounds like [kɑljəm] one may speak of this [j] as an adventitious sound or glide. The same may be said of the off-glide of [k] in some southern American pronunciations of *car, cow*, which sound like [kjɑ·], [kjaɔ]. In French, the release of [ɲ] in a word like *agneau* is commonly through a glide [j] before the vowel. These are not adaptive changes, but sounds resulting from the continuance of breath stream through the shifting speech channel, plus an asynchronism in the onset and release mechanisms. Voice begins too soon in [kjɑ·], [kjaɔ], the velum is raised too soon in [aɲjo].

7.552 From Vowel to Consonant

The transition from a vowel to a consonant in a speech measure will be either from a vowel to the arresting consonant of its own syllable or from a vowel with its own (chest) arrest to the releasing consonant of the next syllable. The second situation is by far the more frequent, but in either event a difference in nexus between the successive sounds may be observed. This difference can be seen in pairs of English words such as *pate*: *paid*, *goat*:*goad*. In *pate* and *goat* the vowels are considerably shorter than in *paid* and *goad*, the difference being something like 20 percent of the length of the longer vowel.[18] This difference is about the length of the diphthongizing diminuendo characteristic of the diphthongal vowels [ei] and [ou]. To put this another way, the vowels of *pate* and *goat* are arrested by the consonant occlusion before the energy of the breath pulse has diminished and the vowel articulation been relaxed to the point where a quality difference in the vowel sound becomes evident, whereas in *paid* and *goad* the consonant occlusion is not made until the energy of the breath pulse has diminished and the tongue position has been relaxed to the point where a difference in the quality of the vowel sound is audible. This diphthongal diminuendo, or vanish, is not confined to the vowels [e] and [o] but may be observed even with the open and usually much briefer vowels [ɪ] and [ɛ], as may be seen in pairs like *bit*:*bid*, *bet*:*bed*. Here too the difference in length is twenty per cent of the duration of the longer vowel and there is a distinct tendency toward a diminuendo or vanish in [ə] in the forms *bid* and *bed*. Jespersen referred to this difference as the difference between "fester Anschluss" and "loser Anschluss,"[19] which may be translated as close nexus and loose nexus, respectively. Salverda de Grave called the phenomena "coupe forte" and "coupe faible."[20] In the fusions of the speech measure many of the syllables which in lexical pronunciation have the loose nexus and diphthongal vowels are cut off more promptly by a chest arrest in preparation for the beat stroke of the following consonant which has shifted by dynamic displacement to the releasing function in the following syllable. In this situation the development of a glide between vowel and consonant is very rare, if indeed it is not physically impossible. Even in the case of word forms which end in vowels, the normal effect of fusion within the phrase when these words come to stand before forms with initial consonants is to speed up the chest arrest of the final vowel and thus to prevent the diphthongal diminuendo otherwise characteristic of words like *blow, go, two, knew, way, play.* This can be seen by comparing *Watch her blow!* with *Hand me the blow-torch, please,* or *He was unable to play* with *He was unable to play the fish carefully.* Here too the development of a glide sound after the vowel is rare if not impossible.

7.553   *From Vowel to Vowel*

When in a speech form or phrase two vowels are made contiguous at the boundary between two syllables, several things are possible. A syllable may be lost by contraction, or crasis, or diphthongization, or apocope, or a hiatus may be produced. A hiatus may be relieved by an intervocalic glide or by a linking consonant.

Hiatus involves the chest arrest of one vowel followed by the even or stopped release of the next, with a cessation of sound between the two vowels. Almost inevitably the cessation of sound is achieved by a glottal occlusion. Potential hiatus is very frequent in English after the article *the,* as one may see in *the angel of the Lord, the easiest way, the ice man, the owner, the outer wall,* but it is also presented by other collocutions involving words of the types represented by *profoundly, draw, knew, blow, free, high, may.* When the glottal stop occurs the release of the second vowel will be distinct, and it may be either the even or the stopped release.

Two types of glide may replace the cessation of voice and thus break the hiatus in English. After the vowels [i], [aɪ], [ei], or [ɪ] the glide [j] tends to appear; for example, *the angel* becomes [ðiʼjendʒəl], *free air* is [friʼjeir], *high altitude* is [haɪʼjæltɪtjud], *may allow* becomes [meijæˈlɑu]. After the vowels [ɔ], [o], and [u] the glide [w] tends to break the hiatus, as in *draw out* [drɔwɑut], *blow in* [blowɪn], she knew all [ʃinjuˈwɔl]. The [j] glide is developed when the chest arrest of the syllable having the final vowel is delayed or weak, and the glide may be a part of the arresting movement, or it may become, by a subsequent dynamic displacement, the releasing movement of the next syllable. The [w] glide is also most likely to appear when the chest arrest is weak, but asynchronism of lip movement may result in a late removal of vowel rounding which will cause the glide [w] even when the chest arrest is not notably lax. In such a phrase as *to go along with him* the [w] glide after *go,* if it occurs at all, occurs rather by asynchronism than by a weak chest arrest.

7.554   *From Consonant to Consonant*

When two consonants become contiguous in a speech form or phrase, they may retain their normal forms, or they may be grouped into an arresting or a releasing cluster by the dynamic displacement of one of them, or they may be fused by various adaptive changes, or they may be separated by a glide.

Asynchronism in the articulation of successive elements in consonant groups may result in the production of a transitional sound between any two of them. One prominent case of this sort results from the closure of the vocal bands for voice before the oral articulation of a following consonant is prepared. The unarticulated voice then sounds like and may develop into a vowel sound, often [ə]. We hear this in English in emphatic pronunciations of *three* [θəˈrij], *please* [pʰəˈlijz], or in slovenly pronunciations of *elm* [ɛləm], or *help* [hɛləp]. This is the phenomenon which has given us Latin *saeculum* instead of *saeclum*, or Pennsylvania German *barik* for German *Berg*. The glide [ə] appears frequently in the attempts of American beginners to pronounce the initial [kn] or [gn] of German words like *Knabe*, *Gnade*, *Vergnügen*. Philologists refer to the vowel thus developed as a svarabhakti vowel, and the process is important in the development of a speech not rigidly controlled by a standard language.

A different type of glide sound may be developed when two dental consonants become contiguous. Usually when [tθ], [tð] or [tt], [td] result in phrases like *that thing, bite this, fit too tight, let down*, English speakers do not execute the back stroke of the [t] but combine the occlusion of [t] directly with the articulation of the next element so that a single release serves for the cluster, regardless of the retention or displacement of the syllable boundary. However, if the first consonant stop is exploded, its release is very likely to be through a close apicoalveolar constriction and hence to sound like [s]. This is likely to be the case also if the first element is [d] rather than [t]. This is the process which gave us Latin *sessum* from *sedeo*, by the contiguity of [d] in *sed-* with [t] in the participial, or supine accusative, suffix -*tom*. It also accounts for the Old English weak past tense form *wisse* (which was soon displaced by the analogously formed *wiste*) beside the present tense *ic wat, we witon*. In both cases the glide sound [s] which developed between the two dentals ultimately became the distinctive feature of the pattern, and the stops were given up as they ceased to be heard. Modern French fails to develop this [s] glide between two contiguous dentals, each of which it is likely to explode, because its stops are glottalized, or at any rate do not have sufficient breathed release to produce an [s] in this way.

Instead of producing a continuant glide sound during the transition between two consonant articulations an asynchronism in the mechanism of one of them may result in the introduction of an intrusive stop between the two articulations. Thus the raising of the velum before the release of the oral occlusion of a nasal consonant may result in an intrusive stop which will be [p] in words like *warmth, comfort, symphony,* or [t] in words like *dense, mince, prince.* Indeed these words with dental nasal are pronounced in American English more often than not as homonyms of *dents mints, prints.* This is the process which produced Latin *exemptus* from *ex-ēmere,* thus giving us *exempt.* It also is the cause of the written *p* in *Hampshire, Hampton,* which with our usual perversity, we now generally do not pronounce.

7.56 *Linking*

Instead of a glide between two contiguous vowels, sometimes a fully formed consonant breaks the hiatus which would otherwise exist. These consonants usually have their origins in doublet forms of lexical units, from one of which the final consonant is lost while it is retained in the other. This situation may be observed in the German doublets *da-* and *dar-*, *wo-* and *wor-* in such forms as *dabei, daran, womit, worauf.* It existed in the Latin forms *a* and *ab,* and to some extent in *e* and *ex,* in forms such as *ab urbe* but *a mari,* or *e curru, e regione,* but *ex parte* as well as *ex urbe.*

In Eastern American speech a final postvocalic [r] is lost from such words as *far,* or *butter,* when these are final in the phrase or when they are followed by forms beginning with a consonant. When in the speech measure they are followed by a word beginning with a vowel, the [r] is not lost from these words. Therefore there are two forms of the morphemes far or butter, namely [fa] and [far], [bʌtə] and [bʌtər]. The first is used in such a phrase as *that's going too far,* the second in a phrase like *that's far and away the best.* The hiatus which might exist in the phrase *far and away* is avoided by the use of the morpheme with a final [r] which is not the usual lexical pronunciation of that word. This final [r] is then usually called the linking [r].

The Latin third person singular present indicative ended in -t, and this ending was preserved in Old and in Middle French. In Modern French the verb has completely lost this -t in forms such as *il a, il va, elle donne, il est, il meurt, elle tait.* Yet if any of these verb forms is spoken before the pronoun subjects *il, elle, on,* the -t is not lost but serves to break the hiatus which would otherwise result from the inversion of the form, as in *a-t-il, est-elle, raconte-t-on des histoires?* The modern French rules for liaison are a description of the phenomenon of linking to avoid hiatus within the speech measure or phrase. Liaison between members of two different rhythmic groups, that is, between two different speech measures, does not occur. One does not carry over a final consonant from an accented final syllable to a following vowel, because the accented final syllable in

French marks the end of the speech measure. For example, one says: *les petits enfants* [lepətizã:fã], but *les enfants ont perdu* [lezã:fãɔpɛrdy], *je me voyais exposé à* [ʒəmvwajezɛkspo:zea], but *je me voyais, en effet* [ʒəmvwajeãnɛfe].

However, the process does not always stop with the retention of these linking consonants in contexts to which they belong etymologically. Eastern American speech uses the hiatus breaker [r] widely in forms in which it is not etymologically justified at all. We find not only *far and near*, but *Emma(r) Eames*, and *raw(r) oysters*. The Greeks developed the use of [n] as a hiatus breaker in much this same fashion. They called it the trailing *-n* (ν ἐφελκύστικον).

If our Eastern speakers were to say *Emma Smith* and *raw fish* it might be said that they have developed doublet forms of these words like those of *far* and *butter*, but many of them do not do this. They attach an [r] to all forms with a final vowel, even when the forms are final or stand before a morpheme with an initial consonant. The most irreproachable speakers will say, when they read it in college chapels, "*The paw(r) of the lion*," (1 Samuel 17:37) and "*The law(r) of the wise*," (Proverbs 13:14), but they will also say *law(r)* when no vowel follows. Many speakers in New England regularly add [r] to words like *soda, piazza, Emma*. To all intents and purposes, for these speakers these words end in a consonant and there is no question of linking [r] in their phrasal fusions. In any event, this phenomenon is one which may give the practical phonetician a problem. We once found it expedient, when trying to teach a singer to pronounce German words like *Knabe* or *liebe*, to write *-er* instead of *-e* for her. She would pronounce a written *Knaber* more or less as German *Knabe* should be pronounced. To persuade her to pronounce *lieber* with final [r] we then had to write the form without *-r*, as *liebe*, and then induce her to trill the *-r* she produced.

The situation in that New England speech in which linking [r] has come to be affixed to words like *raw(r)* and *soda(r)* as a part of the lexical pattern of these words, and thus ceased, strictly speaking, to be a linking [r] or hiatus breaker for these speakers, is an illustration of one of the difficulties involved in maintaining a distinction between synchronic and diachronic phenomena in language. From the standpoint of the larger unity, American English, this phenomenon is a synchronic one and a case in which linking [r] is being used as an epithetic [r]. From the standpoint of the dialect of these New England speakers, this [r] is the result of a phonologic change by analogy and is not a hiatus breaker at all, because in their dialect no hiatus can occur. The reductio ad absurdum of this distinction between language and dialect has been reached in the position taken by some linguists, that each speaker speaks his own dialect. This is undoubtedly true in one sense, but the usefulness of this ultimate dialect is entirely in its nonunique features.

Whether the doublet forms be of pure etymological lineage or whether they be secondarily derived by analogical transfer, the preservation of a final consonant to prevent hiatus, and its loss when this function is not to be served, provide a language with a means of avoiding hiatus which is usually called linking. It may be suggested that when the glottal stop is used between two contiguous vowels it may assume the proportions of an intrusive consonant rather than its usual importance as a form of vowel onset, and that in this case one might regard [ʔ] as a hiatus breaker. Linking may provide a nexus between two syllables through a continued flow of voice, in [r] or [n]. The French continuants in liaison are voiced. The French liaison through [t] and [k], on the other hand, is a case in which hiatus is avoided by preserving a stop which is otherwise lost, and indeed a final [d] or [g] is unvoiced to [t] or [k] in these circumstances. Grandgent used to say that languages abhorred hiatus as nature abhors a vacuum. This may be literally true, since hiatus indeed involves the production of negative air pressure in the chest if the two contiguous vowels are to be respectively chest arrested and chest released. To stop the outward flow of air by movement of the chest muscles, the air pressure in the lungs must be made equal to or lower than that in the pharynx. Closure of the glottis will stop the breath flow regardless of the pressure below the larynx, and the release of the glottal stop may function exactly as does the release of [t] or [k] in the mechanics of the following syllable. The role of the glottal stop in separating contiguous vowels in English, and even more prominently in German, is indeed analogous to that of [t] or [k] in French liaison, though its origin is perhaps rather physiological than etymological. Whether one calls such a glottal stop an intrusive consonant or a linking consonant, or whether one simply accepts the fact that hiatus is made easier by the glottal release of the second vowel will depend upon other factors in the phonological analysis of the language in question.

7.57 *Adaptive Changes*

When two sounds become contiguous in the speech measure one or both of them may in the fusion of the configuration undergo changes which (a) tend to make each more like its neighbor, or (b) tend to make each less like its neighbor. We call the first process assimilation and the second process dissimilation. Indeed, these adaptive changes are not confined to contiguous sounds but may occur when the affected sounds are separated by one or more intervening sounds. It may, therefore, be convenient to distinguish between contact assimilations and remote assimilations, or contact dissimilations and remote dissimilations. The phonetic principles in each case are the same, for these adaptive changes are almost exclusively the result of neuromotor adjustments to promote facility of movement and economy of effort. The nervous "confusion" of speech stumbling, or "anticipation," has been credited with a part in some of the changes classed as remote, but these phenomena are simply neuromotor adjustments within a configuration which are too drastic to be linguistically acceptable. They distort the signal too much to permit their becoming usual. The chap who turned *expedite* into *expediate* on this morning's newscast was suffering from intellectual, not from phonetic frailty.

7.571   *Assimilative Changes of Release*

We have observed the changes of the release of [t] and the onset of [ju] in such forms as *wont you?* or the change of [d] and [ju] in *did you?* By an assimilative change the breathed release of the stop is combined with the constriction of the vowel onset so that a continuant results, which is so like the normal [ʃ] or [ʒ] portion of the affricates [tʃ] or [dʒ] that the fusion is associated with the affricate and this then tends to become a part of the pattern of these configurations. Indeed, most of the affricates in words like *chin, children, bridge, edge* have developed from assimilations of the release of stops from aspiration to affricate by a process sometimes called assibilation. The [tʃ] of *chin, chew, child* is a development from [k] in which the stop has been drawn forward as the blade of the tongue is more definitely raised during the release. The [dʒ] of *edge, bridge* has evolved from a long or double [g] in much the same way. A Latin *gentem* has become Italian *gente*, with initial [dʒ], and in French the stop has been completely lost, so that the affricate has become the significant fricative [ʒ] of *gent*. In the same way, Latin *centum* has become Italian *cento*, with the affricate [tʃ], while French has lost the stop and preserved only the fricative [s] in *cent*. The affricate in French was [ts] rather than [tʃ], as it ultimately became in Italian. English *orchard* results from the assimilation of an Old English [t] and [j] in *ort-geard*, where the open consonant written -*ge*- is simply a [j] which has replaced the stop [g] by a process which the grammarians have called palatalization. When you find *indian* spelled *injun* you have the form in which [dj] has been assimilated to [dʒ], as in *engine* from Latin *ingenium*.

An analogous assimilation may be observed between two open consonants in pronunciations of [ʃ] for [s] and [ʒ] for [z] in such forms as *misuse, this year, cause you, it holds your, it is usually.* Most of these assimilations are frowned upon by champions of good usage, but all are frequently heard in

American speech. We Americans insist upon [ʃ] in *issue*, while our British cousins abhor it. Everyone pronounces [ʃ] in *sugar*, but many speakers pronounce [s] in *sumac*. The case of *sure* is only graphically, not phonetically analogous, for this written *s* before *u* is merely bad orthography for *sh* as in *shoe*, and the [ʃ] results from the assimilation of [sk] in *sure*, no less than in *ship*, *shine*, or *shoe*.

Another adaptive change in the release of stops is the lateral release peculiar to stops before the various [l] sounds. Often these fusions involve still further adaptive changes in the place at which the stop is made and our examples will be cited later in that connection.

7.572 *Assimilative Changes as to Voicing*

Some assimilations are confined to the feature of voicing. The articulatory movements apart from the positions of the vocal bands are not modified by the fusions in context, but one element or the other either loses the voicing normal to its pronunciation or acquires voicing not normal to it in other contexts. For example, [v] is often unvoiced in phrases such as, *he does not have to file*, but voiced in, *you cannot have delivery until*. It tends to lose its voicing in, *we can even live for a while* in the form, *live for a while*, or in the phrase, *the most destructive force*. We voice the final consonant of *news*, but we usually unvoice it by partial assimilation to [p] in the form *newspaper*. We unvoice the final *d* of *used* in *he used to*, but voice it in *he used two*.[25]

Whether the English morphological suffix is [s] or [z] depends upon what precedes it; for instance, *cows, paths, wives, cubs, brides* have [z], but *cats, walks, cups, rites* have [s]. We may leave it to the morphologist to decide what the suffix is, but the matter is of some concern to the phonetician who tries to classify the phenomena he observes. If, let us say, the morphological element which marks the English plural of nouns is [s], then we have assimilations in words like *cows, wives, tubs*. If this morphological element is [z], then the assimilations occur in words like *cats, cups, rites*. If the suffix is the open dental consonant, voiceless or voiced, [s/z], we then have no adaptive change in either set of forms but a selection of one of the two variants, conditioned by the phonetic structure of the movement complex of each word. If the environment of the plural suffix is voiced, [z] is chosen to harmonize with it; if it is voiceless, [s] is chosen. One may then speak rather of a consonant harmony than of an assimilative change in the fusions in which this morpheme appears. Practically, the result is the same in either case; linguistically, and to the science of phonetics, the analysis of the phenomena is different.

We observe that the [ð] of *with* tends to become voiceless in phrases like *with technological advances*. The [ð] of *these* tends to be unvoiced in phrases like *in both these books.* These two cases may serve as illustrations of the distinction between assimilation by anticipation in which the first sound is influenced by the second sound, and assimilation by continuation, in which the second sound is influenced by the first.[26] Anticipative assimilation, particularly as to the factor of voicing, is frequent in French, in words like *obtenir, observer,* where [b] becomes [p], or *anecdote, second,* where [k] is replaced by [g]. Assimilation as to voicing is also anticipative in *chacque jour,* where [g] replaces the [k] of *chacque,* or in *je mange peu,* where [ʃ] replaces the [ʒ] of *mange.*

7.573 *Assimilation of Place of Articulation*

Adaptive changes may also affect the place at which a constriction or a stop is made. For example, the occlusion of [k] in *king* is made much further forward on the palate than that of [k] in *cling.* The long marginal occlusion for [l] influences the position of the stop which precedes it and the breath released by the explosion of this stop flows over the lateral margins of the blade of the tongue rather than through the channel normal to [k]. The same kind of lateral release may be observed in English *booklet,* French *bâcler,* and the lateral release of [t] is characteristic of French words like *atlas.* In English the occlusion of [t] in a word like *atlas* is likely to be retracted considerably and the release is lateral also. There is something of a tendency in English to substitute a [t] for a [k] or a [d] for a [g] in words like *climb* or *glue.* This is not a reversal of the principle by which the [k] of *cling* is displaced to the rear of the hard palate, but is rather the result of an asynchronism in the occlusions. When the movement of the tongue blade for [l] is simultaneous with or slightly anticipates the occlusion for [k] or [g], the first stoppage of the breath stream involves the contact of the middle of the tongue blade for [l] near the front of the palatal region and the occlusion sounds rather like [t] than like [k]. In that event the [t] stop will be heard and may tend to replace the [k] stop in the pattern of the form. There is a factor of perception as well as a motor factor in all such cases, and the influence of the two factors upon the speech form is a composite which usually defies analysis.

Well-known cases of assimilation of the points of occlusion or constriction are those of English *goose*:*geese,* or German *doch*:*Dolch.* The advancing of the stop in *geese* from [g] to [ɟ] is a case of anticipative assimilation. The palatalization of [x] in Dolch to [ç] is a case of continuative assimilation, because the release of German [l] is notably palatal.

An interesting shift in the position of the oral occlusion for the nasal can be observed in the two pronunciations now heard of words like *length, strength.* Standard American speech has the mediopalatal nasal [ŋ] in these words, but many speakers draw the occlusion forward towards the place

where the dental constriction [θ] is formed and pronounce [n] rather than
[ŋ]. The reverse assimilation occurs when [ŋ] is substituted for [n] in words
like *incubate, inquest.*

The [l] which appears before [ju] in words like *evaluate,* or in the form,
I tell you, tends in many cases to be so strongly palatalized that the fusion
might be written [ʎ], or even [j], as in [ɪ'væ·juet]. That is to say, the [l]
first shifts its position as to its central or medial occlusion in the direction
of [j] and then becomes completely assimilated to the [j] of [ju].

7.574 *Assimilation in Manner of Articulation*

Adaptive changes in the manner of articulation may make one sound
more like its neighbor than it was before the change. For example, a voiceless stop consonant between two vowels, as in Latin *ripam,* requires the
opening of the glottis, or at any rate the cessation of voice, at the onset of
the stop and then the resumption of voice for the second vowel. Continuation of the voicing throughout the stop, while it still imposes a major
restraint upon the energy of the breath stream, does eliminate two shifts
in the position of the arytenoid cartilages and the vocal bands. Provençal
made this change of manner of articulation in its form *ripam,* which is
riba. The change in Spanish *riva,* however, was from stop to spirant, and
this is probably a step farther than Provençal has gone, since the Spanish
voiced spirant [β] is most readily understood as the opening of the occlusion, sometimes called the lenition, of a voiced stop [b]. The French form
rive shows the further change of a bilabial spirant to the labiodental spirant,
and this last step is one of those shifts which is rather due in the first
instance to the perception of the sound than to the neuromotor pattern
of its production. It is rather a sound substitution than a sound change.

A very sweeping series of sound changes in which the manner of articulation shifted from that of stop to that of the open consonant is characteristic
of the Celtic languages, where it is a conspicuous part of a group of changes
described as lenition. With a few exceptions, every simple stop in Celtic
became the homorganic open consonant, or specifically, [t] > [θ], [k] > [x],
[p] > [f], and so on. These changes, however, like the quite similar changes
of Grimm's Law in the Germanic languages, occurred at a time so remote
that we have not learned what caused them. We may not regard them as
adaptive changes, because we have no evidence to support such a thesis.
Hence we speak of these shifts as spontaneous sound changes, while we
call those changes for which we can give a certain explanation, like that
of Latin *ripam* to Spanish *riva,* conditioned sound changes, or in our example
specifically, an assimilation.

Also to be classed as adaptive changes in the manner of articulation are those cases in which lip-rounding or nasalization is added to sounds because of their associations within the movement complex of certain forms. We in English are very likely to produce the lip-rounding characteristic of our [w] before we release the velar stop in such words as *queen, Gwendolyn*. The [l] in words like *polo, zulu* is likely to have lip-rounding throughout its entire articulation. Usually this kind of adaptive change is not observed and hence it is not likely to acquire importance in the history of the language. Yet there are instances in which lip-rounding has been added to or taken from the pattern of sounds by assimilations which led to sound changes. This has probably contributed to the development of Middle High German *wirde, wirze* into Modern High German *Würde, Würze*. On the other hand, a Middle High German *küssen* has become *Kissen* by the loss of the vowel rounding peculiar to [y].

Nasality is frequently spread by assimilation over one or more speech articulations which become adjacent to a nasal sound. Thus the [v] of *envoy*, the [w] of the phrase, *this is some winter*, or the [l] of the name of Major Gin'ral *Stanley*, is likely to be nasalized, even by persons not given to a generally nasal form of tone production when they speak.

The vowel of Latin *mensam* underwent a series of changes in its manner of articulation as this word developed into Spanish *mesa*. The order of the development of this change is probably something like this. First, the vowel of *mensam* was nasalized. Next, the nasal consonant was lost and the nasal vowel became longer, say [ē:]. Then the nasality of the vowel was diminished and ultimately lost, and finally the vowel was shortened to [ɛ] as it is in *mesa*. At this stage English borrowed the word in such uses as *officer's mess, mess hall*, and even *mess table*.

Sometimes the assimilation as to manner of formation is more drastic. The phrase, *let me see* is likely to become *le' me see*, which may represent either the complete assimilation of [tm] to [m͡m], the double consonant, or the further reduction of [m͡m] to [m]. The word *interested* is likely to become [ɪnərɛstəd], with the complete assimilation of [t] after [n], if the raising of the velum is delayed until the onset of the vowel [ə]. When this vowel is syncopated, the cluster [n͡tr] results, and in this case the [t] is usually heard. *Something* is regularly *sunthin'* in *The Bigelow Papers*, *dreadful* is *dreffle*, *Demosthenes* is *Demossenes*, all by assimilations as to the manner of articulation of sounds in context.

7.575 *Assimilation of Contiguous Stops*

When two occlusions become contiguous in the speech measure a number of different things can happen. One change is the doubling of like stops by the omission of the release of the first and of the onset of the second, the one occlusion being made to do double duty. French does this usually in phrases like *une grande dame, un bec crochu*. Strictly speaking, this is perhaps rather to be called a form of reduction than an assimilation, but the two classifications are not mutually exclusive and the line between the two phenomena is not easily drawn.

When the two stops are made in the same place but differ as to voicing, we may get a combination of the articulating movements, like the fusion of doubling, either with or without an assimilation between the two stops as to voicing. English phrases such as *a pair of hip boots, he wore a red tie, she baked a big cake, somewhat diffidently*, involve no assimilation as to voicing but show the reduction of lip or tongue movements peculiar to doubling. This produces a dilemma of terminology, because such a fusion as [p͡b] is neither a double [pp] or [bb], nor a simple transition [pb], because the [p] is not exploded and the [b] has no onset of its own. Probably the best thing to call fusions of this sort would be unassimilated double consonants. Stetson calls them abutting consonants.[27] The matter is simpler in French, in one respect at least, in that there is always in addition to the doubling of the oral articulation, an anticipative assimilation of voicing in French fusions of this kind. There is trouble, however, on another score, since it is alleged that the difference between strong and weak, or between fortis and lenis, is preserved in these fused forms. Thus, it is claimed, *une route droite* yields the unassimilated double [t͡d] with voiced fortis [t̬], doubled with voiced lenis [d], while *une grande tasse* is held to yield [d̥t] with voiceless lenis [d̥] doubled with voiceless fortis [t]. In any event, it is clear that the difference between a voiceless fortis and a voiceless lenis occlusion, when neither is exploded, can be heard only in the onset, and that this in turn is most likely to be observable in the way in which the vowel before the stop is terminated. That is to say, the distinctive feature in these situations is likely to be the kind of nexus between the vowel and the stop. Close nexus marks the fortis occlusion, loose nexus marks the lenis.

When the two occlusions are not in the same place there may be a fusion of the release and onset mechanisms, as is usual in English, or each stop may retain its own proper release and onset, as is usual in French phrases such as *un roc très grand*, or in words like *acte, respectueusement*, in which [k] is released before the occlusion of [t] is made. In English the release of [k] in *act*, or in the phrase *we lack time*, is usually omitted. The dental occlusion is made while the palatal or velar stop is still intact, and the result is a fused articulation which has the onset of [k] and the release of [t]. In *act* the fusion is an arresting cluster; in *we lack time* the mechanism is that of a double, in that [k] arrests one syllable while [t] releases the next. One may indicate this graphically by writing [k͡t], but there is no accepted name for the resultant fused stop. One may suggest that such fusions as [k͡t] or [t͡k] might reasonably be called mixed double consonants. I suspect that [t͡k] in such a phrase as *do you want to get kicked?* is frequently assimilated to [k͡k] and, indeed, that it is often further reduced to [k].

Analogous fusion of labial with lingual stops is readily produced. Grandgent's illustrations were *Abgar* and *napkin*. We may add forms like *lab coat drab goings on, they keep talking, deep diggings.* In fusions of this kind, where the labial element is first, the lip closure must be removed before the dental or velar stop is exploded, but the latter stops are occluded while the labial stop is still intact and there is not air pressure enough between lingual and lip occlusion to produce a sound when the labial stop is released. Only the onset of these labial occlusions is audible. When the lingual occlusion is the first element, as in such phrases as *he is a big baby, the rock pile, without protest, the bad boy,* the lingual stop is not released until after the labial occlusion has been formed, and this release is therefore quite inaudible. Often the lingual occlusion appears to be relaxed rather than removed by a back stroke of the lingual muscles.

7.576   *Assimilation in Clusters*

When more than two consonants become involved in fusions, various assimilatory adjustments may occur, but each of these is identical in principle with one or another of the phenomena we have already cited. Illustrations are easily found in English. For instance, an internal [t] is likely to be drastically reduced in such groups as these: *he left the United States,* where [ft͡ð] becomes [f t͡ð] or [fð]; *softness* where [ftn] becomes [f t͡n] or [fn] as is usual in *soften; can affect that movement* yielding [kt͡ð] or [kð]; *if the locked door* with [kt͡d] or [kd]; *perfectly* becoming *puffickly* (Lowell), with [k͡tl] becoming [k͡kl] and then [kl]; *which attempt to* with [mpt͡t] becoming [mt͡t] or [mt]; *in a violent time* with [nt͡t] becoming [n͡t], but *want to* often yielding [n͡n] or [n] [wʌnə]. In combinations after [s] the dental stop is subject to assimilation in phrases such as *the most delightful one, he must get out, almost completely, for the most part,* and *listen,* in which the loss of [t] is now regular. Out of such assimilative combinations we get colloquial forms of words like *just, most, must* with no final stop, or as is the case in *The Bigelow Papers,* with a final stop before a vowel but none before a consonant, thus: *jes' like, jes' for,* but *jest a kind.*

Nasal consonants are sometimes assimilated to the motor context in such clusters as occur in the phrase, *what happened to you?* [hwɔthæpm̩dt͡ə'ju], or in a word like *pumpkin,* when it becomes [pʌŋkən]. In German, *wir haben* is frequently pronounced [viːr haːbm] and in less careful speech this may become even [mrḥaːm], beside the inverted form, *haben wir,* which is reduced to [hɑm̂mr] by the assimilation of [b̂mv] to [m̂m] or even to [hɑmr] with [m].

We have observed the loss of [d] from the group [nd] in words like *and*, when these fuse with a following morpheme beginning with a dental, in collocutions such as *and degrees*. There is a tendency for [d] to be completely assimilated, or lost, between [n] and a following [l] or [r] in words like *kindling, swindler, laundry, hundred, handle*. The oral occlusions for (n) and for [l] are made in the same general region and so, when they fuse, the stop once set up for the nasal is not shifted until the lateral release of [l] is made. If the velum is raised before this lateral release of [l] begins, a [d] will be heard. When the raising of the velum comes after or simultaneously with the lateral release, the stop [d] will be assimilated completely with the nasal. The result will not be a double nasal in such cases, but it may be a long [n:]. When *candidates* is pronounced *canidates*, the cause is probably the assimilation of the first dental stop to the nasal; when it is pronounced *candates* we may speak of haplology, which is a form of dissimilation, but the path to that end may well be first the assimilation of [nd] to [n], and then the loss of the unstressed vowel of *canidates* by the same sort of syncope that gives us *pop'lar* for *popular*, *guv'ment* for *government*, *reg'lar* for *regular*.

7.577   *Vowel Adaptations*

Adaptive changes which involve vowels are somewhat less readily cited from materials generally known. We have in some American pronunciations a levelling of the diphthongs [aɪ] and [ɑʊ] which probably results from assimilation. In some southern American speech the diphthong of words like *I, buy, aisle* is monophthongized to [ɑ:]. This may be regarded as the assimilation of the second element of the diphthong to the first, though the first element itself has been lowered and retracted. Latin had the diphthong [aɪ] which it wrote *ae*, for instance in *paeniteo* (to make, or to be sorry). This diphthong was ultimately assimilated to [ɛ:], and then in some words, shortened to [ɛ], as we have it in English *penitentiary, penitent*. In this case each element of the diphthong has been changed in the direction of the other and the two have met in a compromise more or less midway between the two original positions. The Germanic diphthong [aɪ], on the other hand, was monophthongized in English to [ɑ:], apparently by the same sort of levelling or assimilation as that now current in Southern speech.

The various pronunciations of the diphthong [ɑʊ] show some cases of partial or complete assimilation. In parts of Canada, for example, the diphthong of words like *house*, where [ɑʊ] stands before a voiceless consonant, is pronounced approximately [ʊu], and at times seems even to approach monophthongization to [u]. The same sort of assimilation can be heard in eastern Virginia, and elsewhere in our eastern southern states. The Germanic diphthong [ɑʊ] remained [ɑʊ] in some German dialects, except for two conditioned changes by which it became [oː], but in other dialects the diphthong has been wholly levelled to [oː]. In English the present reflex of that diphthong is [iː] in *leaf, cheap, neat* (ox). This [iː] is in turn a reflex of an earlier [eː], which resulted from the monophthongization of a still earlier diphthong, possibly something like [æə], which resulted from the Old English reflex of Germanic [ɑʊ] and was usually written *ea*. An [æə] from [ɑʊ] is thus not too remote from the [æʊ] which can be heard now in southern American pronunciations of words like *how, houses, found*, where the diphthong is final or before a voiced sound.

Perhaps the pronunciation [ɪ] which can often be heard in American speech for [ɛ] in words like *men, pen, when* is the result of the assimilation of the tongue position of [ɛ] to that of the oral occlusion of the dental nasal. This would involve only a slight raising of the forward portion of the tongue blade plus a pharyngeal adjustment which would slightly enlarge the cavity behind the tongue. In any event, the vowel [ɛ] before a single nasal, or before a nasal plus consonant has always tended, in English at least, to become [ɪ], and at times this tendency produces an assimilative shift.

Two cases of remote assimilation may be cited. The first is demonstrably an adaptive change. The Old English antecedents of *foot:feet* were *fôt:fêt* and this word along with *tôþ:têþ* was already an irregular form in Old English. It is clear, however, that the vowel [eː] of the plural of these words is the result of an assimilative change by which the vowel of the base, [oː], was made more like the vowel of the plural morpheme [i]. The analogous forms in Old High German are *fuoz:fuozi* and this *uo* is the regular Old High German reflex of a Germanic [oː]. This kind of remote assimilation is so important in the historical explanation of modern language forms that it has acquired its own name. In English it is called vowel mutation, in French it is called either metaphonie, mutation vocalique, dilation vocalique or inflection. In German the process is called Umlaut, and this term has considerable currency in English usage.

It is clear that when such an assimilation affects the vowel of the base of a word in some of its forms but not in others, for instance in the plural but not in the singular, the "same" word, or morpheme, will occur with two different forms. One form has resulted from a sound change, let us say the Umlaut of [oː] to [eː]. The two forms of the same morpheme then show a sound interchange [oː]/[eː], or ō/ē, as it is usually written, and this sound interchange may ultimately come to be the distinctive mark of a functional difference, as it has in English *foot:feet, tooth:teeth*, or it may exist with no discernible functional importance, as must have been the case in twelfth-century German, when either *kraft* or *krefte* could be used by the same author as the dative singular of *kraft*.

The sound interchanges observable in English verbs like *drive:drove: driven, hang:hung, sing:sang:sung* result from very ancient sound changes about which we know very little, but which once considerably affected the form of many words in all of the Indo-European languages. One of the major characteristics of the Germanic languages is the fact that they made of this interchange a functional feature in the tense system of their so-called strong verbs. The phenomenon represented by these sound interchanges is called in German Ablaut, in French apophonie or alternance vocalique, and in English vowel gradation. The German term Ablaut is also current in English usage, although it sometimes suffers a hideous anglicization to [æblaɔt].

There are numerous languages in which our second case of remote assimilation may be observed. These languages have morphological elements with two or more quite equivalent forms, the choice between which, when words are formed, appears to be determined entirely by a tendency to make the vowel of one component as nearly like that of the other as is possible. A case may be cited from the African language Moru, which belongs to the group called the Eastern Sudanic languages.[28] There the vowel of the first person pronoun, for example, is made to harmonize with the first vowel of the verb stem, so that one hears má-lása (I wash), mó-lósó (I sewed), mí-lii-te (I wept), mú-túri (I fear). In each case *m* plus a vowel is the pronoun "I." Other examples of this kind of sound interchange with remote assimilation can be had from Turkish, or from the Finno-Ugrian languages. The name usually applied to the phenomenon by the grammarians is vowel harmony. What adaptive changes may underlie the existence of the several forms of the morphemes concerned is a question for the historian of the language, and the propriety of citing any case of vowel harmony under the rubric of assimilation derives not from the origin of the forms but from the principle of their selection for use.

7.578 *Dissimilation*

Under some conditions of fusion the constituent sounds of a linguistic form suffer adaptive changes which make them less rather than more like their neighbors in the configuration. This phenomenon is called dissimilation. Whereas the phenomena of assimilation result from the anticipation of some portion of a movement required for a subsequent sound in the complex, or from the continuation of some feature of one sound into the articulation of a subsequent one, dissimilation is due to the avoidance of the difficulty of execution of two identical or closely similar movements within a very brief period of time. Every muscular movement has a minimum repetition time (or a maximum repetition rate), that is, a minimum period within which it cannot be successfully repeated. If new nervous impulses calculated to repeat the movement are initiated before this minimum interval has elapsed, the result is likely to be to lock the moving organ into its position rather than to repeat a movement. It appears to be possible to avoid this disturbance sometimes by what seem to be quite small modifications of the gross movements, if these are changes which involve a different array of neuromotor units in a different time pattern. Thus, two [θ] sounds in quick succession are much more difficult to enunciate than a [t] and a [θ] in the same time interval (cf. below). When one becomes confused by such a tongue twister as *the seething sea ceaseth and thus the seething sea sufficeth us*, it is because the repetition time of the spirants is such that the muscles become locked in the attitude required for the slit fricative [ð] and the hole fricative [s] cannot be produced, although the whole tongue can be moved up and down for the syllabics which intervene.

There are a number of classic examples of dissimilation in the history of various languages. There is, for instance, Grassmann's law for the dissimilation of aspirates, which is valid for Indic and for Greek.[29] This law shows that when, by composition or otherwise, two syllables each with an initial aspirate, such as Sanskrit [dh], [bh], [gh], came to succeed one another in the form or phrase, the first aspirate was changed to the homorganic simple stop without aspiration. Thus a form *dha-dhâ-mi would become da-dhâ-mi. Greek τίθημι is the reflex of an earlier *θίθημι. Many words were affected by this kind of dissimilation and the law is important to the etymologist who must compare English and German word forms with Greek and Sanskrit forms.

The liquid consonants [l] and [r] are subject to dissimilative changes when too many of them come too closely together in the word form or phrase. Latin *peregrinus* has become Italian *pellegrino* by the dissimilation of the two [r] sounds. English *marble* is our choice between Middle English *marbre* and *marbel*, the latter being the form by dissimilation of the two [r] sounds in French *marbre*, which in turn has its [b] by dissimilation of the two [m] sounds of Latin *marmorem*. English *heaven*, beside German *Himmel*, represents a twofold dissimilation, since *heaven* results from the dissimilation of the nasals [mn] to [βn], which became [vn], while *Himmel* represents the dissimilation of *himin* to *himil*. The adaptive change of [n] to [l] may have helped or been helped by the analogy of *esil* from Latin *asinus*, or *kumil* from *kumin* from Latin *cuminum*. French turned a late Latin *caminata* into *cheminée*, which we borrowed as *chimney*, but popular speech has often dissimilated the two nasals and produced *chimley*, or even, with an intrusive stop, *chimbley*.[30]

A type of dissimilation as to voicing, which appears to be characteristic of English, was first commented upon by Henry Sweet. When the voiced stops or constrictives [b], [d], [g], [v], [z], [ʒ] are preceded by another consonant and followed by a word beginning with a vowel they are regularly unvoiced, or whispered. Examples are the following: *the barb of the hook*; *he proved it conclusively*; *the morgue is closed*; *twelve are needed*; *the beds are ready*; *the hedge is burning*.

The repetition of two consonant movements which become successive in a word or phrase but which are separated by a vowel so that no form of doubling is convenient, is often avoided by omitting one of the articulations and with it frequently, but not always, one of the syllables of the word. This is essentially the definition one finds in books for the term ecthlipsis, and it also is the definition of haplology. One may suggest a differentiation between the two terms in this sense. When the entire syllable is lost, we have haplology, which is a form of syncope. We have cited *abanding* for *abandoning*. Classic examples of haplology are Latin *nutrix* for *nutritrix*, *stipendium* for *stipipendium*, French *idolâtre* for *idololâtre*. Probably J. R. Lowell's *substutes* for *substitutes*, and perhaps his reduced form, *an 'tone it* for *and intone it* are haplologies also. However, if the reduction results in the squeezing out of a vowel and the doubling, either true or unassimilated, of the consonants which then become abutting, one might rather call the phenomenon ecthlipsis. Thus an Old High German comparative *hêriro* became first *hêrro* with double [r], we suppose, and later *hêro* with single [r]. The first stage of the reduction may be called ecthlipsis, the second haplology. In the same way a superlative *bezzisto* is dissimilated to *besto*. But the thing also happens in the phrase, as well as in the word. Walther von der Vogelweide (20,15) probably said [daʃtyənd͡dox] with double [d͡d] for *da stüende doch*. Many other cases could be adduced.

7.6 *Boundary Marks*

Within the breath group, which constitutes the largest physiologically determined unit of an utterance, the speech measures, or phrasal groups, are set off from one another by various means in various languages. One essential feature of the marking of these groups, however, is the failure of the phenomena of fusion to take place across the boundaries between them. There is a cessation of the commingling of movement patterns at the end of a speech measure.

Within the phrasal group or speech measure usually a number of morphemes have been fused into a single movement complex or configuration.

Out of such fused forms it is possible by the processes of linguistic analysis, by comparison of minimally different forms, to abstract the several morphemes represented in the whole. The phonetic form of each morpheme will be different in different configurations (a) because of different opportunities for one or another of the phenomena of fusion to occur, and (b) because of different conditions of tempo and stress. That these two factors are often interdependent should be self-evident. In some phrases the beginning or the end, or both, of a morpheme may be marked; in other phrases these boundaries may be obscured and the morpheme may be reduced, as the morpheme *not* is reduced in the form *can't* by the loss of its syllabic and the fusion of its release with the arrest of the morpheme *can*.

The delimitation of the morpheme is usually achieved by marking its beginning with the characteristics of an initial element (cf. pp. 165–68). This means that changes due to fusion between this initial element and what precedes it are prevented. Initial elements may be marked by peculiarities of their onset, of their release, and of their nexus with what follows. In addition to these features, there may also be certain peculiarities of pattern which mark the boundaries of a morpheme. No English form begins with [ŋ], no German form ends with [j]. Only initial elements have the stopped beginning in German. Phrasing is achieved by pauses and by musical and dynamic patterns known as intonational and accentual patterns. The kinetics of the speech measure is a subject which greatly needs extensive study. Progress has been made with the study of the syllable as a movement complex, but the larger patterns of groups of syllables are only beginning to be understood. The study of rhythm is a difficult business.

It is evident that the features which we have called close nexus and loose nexus, since they are phenomena of the relationship between speech sounds within the syllable, are not likely to serve as a mark of the end or of the beginning of a new morpheme. Lack of nexus, on the other hand, indicates an interruption in the flow of movement peculiar to the fused form, and the essential quality of the absence of nexus is precisely that the speech sound immediately preceding it will end as that speech sound normally does when final and that the speech sound next after it will be a characteristic morpheme initial, marked by whatever peculiarities of onset, of pattern, and of accent may be normal to the sound or form when it is initial. The difference between the movement patterns of the phrasal units, *an ice man* and *a nice man*, is precisely the lack of continuity of movement after the article *a* or *an*, and the marking of the onset of the first sounds of *ice* and *nice* by the onset normal to these words when they are uttered alone, or as initial elements. This implies that the tempo of utterance of these words when they are phonetically discrete forms is approximately the tempo of lexical pronunciation. As a matter of fact, the distinction is commonly not at all clearly marked in this way unless the level of presupposition requires it to be, and this is rarely the case because the intonational patterns of two such utterances as *Oh, he's an ice man* and *Oh, he's a nice man*, are quite different. The form *ice man* tends toward the pattern of compounds like *warehouse, ball bat, cookstove*, whereas *nice man* usually has a contrast pattern of intonation, either *nice* vs. something else, or *man* vs. *person*, let us say. Negatively, the two are marked by the fact that *man* may not be stressed in *ice man*, but may be stressed in *nice man*. This all means that the same pattern of articulatory movements may serve as two different signals which are distinct, not because of any interruption of the flow of these movements, but because of differences in the incidence of stress or differences in the musical pattern of intonation.

7.7   Allegro and Lento Forms

As the morphemes of a language occur in speech the phonetic form of each is certain to differ in different utterances. One may say that a given morpheme has a number of different phonetic forms, and of course one may not call abnormal any speech form which regularly occurs and is identifiable by the processes of linguistic analysis. It is also certain that differences in the rate of utterance and in the degree of stress can be correlated with differences in the phonetic form of a given morpheme. The problem of analysis here is to determine the relation of the several forms one to the other. Consider first the forms of the morpheme *have* in the English phrasal group, *I have seen it there*. One form of *have* is [hæ:v], another is [hæv], another is [həv], another [əv], another [v], another [f], and then there is the form from which *have* is omitted: *I seen it there*. This is substandard, to be sure, but it is a real form. Evidently, the expression "from which *have* is omitted" begs the question, unless one is willing to admit that the forms with *have* represent a norm from which the form *I seen it there* can be said to deviate. The correlations of tempo and stress with the forms of *have* are such that slow tempo and strong stress go with [hæ:v], the lexical form; and faster tempo and less stress go progressively with the forms [hæv], [həv], [əv], [v]. Still faster tempo and less stress produce [f] and ultimately the omission of any phonetic representative of the morpheme *have*. This can happen to good speakers if they accelerate their speech too greatly. It is then sometimes alleged that these variations are "reversible." That is to say, if one reduces the rate of utterance and increases the stress, the morpheme will appear progressively as [v], [əv], [həv], and ultimately in its full lexical form. It is clear, however, that for those speakers who habitually "omit" *have*, and say, *I seen it*, no amount of retardation or of stress will "restore" the missing morpheme. For them the process of reduction is no longer "reversible" and a linguistic change has occurred.

But this term "reversible" has in it the necessary premise of a direction away from or toward something, and if we wish to remain entirely objective in our analysis we must choose one of two alternatives. One is to assume that the pattern of innervation and of movement, the neuromotor, auditory, and kinaesthetic pattern peculiar to the morpheme in unhurried or deliberate utterance is the starting point away from which deviations may occur as a result of purely physiological and mechanical necessities produced by changes of tempo and of stress. I have operated with this kind of assumption of a norm. The other of the alternatives is to assume that the morpheme is a class of forms, each of which occurs under its own conditions of tempo and stress. If that be assumed, then the morpheme may not be said to occur: it is represented by one of its members. Under the first assumption the various forms in which a given morpheme occurs have been derived from the lexical form of that morpheme by reductions or reinforcements which can be accounted for by physiological necessities correlated with tempo and stress. This is true whether the individual speaker makes the reduction or merely repeats a learned reduced form, i.e., whether the reduction is for him reversible or not. Under the second assumption no form of the morpheme is derived from any other form thereof and the correlations with tempo and with stress indicate which form is to be expected but not why. A neurological account of a norm from which deviations may be produced by physiological and mechanical forces is exceedingly difficult: a neurological account of the persistence of a morpheme class which has several forms, none derived from the other, requires a neurological account of a number of higher units, or phrasal groups, and is prohibitively difficult.

Whatever one chooses to assume as the basis of an explanation of the facts, there are in many languages, particularly in those with strong dynamic accentuation, many morphemes which may be said to have two forms, one found regularly under strong stress and at slower tempo, the other found regularly under weak stress and at faster tempo. This difference is fully exemplified in Kenyon's lists of stressed and unstressed forms.[31] I need only illustrate the phenomenon. Compare the forms of *who* in the phrases, *who did that?* and *the men who did the fighting.* Observe the forms of *can* in *I'll come if I can*, and *I'll see if I can come.* The form of *has* is a lento form in *Oh, he's an old has-been.* It is an allegro form in *That has been proved again and again.* I remember Meillet's lento form of *parce que* [parsəkə], beside the more usual allegro form [parskə]. Words which are peculiarly susceptible to modification under slight stress and rapid enunciation are connectives, adverbs, conjunctions, prepositions, pronouns, articles, and auxiliary verbs. Many of these occur usually in their allegro forms and only under contrastive emphasis in their lento forms. Adjectives, nouns, and principal verbs may have allegro forms but are usually found in their fuller lento forms.

8.1 *Duration and Tempo*

Since every utterance occurs in time, duration is one of the dimensions of speech forms. The only difficulty involved in the accurate measurement of the duration of speech forms is the definition of their limits. The reciprocal relation between duration and tempo is self-evident. If I utter the morpheme *food* in 0.5 second I have uttered it at the rate of 1 ÷ 0.5 or 2 per second. The term tempo is used also to describe the rate of utterance of larger speech units. When we say that the tempo of an utterance is rapid or that it is slow, we mean that the speaker utters relatively many or relatively few words or syllables per unit of time. When we call a specific form an allegro form we mean that it is that form of the morpheme which appears when the rate of utterance is greater than usual, or that it is a form which has become the usual one as the result of the frequent occurrence of that morpheme at relatively rapid rates of utterance. Lento forms are forms which have maximum duration because they are uttered at a slow tempo.

Information as to the tempo of utterance of larger speech units may be given in terms of words per minute, syllables per second, or speech sounds per second. For example, two samples of one minute's duration each from the last inaugural address of the late President Roosevelt show that he spoke in the first at the rate of 105 words per minute, 2.5 syllables or 6.4 speech sounds per second. In the second sample the tempo was 90 words per minute, 2.1 syllables or 5.9 speech sounds per second. Two samples from the radio address of President Truman, August 9, 1945, show rates respectively of (1) 163 words per minute, 3.9 syllables, 8.2 speech sounds per second, and (2) 147 words per minute, 4.1 syllables, 12.3 speech sounds per second. These computations include all pauses as parts of the total duration of the utterance. Such pauses probably occupy something like 24 per cent of the total time of the utterance.[32] The form of each utterance may be described as that of deliberate, careful, expository speech.

The effect of including or excluding pauses in compiling such data can be seen from measurements of two recordings of a short German lyric poem. The rates for the two speakers, computed as were those for the speeches of Presidents Roosevelt and Truman, are these: Speaker A, 2.17 syllables, 6.2 speech sounds per second; Speaker B, 2.33 syllables, 6.6 speech sounds per second. When the duration of the pause at the end of each line is deducted from the whole, the rates become these: Speaker A, 3.13 syllables, 9 speech sounds per second; Speaker B, 3.08 syllables, 8.7 speech sounds per second. In both cases the data represent the tempo of deliberate careful utterance.

Some time ago I recorded a group of sentences which may be cited in this connection.[33] Four of these sentences made up the little colloquy represented by this series: A. *Did you bring the food?* B. *What? No food?* C. *Where is the food we bought?* D. *Isn't there even any food for the cat?* The data used are the mean values of more than 30 measurements of each item. The average tempo of these utterances may be described thus: A. 4.3 syllables, 12.0 speech sounds per second, B. 2.1 syllables, 5.5 speech sounds per second; C. 4.2 syllables, 10.6 speech sounds per second; and D. 5.4 syllables, 12.3 speech sounds per second. The discrepancy of tempo observed for B is due to the inclusion of the pause after *What?*

Mr. George Baker, the Lord Chancellor of the D'Oyly Carte recording of *Iolanthe*, provides an illustration of the possibilities of acceleration of tempo. In the first minute of the song, "When you're lying awake, with a dismal headache . . . ,"[34] the text sung comprises 258 words,[35] or more accurately 314 syllables. This means that he is singing at the rate of 5.2 syllables per second, pauses included. When the last section of the song is reached, real acceleration occurs. In the first breath group, beginning, "You're a regular wreck . . . ," Mr. Baker enunciated 59 words, or 62 syllables in 8 seconds and he goes on to complete the whole section of 86 words, or 95 syllables, in 12 seconds. The tempo of these breath groups is therefore 7.75 syllables per second for the first, or 7.9 syllables per second for the whole. The number of speech sounds represented is 258, and if he uttered all of them he spoke at the rate of 21.5 speech sounds per second. Fusions reduce considerably the number of speech movements produced, but the utterance is notably distinct and the rate is high. If the number of words indicated is taken as the basic datum, the rate of this utterance may be described as 430 words per minute, which is 1.66 times the 258 words of the first minute of this song and about four times the rate of the first unit measured from President Roosevelt's address. One would have to describe Mr. Baker's utterance as very rapid and as very careful. There is no necessary correlation between rate and care in enunciation, and careful *vs.* careless is quite as important a descriptive opposition as slow *vs.* rapid.

The tempo of speech in English, then, may be said to range from that of deliberate, formal utterance at something like 2.0 syllables and 5 speech sounds per second through the tempo of animated conversation at 4 to 5 syllables and 10 to 12 speech sounds per second to the tempo of a highly accelerated utterance, which may reach at least 8 syllables and 21 speech sounds per second. These values are all average values, and any one syllable may be uttered at a rate quite out of harmony with the general tempo.

It is not likely that the syllable rate achieved by Mr. Baker in the last portion of his recording, which ranges from 7.5 to 8.2 and averages 7.9 syllables per second, could be greatly increased. Stetson says[36] that the maximum rate for syllables is nine to ten per second. The maximum repetition rate, that is, the maximum number of times per second a given articulation can be repeated, for my own speech mechanism, is for labial stops 8.5, for dental stops 8, and for velar stops 7 per second. I can manage to repeat only 6 vowels per second. But when I add the vowel [ɑ] to initial stops I can repeat [bɑ] 8.5, [pɑ] 8, [gɑ] 7, [kɑ] 7, [dɑ] 8, and [tɑ] 7.5 times per second. That is, the addition of the vowel to the stop does not diminish the repetition rate at all. The maximum repetition rate I can manage for *food* is 6 syllables per second. I can repeat *bring* 6.5 times, *trip* 6 times, *sprint* 5 times, *tough, gas, cuss* 6 times, *pass* 5 times per second. This is not the performance of a practiced virtuoso at this activity, but it is about average.

Data which give the tempo of an utterance in terms of the number of syllables per second may or may not indicate the approximate tempo of any given syllable in the utterance. In languages with minimal differences between the lengths of syllables, rate given in these terms may indicate approximately the length of any one of the syllables of the utterance. I do not know any such language. In English or French or German, the description of an utterance in terms of syllables per second says nothing whatever about the probable length of any one of the component syllables. That is contingent upon the incidence and the degree of stress upon the syllable in question. In the sentences of the little colloquy just cited, the duration of the word *food* was measured, and the comparison of this data with the syllable rates for the utterances as wholes shows a complete lack of correlation between the two events.[37] In sentence A, *Did you bring the food?* the syllable rate was 4.3 per second, the duration of *food* was .473 seconds. In B, *What? No food?* at 2.1 syllables per second, the duration of *food* was .492 seconds. In C, *Where is the food we bought?* the syllable rate was 4.2 per second, the duration of *food* .299 seconds. In D, *Isn't there even any food for the cat?* the rate was 5.4 syllables per second, the duration of *food* .320 seconds. The strongly stressed forms of *food* in A and B are relatively long, the weakly stressed forms in C and D are relatively short. Or, to put this more sharply, the syllable rate of sentence A, compared with the syllable rate of *food* (that is, the reciprocal of its duration) shows the relationship 4.3 *vs.* 2.1 syllables per second. In B the rates are 2.1 *vs.* 2.0; in C, 4.2 *vs.* 3.3; in D, 5.4 *vs.* 3.1. The full form of *food* under strong stress in A and B has a tempo of about 2.0 syllables per second, the reduced form under reduced stress in C and D has a tempo of about 3.0 syllables per second.

Almost all studies of duration have concerned themselves rather with the length of speech sounds than with the length of morphemes or of syllables. One very good reason for this is the fact that it has been thought to be much easier to discern the limits of a speech sound than to discern the limits of a syllable. Another reason for this interest in the length of individual speech sounds is the conventional distinction made by descriptive phoneticians and by grammarians between long and short vowels, long and short consonants. It is evident that the two categories, long and short, are based on relative rather than on absolute durational values. Sounds which are classed as long sounds in one context may be no longer, absolutely, than sounds which are classed as short in other contexts.

The auditory evaluation of differences of duration of speech sounds has long been practiced. The best such analysis of American English quantities known to me is that of Grandgent.[38] He divided our vowels into two categories, which he called heavy and light. He described the stress on these vowels in the terms, accented, half-accented and unaccented, and he called the resulting quantities overlong, long, half-long, and short. He described as overlong those heavy vowels which are accented and stand before a pause, e.g., *high, low, raw*, or before a voiced consonant, e.g., *hide, load, bawd*. A light vowel under these conditions is long, rather than over-long, e.g., *pshaw, pooh*, or *beg, pull, buzz*. A heavy vowel is long when it stands in an accented syllable before a voiced consonant followed by an unaccented syllable, e.g., *rising, tunic*, or before a voiceless consonant followed by a pause, e.g., *fast, nice*. Light vowels under these conditions are half-long, e.g., *ever, beggar, pullet*, or *puss, hiss, bit, but*. Heavy vowels are half-long when they are accented and stand before a voiceless consonant followed by an unaccented syllable, e.g., *faster, nicely*, or when they stand before a vowel, as in *fear, fare*, or *fire* [fiər], [feər], [faɪər]. Light vowels when stressed before a voiceless consonant and followed by an unaccented syllable are short, e.g., *bitter, butter*. When half-accented, the heavy vowels are long when final, or when they stand before a voiced consonant, as in *fortify, Mayday*, or in *hay-ride, homogenize*. They are half-long when they stand before a voiced consonant followed by an unaccented syllable as in *matrimony, homogenizing*, or before a voiceless consonant before a pause, as in *eliminate*. They are short when they stand before a voiceless consonant followed by an unaccented syllable, as in *culminating, refrigerator*, or when they occur before a vowel, as in *emulsifier*. Heavy vowels, when unaccented are short, as in *so I do, follow*. Light vowels either half-accented or unaccented are short.

Clearly, the duration of American vowels is correlated with the degree of accent by stress and with the kind of nexus between vowel and consonant, but Grandgent's distinction between heavy and light vowels implies a difference due to the nature of the vowel. Some vowels, by this implication, are naturally longer than others. His heavy vowels are the only vowels which he finds to be overlong. If this distinction between heavy vowels and light vowels is founded upon a difference in the nature of the vowels rather than upon a difference in the usual stress or contextual influences exerted upon them in the speech measure, it should be possible to divide the American vowels into two classes upon the basis of their duration when put into the same phonetic context under the same accentual conditions. This has been tested experimentally.[39]

The instrumental measurement of duration requires the delimitation of the entity to be measured, and the problems involved are difficult of solution. The records measured are usually graphic or photographic recordings which permit the linear measurement of the trace produced when movements of the air or of the organs of speech displace the writing elements of the instruments into which words or sentences are spoken. One thing is abundantly clear: the movements which produce the speech sounds of such a word as *food* are not produced independently, one after the other. The innervations are fused to provide an integrated movement pattern for the morpheme. When I repeat *food* five times per second, I produce fifteen speech sounds per second; when I repeat *sprint* five times a second, I produce thirty speech sounds per second. The number of speech sounds thus produced is therefore at least three times the number of times I can repeat any one of these articulations in one second. It is clear enough that the performance of a series of movements can be much more rapid than the repetition of the same movement. The transition from one speech movement to another is easier in proportion as the same muscle fibers do not have to be relaxed and then immediately reactivated. When the same sound is to be repeated this requirement is maximum; in sound sequences such as those of *fib*, it is approximately minimum because the time required for the relaxation of one group of muscle fibers can be occupied by the contraction of those required to produce the next speech sound, since this is articulated by wholly different organs. Parts of two articulations can thus be produced simultaneously. Indeed, it is evident that when, in the flow of speech, the sequence of speech sounds represented is uttered at rates like 20 to 30 per second, either some of the articulatory movements observed to occur when the sounds are produced alone are omitted from the movements which produce the fused or integrated form, or some of the articulatory movements which belong to one speech sound are accomplished while its neighboring sounds are being articulated. There is no doubt that both of these things occur. We have discussed some of the usual phenomena of fusion; the overlapping in time of several articulations of the speech form has been called coarticulation.[40] Because of overlappings of this sort, measurements of duration which are based on phonographic or oscillographic recordings do not attempt to consider movements of articulation but determine the beginning and the end of each speech sound by purely acoustic criteria. It is therefore impossible directly to compare the data of measurements made by these methods with those which are based upon the characteristic movements of articulation. Both represent facts, but the relationship between these facts is not a simple one.

Some languages appear to mark the difference between two speech forms by a difference of duration between two otherwise identical speech sounds. German does so in contrasts like *Bann:Bahn, Kamm:kam*, at least in those regions in which the difference in the quality of the long [ɑ:] is not distinctive.[41] French in its standard form uses the difference of duration to distinguish between [ɛ:] and [ɛ] in pairs of words like *bête:bette, maitre* or *mètre:mettre*. English does not now use the factor of duration as a distinctive mark of any of its speech sounds. What we conventionally call long vowels are distinguished from our so-called short vowels by distinctive differences of quality. This was true of classic Greek in its distinction between *eta* (η) and *epsilon* (ε) and between *omega* (ω) and *omikron* (o). *Epsilon* and *omikron* were close short vowels, *eta* and *omega* were open long vowels. This is just the reverse of the situation in English and in German, where the vowels of *bait, hope, stehlen, Ofen* are long close or tense vowels and those of *bet, hop, stellen, offen* are short open or lax vowels.[42]

Sievers describes short vowels as vowels which cannot be lengthened without destroying the typical form of the word.[43] Long vowels, he says, may be lengthened ad libitum without disturbing the form of the word. This definition is valid, certainly, for those languages in which the brevity of a vowel is the distinctive mark of a difference between forms, but its applicability to languages like English or German appears to be slight. The prolongation or reduction of any element in any morpheme will change the form from its "typical" or usual form but this will not prevent the functioning of the form in English.

In words in their lexical pronunciation there is a notable difference in the duration of all English vowels which is correlated with the nature of the consonant which follows them.[44] Vowels before a voiceless stop are regularly shorter than they are before the homorganic voiced stop. The same relationship appears to exist for the vowels before continuants. The average duration of the several vowels of English when they are produced in similar phonetic contexts, as in such a series of words as *pit, put, cut, pet, pot, peat, pat, caught, coot, curt, Kate, kite, coat, pout*, ranges from 0.15 second to 0.27 second before [t] and from 0.20 second to 0.33 second before

[d]. These, at least, are average values for Midwestern speakers. It is not possible, however, to divide these series into two classes which might be called short vowels and long vowels. The most that may be said is that in each of these series the vowels [ɪ], [ɛ], [ʊ], and [ʌ] head the list in order of brevity. The vowel of *bid*, however, is as long as the vowel of *beat*, and the vowel of *big* is even longer. That is to say, the relative shortness of these four vowels is real only within each type of phonetic context and cannot be shown to be a characteristic of the vowels only. To contend that these four vowels must be called short because they cannot be lengthened without destroying the typical form of the words in which they occur is to ignore their occurrence in such forms as *never, oven, difficult, pulley*. The length of a vowel in English is not determined by the nature of the vowel but only by its phonetic environment, that is, its relation to its neighbors in the movement complex and its place in the accentual pattern.

The Zwirners found[45] that if you ask a group of trained observers to describe the length of speech sounds as these are heard from the phonographic record of speech in standard German, only two classes of sounds will be set up with assurance, long sounds and short sounds. Approximately 85 per cent of the sounds observed were classed as short, while the remaining 15 per cent were called long. Subsequent measurements of these recordings showed that the sounds thus classified as short had durational values which clustered around a mean of 0.072 second, while those which were classed as long had a mean duration of 0.149 second. Parmenter and Treviño found[46] that in Midwestern American speech stressed vowels have an average duration of 0.154 second, unstressed vowels an average duration of 0.089 second. Stop consonants were a trifle shorter than continuants, voiceless stops averaging 0.073 second, voiced stops 0.077 second, voiced continuants 0.082 and voiceless continuants 0.086 second. Consonants and unstressed vowels are short sounds; stressed vowels are long sounds in this classification. English is very much like German in this respect. Any vowel may be long if it is strongly stressed; and any vowel may be short if it is not stressed.

The question of classification by duration is probably best solved, then, by recognizing two major groups: short sounds and long sounds. We then observe that the range of variation in the length of long vowels is greater than that of short vowels and that there are many fewer of them in any utterance of considerable length. In general, it is unlikely that in any language there will be much deviation from the averages indicated, by the Zwirners for German and by Parmenter and Treviño for English, for the mean length of short and long speech sounds. These values result, after a certain minimum rate of utterance is reached, largely from sheer physiological necessity and the factors of that control are the same every-

where. Since variations within the group of long sounds are readily observable without instruments, such distinctions as those made by
Grandgent's classes of overlong, long, and half-long vowels have a practical usefulness which makes them worth retaining. We may indeed say,
without distorting the facts, that certain vowels which are long in most
of their contexts are lengthened in others and may be described then as
overlong. They may be reduced in still other contexts, either to half-long
vowels, when they have a secondary stress, or to short vowels when they
are unstressed. Similarly one may say that vowels which are short in most
of their contexts may be lengthened in others so that they will be either
long or half-long. Any vowel may in still other situations be reduced to
zero, or to a whispered vowel, or to [ə]. Loss of a vowel or its reduction
to zero may be regarded as a quantitative phenomenon: change of a
vowel to a whispered vowel or to [ə], although it may come with a reduction, is essentially a modification of quality rather than a reduction of
quantity.

Grandgent's division of the English vowels into the two classes, heavy
and light, appears to be founded upon facts involving considerations other
than mere duration. Perhaps this classification can be justified on the
grounds of differences in the usual contexts of these vowels, or upon the
relative burdening of the vowels in English morphemes. This point merits
further study. English vowels may not be classed as long or short because
of their nature, their type, or their quality. They may be long or they may
be short according to the tempo of their utterance, and this is a function
of their place in the movement and intonational pattern of the speech
measure.

The duration of any speech sound is correlated with the tempo of the
syllable of which it is a part, but the behavior of consonants is not identical with that of vowels when the tempo is accelerated, and the minima for
the two classes of sounds are different.

It is a fact of experience that any morpheme of his language which a
speaker can be induced to pronounce in isolation will have a patterned
form in which the durational values of the several components are stable
and can be determined experimentally. This same morpheme, when it
occurs in speech forms with the stress and at the tempo natural to the
idiomatic utterance of these forms, may be shorter than it is in isolation,
or it may be longer. When the tempo of an individual syllable is reduced
by the incidence of heavy stress and the accentuation of differentiation or
some emotional mark, such as surprise, the length of the entire form is
increased. In that event the length of each of its constituent sounds may
become greater, the constrictions of open consonants or the occlusions of
stops are maintained longer, the vowels or syllabic elements are prolonged,

and the intersyllabic spaces of the speech measure may be increased. When the tempo of the individual syllable is increased by virtue of its lack of stress, the duration of the constituent elements is reduced. The initial reduction is likely to affect all elements of the configuration, but the minimum of duration of consonant movements is soon reached and it is then the vowel which suffers a disproportionate shortening. In such forms as Sanskrit *pita*, French *petit*, English *petition* the vowel after [p] may even completely disappear. Usually, it is represented by the unvoiced breathed release of [p] and grammarians then speak of a whispered or voiceless vowel. Reduction of duration does not need to imply change of quality unless it becomes extreme. The shift of the quality of unstressed vowels to that of [ə] is not due solely to the reduction of the duration of these vowels. In fact, the vowel [ə] is usually quite as long as any other short vowel. The shift to [ə] is merely one more feature of the reduction of all articulatory effort to the minimum acceptable for the purposes of communication. All vowels tend to become [ə] but are prevented from doing so by the principle of distinctive forms for different meanings. In the Germanic languages generally the requirements for distinctive vowel quality have come to be confined to stressed syllables. Therefore the way is open for lassitude to produce and intelligibility to permit unstressed vowels to suffer this reduction, even when the tempo of utterance permits full vowel duration to the syllable or form. Consonants, on the other hand, can suffer only a limited reduction in duration. Any reduction of the total length of the form beyond the minimal consonant durations comes either at the expense of the vowel or by the omission entirely of one or more consonant articulations.

Consonants may be long as well as short, and in some languages long consonants are the distinctive marks of differences of meaning. Long consonants are not double consonants, for double consonants have a twofold function. Long consonants may be either releasing consonants or arresting consonants; double consonants serve both functions in the same form. The duration of double consonants is likely to be notably greater than that of single releasing consonants, but the distinctive feature of double consonants is not this greater length, but their double function. Long consonants when they are the distinctive features of morphemes, are so because of their length. Final consonants, notably the nasals and the liquids, [m], [n], [ŋ] and [l] or [r], tend to have increased duration when they are syllabic in unstressed syllables, as in German *Leben* [lebm] or [lebn], English *taken*, [tekn] or [tekŋ], *table* [tebl]. Length in these instances is not significant.

9.1 *Pitch, Intonation, Melody*

Every speech sound during the production of which the vocal bands vibrate, every buzz, hum, or tone, has a fundamental pitch. Pitch therefore is one of the qualities of speech sounds. Often it is a very important factor in the functioning of the linguistic signal. No speech can occur without variations in the pitch of its sounds. In some languages these variations are a part of the total pattern of the speech sound; in others they are a part of the total pattern of larger units of morphemes. In still others, the pitch patterns are adjuncts to rather than parts of the linguistic signal.

The actual physical rate of the vibration of the vocal bands is likely to change as the articulation of any sound progresses. Sometimes no two successive sound waves of a speech sound have precisely the same length or period. The variation in pitch may either be up and down about a more or less stable mean frequency, or it may have direction, progressively either falling or rising. The human hearing mechanism tends to smooth out or to fail to hear minor changes from vibration to vibration if the general level of pitch remains constant, though it is quick to perceive any drift or tendency to rise or to fall. We need consider for linguistic purposes no more than can be heard. The absolute pitch of speech sounds is never significant in a language; if it were, men could not converse with women and children in that tongue. It is the relative pitch of speech sounds which is a linguistic means of differentiation between meanings.

Essentially, those features of pitch which require consideration by the phonetician are (a) the relative pitch of the initial fundamental tone, which may be described as high, medium, or low,[47] (b) the direction of any characteristic changes in pitch, which may be described as rising, falling, rising-falling, falling-rising, or level, (c) the mode of change, which may be described as abrupt (detached) or slurred (portamento), (d) the degree of change, which may be described in terms of musical intervals, or merely as large or small. The two intonational changes falling-rising and rising-falling are sometimes called circumflex.

Insofar as it is important linguistically, pitch is an integral part of some meaningful unit, the morpheme, the speech measure, or the clause. The production of significant pitch characteristics in any speech form may be called intonation, and this term is then applied to the characteristic pitch patterns themselves. The term melody is usually restricted to pitch patterns used to mark larger units, such as phrases or clauses.

Languages such as Chinese, Thai, Anamese, which use pitch as the distinguishing mark of morphemes are sometimes called "Tone Languages." The term is not an altogether happy one, since no language can be devoid of tone and most, if not all, languages use variations of pitch significantly. In any event, there are numerous languages in which the distinctive mark of a different linguistic reference may be rather the pitch or intonation than the articulatory movements of the morpheme. As Bloomfield pointed out,[48] English can use different intonational patterns to distinguish between *John! John?* and *John.* But these different tonal patterns do not indicate a change of the reference of these forms from one object to another. They indicate, as a syntactical setting might indicate, differences in the relationship between this object and the speaker. When such changes of pattern occur with morphemes which have no clear objective references, such as English *Yes! Yes? Yes.* (not to mention the varieties of *Yeah!*),[49] or with German *So? So! So.* their share in the distinctive quality of the utterance only seems to increase. They are still marks of relation with a kind of reference which is quasi-pronominal.

In Swedish and in Norwegian, which are on the whole very much like English and German in this particular, there are a number of pairs of forms which are homonyms except for the intonational patterns. That is, there are some cases in which the intonational pattern is the distinctive mark of a semantic difference in these languages. To be sure, this distinction is also associated with the stress pattern, and may be obscured by sentence intonation. Indeed, the number of times when the intelligibility of a Norwegian utterance hinges upon the proper intonation of one of these words is not large. Two patterns suffice to describe the phenomenon in either language. In Norwegian (of Oslo) the first tone, also called the simple tone or the monosyllabic tone, is essentially a rising tone, since the stress is incident upon the portion of the pattern in which the tone is notably rising. This rise is usually preceded by a brief fall of pitch, and the termination of the pattern may also drop off slightly from the top of the rise. It may be exemplified in the words *gassen,* "the gas," *anden,* "the duck," *jernet,* "the iron," *skallet,* "the shell." The second tone, also called the compound tone or the polysyllabic tone, has two rises, but the stress is incident upon the part of the pattern which is falling after the first rise. In Oslo, then, it is a rising-falling-rising tone and its termination may be very much like that of the first tone. It may be exemplified in the words, *gassen,* "the gander," *anden,* "the second," *gjerne,* "gladly," and *skalle,* "skull."[50]

9.11 *Chinese Tones*

In North Chinese, however, the forms [ʃjī], [ʃjǐ], [ʃjì], and [ʃjí] are distinct only because of the intonation of the syllable: [ʃjī] with a high level tone means "a small group of," [ʃjí] with a high rising tone means "a shoe," [ʃjì] with a falling tone means "thank(s)," and [ʃjì] with a low tone means "to write."[51] Or [měj] with low tone means "to buy," [mèj] with falling tone means "to sell," [ʃf] with high rising tone means "to pick up," [ʃì] with falling tone means "to try on." The whole repertoire of isolated words in Pekin is comprised in 411 syllables[52] (or in about 600 in Po-Pei), and it is only by means of the intonational patterns of these syllables that sufficient multiplication of morphemes is achieved to permit intelligible speech. Given four such intonational patterns the resulting number of morphemes is 1644 and with that many monosyllables facile communication is achieved. Jespersen once calculated the number of monosyllables actually in use in English to be some 8,000.[53]

The analysis of the kind of intonation shown by Chinese into the categories (a) high, medium, low, and (b) level, rising, falling, rising-falling, falling-rising gives fifteen patterns, and it is not likely that any one language uses all of them. North Chinese can be learned with four patterns, or "tones," (1) the high level, (2) the high rising, (3) the low level, and (4) the medium falling tone. Cantonese combines duration with inflection and pitch to produce nine "tones." High, medium, and low pitch with long syllables (fermata), and high, medium, and low pitch with short syllables (staccato) account for six, and the other three are a high rising, a low rising, and a medium falling tone. The tonal patterns of the dialect of Pekin are described in detail by Mr. Wang.[54] The first Pekin tone is usually described as a high level tone. Mr. Wang finds that it has a rising portion, both before and after the main level portion of the tone. The general pitch of the level portion is properly called high, as it was approximately g above middle c (or 194 c.p.s.). The two rising portions are relatively brief. The second Pekin tone is usually called simply a rising tone. Mr. Wang finds an initial brief descending portion, after which the rise begins. The range of this rise is about six semitones, or an augmented fourth, from $e♭$ (154 c.p.s.) to a (218 c.p.s.). The third Pekin tone is usually described as falling-rising, but beyond that the aural descriptions are divergent. Mr. Wang finds various modifications of a typical form, which might be called undulating, since it rises from about $e♭$ (154 c.p.s.) to a (218 c.p.s.), then falls an octave to A (109 c.p.s.) and rises again to a (218 c.p.s.), after which it falls to about d (145 c.p.s.). The four portions of this tonal movement are found by Mr. Wang to be about equal in duration. The fourth Pekin tone may be called a falling tone, although Mr. Wang finds here a brief rise at the beginning. The range of pitch in the fourth tone is maximum, beginning about d (290 c.p.s.) and falling more than an octave to G (97 c.p.s.). Duration and emphasis seem to join with pitch to mark a fifth tone in Pekin. This is a rare, brief, rather lightly stressed falling tone, which has nothing to do, apparently, with the historical fifth tone of North Chinese, which has been lost in Pekin.

The range of pitch variation in tones described as rising, falling, or circumflex, may be considerable, as it is in Mr. Wang's Pekin tones, or it may be narrow. The falling tone in some Anamese words of which I have recordings ranges only two or three semitones, say from 149 c.p.s. to 129 c.p.s. or from 130 c.p.s. to 108 c.p.s. All of these intonational patterns suffer more or less modification in contexts where sentence melody affects their pitch. Apparently, all that is required for successful communication is that they keep enough of the intonational form to suggest the morpheme to auditors whose level of presupposition is high.

Tones of any type may be extended over the whole of a disyllabic form. For example, a rising tone on a disyllabic form may rise gradually (portamento) throughout the first syllable and the rise may be continued in the second from the point where the first left off. More often, probably, the rising tone in disyllabic forms is detached, in the sense that the first syllable has a more or less level pitch pattern and the second syllable is a step-up of perhaps a whole tone or more. Slurred pitch changes (portamento) are more likely to be found in monosyllabic than in disyllabic forms.

9.12   *Word Pitch Patterns*

Patterns of pitch variation may attach themselves to words rather than to syllables. The distinction between the English nouns *abstract, affix, alloy, ally, conduct, confine, conflict, conserve, consort, convict, convoy, digest, discard, discourse,* etc., and the verbs which we write in the same way is marked by the incidence of stress. This falls on the first syllable of the nouns and on the second syllable of the verbs. But there is also a pitch pattern, in that the nouns have a higher pitch on the first syllable than on the second, or a falling intonation, while the corresponding verbs have a lower pitch on the first syllable and a higher pitch on the second, or a rising intonation. In the nouns *counterattack, counterbalance, countermarch,* the intonation may also be described as falling, but in the verbs which we write in this way the intonation first falls from the initial syllable somewhat and then rises notably on the syllable which has the major stress. Indeed, the pitch pattern of the verb *counterbalance* may be said to be falling-rising-falling. However, these pitch patterns are correlated with the more prominent variations of stress in English, in the sense that the stronger the stress the higher the pitch, and the less the stress the lower the pitch will be. It is not necessary to learn pitch patterns of words as such in order to pronounce these words acceptably in English. Stress patterns of words in English must be learned, and these bring with them the normal pitch variations. Deviations from the normal pitch patterns, if the stress pattern of the word is preserved, are not distinctive.

9.13 *Phrase Patterns, Speech Melody*

When one set of morphemes fused into a speech measure has two or more different meanings, each significantly correlated with the different intonational pattern given it in different utterances, one may speak of the distinctive use of speech melody, or of distinctive intonational patterns of the phrase. Whether or not our English phrase melodies are distinctive in this sense depends upon what a meaning is, and this is a question which has not yet been dealt with adequately by linguists. What one says in English is probably never contingent upon the melody of one's utterance, but what one thinks about what one says is often implicit in the tune to which one says it, and frequently this, rather than the literal sense of the speech form, is the real gist of an utterance. Whether this is then the meaning of the utterance or not, and whether these tunes are therefore distinctive or not, they are in any event characteristic of normal English speech and indispensable to an acceptable pronunciation. The same thing may be said of German, French, or Italian; all languages have their own typical phrase patterns of intonation.[55] English spoken with the normal Swedish tunes may be grammatically impeccable but still "foreign" and often inadequate as to "shades of meaning." Germans who speak English with North German tunes often create the impression of undue violence of speech and temper. Therefore the study of the intonational patterns of the phrases of a language is a necessary part of its full description.

To describe the intonational patterns of the larger units of morphemes in the speech measure or phrase we need the same terms and categories we have used to describe the intonation of syllables. We need to designate the relative level of the pitch, the direction of change, the manner of change, and the degree of change. A great deal of descriptive work has been done with British intonation patterns, considerably less with American patterns. Most of the continental languages have been studied from this point of view, to some extent at least. All that can be undertaken here is to indicate the nature of these phenomena; the detailed description of the facts for each language must be left to the books dealing specifically with one language.[56]

9.131 *Finished or Unfinished*

In the first place, we may observe that the same phrase may have two different intonational patterns. Compare the tunes of "occurs to us" in these two sentences: (1) *"It apparently never occurs to us that such a search might merely lead to new strife.*" (2) "*That such a search might merely lead to new strife, apparently never occurs to us.*" In both cases *occurs to us* is the end of a speech measure, but in (1) the intonation pattern of the phrase is rising from the accented syllable of *occurs* to the syllable *us.* In (2) the intonation pattern is falling, for the tone of the accented syllable of *occurs* is lower than that of *never* and the tone of *us* is still lower. The same comparison may be made of the intonation patterns of the word *strife* in these two sentences. These facts can be shown graphically in a number of ways. Probably the best is a compromise between an accurate physical notation of the absolute pitches involved and the rather gross notation which isolates only four levels of pitch. The range of pitches used is astonishing. A compass of two octaves is not unusual for speakers who could not possibly sing through that range.[57] The system devised by Mr. H. O. Coleman,[58] which shows intonation by means of the numbers 1 to 9, representing a rising scale of regular but undefined musical intervals, is probably the most satisfactory means for a careful notation of the pertinent facts. Actually, I often find pitches beyond the extremes of this nine-point notation and these may be noted if they seem significant. Simpler notations, such as those used by Daniel Jones in his *Outline,*[59] or by Klinghardt[60] in his various books on intonation, may well be used for the purposes of teaching. The two tunes of *occurs to us,* then, may be indicated by writing them with numerals:

$$6 \quad 8 \quad 8 \quad 7\text{–}6 \quad 3 \quad 5\text{–}7\text{–}8$$
(1) nev -er -oc -curs -to -us

$$6 \quad 6 \quad 6 \quad 5\text{–}3 \quad 2 \quad 1$$
(2) nev -er -oc -curs -to -us.

Or we may write this on a quasi-musical staff as in Figure 1 of Plate 25. The word *strife* in the same two sentences also has two tone patterns, the "unfinished" intonation being 6-5-9, and the "finished" intonation pattern of the first sentence being 4-3, or it may be expressed in diagram form, as in Figure 2, of Plate 25. The two patterns in disyllabic words are illustrated in these sentences: (1) "*It would probably serve us better to insist upon a complete review.*" (2) "*To insist upon a complete review would probably serve us better.*" Here the patterns of *serve us better* and *review* are something like the representations in Figures 3 and 4 of Plate 25.

Comparison of numerous other complete and incomplete oppositions of this nature appears to indicate that it is the manner of the change of intonation and the direction of this change on the last accented syllable, or on the two syllables of a final disyllabic form, which indicates to an

Plate 25. INTONATION PATTERNS

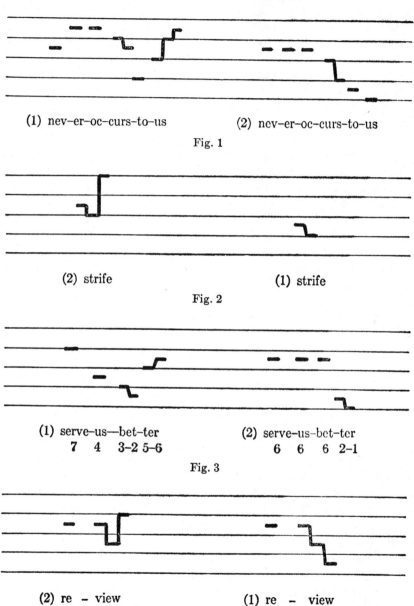

(1) nev–er–oc–curs–to–us   (2) nev–er–oc–curs–to–us

Fig. 1

(2) strife   (1) strife

Fig. 2

(1) serve–us—bet–ter   (2) serve–us–bet–ter
    7   4   3–2 5–6   6   6   6 2–1

Fig. 3

(2) re – view   (1) re – view
    6   6–4–7   6   6–4–2

Fig. 4

auditor the difference between a finished and an unfinished utterance. The manner of change in English is gradual; that is, a glide from one pitch to another marks the change. The direction of the change for an unfinished utterance is rising; for a finished utterance it is falling. In French the same result is achieved by an abrupt, or detached, change of pitch, a step-up or a step-down from the stressed to the unstressed syllable of a final disyllabic form such as *question*, or by a step of considerable proportions from an unaccented to a final accented syllable, as in *occupe*. Thus, "*Revenons à la question qui nous occupe*," will have a distinct step-up to the last syllable of *revenons* and of *question*, and a long, abrupt step-down to the last syllable of *occupe*. None of these changes is slurred.[61]

The kind of intonational pattern which we have observed in our English sentences may not be said to change the meaning of the words *occurs to us, strife, better*, or *review*, but serves rather as an additional signal, not made with words, to influence the behavior of an auditor. The situation borders on that of gesture, and it is difficult to draw a line between linguistic and nonlinguistic means of communication in this particular. A rising intonation appears to be correlated with intentness and stimulation, a falling intonation with relaxation and quiet.[62]

9.132 *Declarative, Imperative, Interrogative*

Anyone who listens to English as it is spoken will observe that there are different melodic "tunes" at the ends of simple statements, commands, and questions, particularly those which can be answered with "yes" or "no." The terminal cadence of a simple statement is falling, e.g., *He has gone home.* Any simple statement may have one syllable set out by a higher pitch for reasons of emphasis of some kind, after which the general melodic line is steadily downward to the last stressed syllable, where we find the downward slur which is characteristic of finished utterances in English. This cadence is likely to be a low falling slur of relatively small interval. An example of greater length is the present sentence. Here, since the word *length* has the major stress, the intonation is either about level or slightly rising until the word *length* is reached. This is emphasized somewhat and has a moderate or a medium high pitch. The tone of each succeeding syllable is progressively lower and the fall from the first to the second syllable of *sentence* is a little greater, with a slur downward on the final syllable. One may indicate all this graphically with a modification of the method of Klinghardt, which has been used by Daniel Jones. This involves somewhat less precise indication of pitch than that called for by Coleman's method.

An-ex–am – ple – of –great – er –length – is – the – pres–ent – sen–tence

The intonational patterns of commands vary considerably. Some have the same cadence as declarative sentences, for example, *"Give them each a book and a pencil."* Indeed, some commands have the outward form of statements, e.g., *"You will appear, properly dressed, at four twenty."* Other commands are characterized by a rise in pitch, usually an abrupt rise, to the last stressed syllable. The final syllable, whatever its level, will have a downward slur. Thus the command, *Go home!* will show a step-up of pitch between *go* and *home*. Sometimes the interval is great, sometimes it is small. The pitch of *home* may be either medium high or high, and there is usually a downward slur at the end of the form. A command such as, *Now you go straight home!* will have the maximum pitch on *straight*, with a step-down from this to *home*, and *home* will have the expected downward final slur. A rising slur on the final element turns such commands as *Go home! Now you go straight home!* into admonitions, presumably with an added implication, which might be put into words after such a connective as *or*.

Questions such as *When did he go?* or *Where, Why, How, With whom did he go?* that is, questions with an interrogative adverb or an interrogative pronoun which look for some answer other than a mere "Yes," or "No," also have a falling terminal cadence. In the case of *When did he go?* the major emphasis may be on *when* or it may be on *go*. If the main stress is on the adverb (or a pronoun) the cadence of *go* will be a low falling slur of slight interval. If the main stress is on *go* this form will have a relatively high pitch and the downward slur at its end is likely to be a little longer.

Questions such as *Has he gone home?* that is, questions which may be answered by a simple "Yes," or "No," normally have a rising final cadence, which may be described as a low rising slur of moderate interval. An element of enthusiasm or of surprise in such a question may lead either to a higher starting pitch for the final element or to a longer upward slur. Alternatives in question form show interesting patterns. A question such as *Shall we go to a movie, or shall we go home?* is likely to have the rising cadence of a yes-or-no question on the word *movie*. The end of *home* will have the downward slur of a finished utterance rather than the upward slur of an interrogation, such as belongs to the simple question, *Shall we go home?* Either *go* or *home* may be higher than the other, probably because different speakers integrate the contrasting speech forms differently. To some, the contrast is between *movie* and *home*, and *home* will have a higher pitch than *go*. To others, the contrast is between *go-to-a-movie* and *go-home*, and in that case, *go* may have a higher pitch than *home*, simply because it precedes *home* in the integrated phrase. Of course, the two elements *go home* may also have level intonation, that is, both may have the same starting pitch and only *home* may have the final slur downward. Downward slurring of *go* occurs in the speech of one of my subjects whose utterance was relatively deliberate. Perhaps the rising cadence of *movie* is merely the signal that the utterance is unfinished. We get the same intonational form in enumerations, such as *He lost his hat, his coat, his money, and his keys.* Here the words *hat, coat, money* have the rising cadence of unfinished utterances, while *keys* has the falling tune of a declaration. But it is clear enough also that the person who asks, *Shall we go to a movie or shall we go home?* can indicate to his auditor what his own desires are, or he can refrain from giving this indication. This means that he can make his question carry, or have the effect of, a statement as well. This, however, is managed by a combination of all the expressive factors of which the speaker has command: pitch changes, stress changes, tempo changes, quality changes. Certainly intonation alone is incapable of these differentiations in English. No two of my five subjects manage the distinction in quite the same way, and an analysis of the several procedures leads to no useful generalization beyond the fact that lively tempo, high-rising intonation, active stress, and clear voice quality suggest animation, interest, and the answer "Yes," whereas retarded tempo, low level or falling intonation, slack stress, and dull voice quality suggest lack of interest and the answer "No."

9.133 *Implications*

In situations in which the words uttered comprise less than the whole communication made one may speak of implications, or of implied meanings, or probably, of "shades of meaning." Many of these emerge from the situation or inhere in the mutual level of presupposition which has been established between speaker and auditor. As such they are nonlinguistic. Our problem is whether or not there are conventionalized patterns which may serve to communicate something more than the words uttered and something more specific than merely the finished or unfinished nature of an utterance, or something which goes beyond the invitation to reply which is conveyed by the rising pattern of the yes-or-no question. The probable insolubility of this problem is intimated by the pattern of the yes-or-no question. We use the same intonational pattern for this type of interrogation that we use for an unfinished utterance: that is, we invite our auditor to answer, and we ask him to refrain from interrupting us by means of the same tune. The meaning, or the signal value of this intonation pattern is evidently not distinctive, since its function as a signal is contingent upon factors outside itself.

The most which may be said with assurance in reply to this question appears to be (a) that there is no evidence that a conceptual meaning (such as the meaning of a word or of a phrase) is expressed in English speech by means of any given intonational pattern uniquely associated with it; (b) that there are at most four types of intonational cadence in general use, the falling, the rising, and the two circumflex, rising-falling and falling-rising patterns; (c) that the falling type is associated with completed utterances as a sign of completeness and finality, while the rising type is associated with incompleteness of utterance and the expectancy of further speech, as in the case of some questions, (d) that there is no correlation between the kind of hedonic tone, pleasant or unpleasant, and the type of intonational pattern; (e) that there is a correlation between the intensity of the hedonic tone and the range of intonational change in the expression of it, if the stress pattern is constant in the utterances compared; (f) that the difficulty encountered in endeavoring to isolate a meaning which may be uniquely expressed by an intonational pattern stems mainly from the fact that English accentuation is not by intonation alone, but involves the interplay of intonation, stress forms, and durational patterns, plus the fact that the hedonic tones of more intense displeasure or pleasure usually are reflected rather in difference of voice quality than in differences merely of pitch. There is little doubt that in some circumstances the hedonic tone of pleasantness is associated with the active rising intonation and the act of seeking, while unpleasantness is associated with a falling intonation and the act of avoiding, but these relationships are by no means simple and many factors can cause them to be nullified. Seeking itself may be associated with either type of pattern, as in the utterance, *May I have one?* vs. *I wish I had one!* either of which forms may be used in an endeavor to get "one" from the person addressed. The problems here hinted at are not likely to be solved by a study merely of pitch patterns of speech: what is required is the analysis in detail of the accentual patterns as these combine pitch, stress, and duration to produce the effects we too often attribute to pitch changes alone.

10.1   *Quality*

What we understand by quality is the timbre (le timbre, die Klangfarbe) of the speaker's voice apart from the characteristic modifications of the vocal note peculiar to each of the several speech sounds, notably to the vowels. We are in the habit of describing vocal quality by means of metaphors, such as thin, rasping, shrill, harsh, heavy, nasal, dull, smooth, or soft. In so far as the various component sounds which produce these qualities result from permanent conditions in the structure of the sound producing mechanism of the individual they are of no importance to the linguist. Yet it is a matter of every-day experience that the changes of voice quality which accompany changes of mood and of temper are very effective signals to the animals about us. Probably everyone has amused himself at one time or another by saying utterly blasphemous things to his dog in a persuasive, amiable tone and smiling when the poor creature reacts to the quality of the sounds and not to the words. The difference between dogs and humans in this respect, however, is one of degree rather than of kind. This fact is precipitated in the saying, "It isn't what he says, it's the way he says it."

These changes of voice quality go with and probably in large measure result from the muscular changes incident to changes in facial expression. The ramifications of the mimic musculature are extensive and important for the understanding of the phenomena of the emotions. These matters must be left out of a consideration of phonetics, since they involve far more than mere linguistic signals. However, there is some evidence that changes of voice quality are used in some languages as the significant marks of meaningful differences. In a brief note in 1937, Miss Ida C. Ward reported[63] that in the African language Abua, words having the mid vowels [e] and [o] were found in oppositions in which the distinctive feature was the tightness or the relaxed state of the pharynx.[64] I believe the same phenomenon can be shown to exist in Anamese, but I am unable to investigate the matter further and my notes are wholly inadequate to prove the point. As a name for the peculiar voice quality produced by the extreme compression of the walls of the pharynx, and this includes beyond doubt the increased pressure of the laryngeal muscles as well, one might suggest the term tight, and one would then have to speak of tight vowels (vocales tendues, gepreßte Vokale) as compared with relaxed vowels (vocales relâchées, schlaffe Vokale) in the special sense here indicated, and only when the contrast between the two qualities is distinctive.

11.1　Stress

Stress in speech is in one respect like heat: everything has some of it. For stress is the term we use to refer collectively to those phenomena of speech which are correlated with our sensations of muscle movement in the production of speech articulations. Stress is reflected in the quantum of muscular energy which goes into each articulatory movement, but we have not yet found a way to measure this satisfactorily. Stress is reflected in the amount of sound a given speech articulation makes, unless, of course, it is a speech sound which by definition makes no sound at all, such as an unexploded [p], [t], or [k]. However, the acoustic energy of one sound may not be compared with that of another sound of different articulation as a measure of the relative stress of the two articulations. The vowel [ɪ] of *hit* may be articulated with much greater stress than the vowel of *hot*, yet the latter is likely, unless conditions are extreme, to have considerably more acoustic energy than that of *hit*. The sound [ɑ] will always, under equal stress, move the indicator of a microwatt meter much farther than the sound [ɪ], not because it is produced with greater expenditure of energy, but because it is inherently more sonorous, or less damped. Acoustic measurements of speech energy are useful indicators of stress only when the energy of a given sound is compared with the energy of the same sound under different circumstances. Then again, we sometimes find that a syllable which is produced with particularly strong stress may be whispered. In such a sentence as *Our obvious course is now to hide!* the word *hide* will have the strongest stress of the whole utterance, but it may be spoken without voice and so have relatively little acoustic energy.

Every speech articulation involves the expenditure of its own peculiar quantum of energy. There is undoubtedly a minimum expenditure which must be made if the sound is to be recognized as itself. Less energy expended upon it will change its character. Probably there is a maximum expenditure of energy beyond which further effort will produce a change in the character of the sound. Between the two limits thus defined there is a considerable range for most sounds through which they may be produced with greater or less expenditure of energy according to the momentary disposition of the speaker. Within this range the speaker probably is not aware of any effort to produce the sounds of speech. But he does expend energy and this is recorded in his nervous system by the kinaesthetic sensations which go with speech movements. We know whether the ballistic stroke of these movements is strong, moderate, or weak.

Since the usual minimum unit of speech is the morpheme rather than the speech sound as such, and since the minimum morpheme is a monosyllable, it is clear that the minimum unit of stress will be the syllable. Certainly the most prominent energy component of the syllable movement is the breath pulse which defines it. For this reason it is customary to consider stress as a quality of a syllable. Every syllable has some stress. Traditional terminology recognizes three degree of stress and says that syllables may be fully stressed, half stressed, or unstressed. The term unstressed is used loosely for minimally stressed and must always be understood in that sense.

11.2   Word Stress

There is no problem as to the incidence of major stress on a mono-syllable. Whatever stress the word has is centered in the release of its one syllable. Words of more than one syllable may have a stress pattern which is quite as much a part of the total pattern as any of the component articulations. For disyllabic words it is often sufficient to distinguish between stressed and unstressed syllables; for polysyllabic words it is often necessary to distinguish between primary (or full), secondary (or half), and minimal stress. English, like the other Germanic languages, has made large use of stress as a means of giving distinctive form to its words. We have cited (pp. 216–17) forms such as 'content vs. con'tent, 'convict vs. con'vict. In words of this kind we have only the contrast between stressed and unstressed syllable. In a large number of words such as 'fire₁place, 'brick₁bat, 'apple₁tree, 'shirt₁sleeves, ₁home'made, ₁second'hand, we have syllables with primary stress and syllables with secondary stress, plus, in some cases, syllables with minimal stress. German has a number of pairs of words in which the relative position of primary and secondary stress is distinctive. This is notably the case in compounds such as 'unter₁laufen (to slip in), or ₁unter'laufen (to show on the surface), 'durch₁ziehen (to draw a line through), ₁durch'ziehen (to travel through), 'um₁gehen (to rotate), ₁um'gehen (to avoid). French words in their lexical forms usually have their maximum stress on the last syllable. English polysyllabic words usually have three levels of stress, as one may see from such examples as ex₁amin'ation, ₁periton'itis, ₁alco'hol, ₁alco'holic, though it should be said that the tendency in British English is to reduce many of these forms with secondary stress to single stress patterns. The words appletree, keyhole, pickpocket, for example, are single stress forms in Britain and compound stress forms in America. For some languages certain useful rules for the incidence of word stress can be formulated. For others word forms simply have to be learned as patterns. This is largely true of English and of Russian, while in Czech the stress is on the first syllable, in Polish it is on the next-last syllable. Latin word stress was on the next last syllable, if this was long, and if this was short the stress was moved forward one syllable, so we had puellae, puellârum, but domini, dominôrum. The Germans still observe this "rule" in forms like Pro'fessor, Profe'ssoren, 'Doktor, Dok'toren, but 'Doktorin.

11.3 *Group Stress*

When a number of words are fused in a speech measure the distribution of syllabic stress throughout the group may or may not coincide with that stress which characterizes the word forms in other contexts, or in their lexical form. The stresses on *wastepaper* and *wastepaper-basket* are not identical, and it is particularly *paper* which undergoes a change. There is a difference between '*second₁hand* and ₁*second'hand*, but we say '*second₁hand'books* without implying that the books deal with watchmaking. Shifts of this kind are probably the result of rhythmical tendencies.

Apart from and sometimes opposed to the influence of rhythm, considerations of accentuation are likely to determine the location of the major stresses within a fused group of forms. The principles of rhythm are probably independent of national characteristics and much the same in all languages; the principles of accentuation are more a matter of convention than of physiological necessity and therefore vary from language to language. English accentuation is primarily a stress accentuation and the location of the principal group stress is likely to be due to the requirements of accent. Languages with strong stress accent are likely to have rhythms of no subtlety whatever; languages which make less use of stress contrasts have rhythms which are less obvious. The rhythms of English and of French, for example, are in many ways comparable to the rhythms of Sousa and Debussy. One of the features of English stress which baffles those who have to try to learn it is the almost completely level stress, with no intervening minimally stressed syllables, which is found in many English utterances, such as *John bought one cow, two sheep, five hogs, and two young horses*; or *Carl knows where ten cans of gas are*. Rhythmic units of about level stress are frequently found in English from *Beowulf* to our own time: *wael-rapas* (1610), *driht-guman* (1388), *guð-searo* (328), *stan-fah* (320) have the same general form as *white wrapper, good going, pure oil, bad boy*.

12.1 *Rhythm*

When used precisely, the term rhythm designates an experience: rhythm is the perception, the recognition of groups or patterns of successive events.[65] When we experience rhythm we become aware of a regularity, a consistency of patterning within each group of events, and this regularity relates usually to differences in the relative intensity and the relative duration of the sensations which are correlated with the several components of the pattern.

When we speak of the rhythm of a language we have usually transferred our attention from the experiences to the stimuli which produce them and we discuss word patterns or group patterns rather than our perceptions of them. This shift of attention is likely to mislead us only in questions of intensity, and even here the danger is chiefly to those who work with instruments. Those who observe rhythm directly will refer their impressions of intensity to their sense of the muscular effort required to produce the same intensities in their own organism and they will thus arrive at intensity patterns which correspond closely to those of the speaker. Measurements of acoustic intensity in decibels may or may not correspond to the quantities of physiological energy which have gone into the factors which produce rhythm. Measurements of duration are more reliable indices of the durational characteristics of a rhythmic form.

Rhythm is normally important rather as a stylistic than as a semantic factor in language. The characteristic forms of a language, however, when they comprise several syllables, as they do in *typewriter, conscientious objector,* or *second-hand store,* are potential units of a sequence which may produce rhythm and we may then speak of the rhythmic qualities of these forms individually. In English, at any rate, rhythm is primarily correlated with the incidence of stress, or perhaps more precisely, of accentuation.

12.2 *Accentuation*

The process by which any one syllable is uttered with greater emphasis than its neighbors in the sequence of speech forms is called accentuation. A syllable thus emphasized may be said to have the accent, or to be accented. Insofar as accentuation is achieved by phonetic means it is the result of changes of dynamic stress, of pitch, of duration, and of quality in the sounds or syllables which bear the accent. English accentuation always involves at least two of these factors; frequently three contribute to the accent. I have never heard a language in which dynamic stress did not contribute to the accentuation, but some languages use stress more prominently than others.

The terms accent or word accent are often used to describe the incidence of stress in words in their lexical forms, such as *con'vict* vs. *'convict, durch'schnitt* vs. *'Durchschnitt.* In this sense the term accent designates a regular feature of the phonetic pattern of a form and not a feature of phrasal or sentence modulation. That this incidence of stress is correlated with an intonational pattern in each form should be abundantly clear. Word accent is usually subject to modifications dictated by the larger patterns of the speech measure or phrase. Some languages have important differences in the patterns of word accent, others have very few such differences. English and Russian are instances of the first, Polish and Czech of the second kind of languages.

The terms acute accent, grave accent, and circumflex accent, or accent aigu, accent grave, accent circonflexe: Steigton, Fallton, or Hochton, Tiefton, zweigipfliger Ton, have been used also to designate respectively rising intonation, falling intonation, and rising-falling or falling-rising intonation. For example, the first tone of Norwegian or Swedish, which is often called the simple or monosyllabic tone and which is a rising intonation, is sometimes called an acute accent. The second tone of these languages, the compound or polysyllabic tone, which has the main stress on the falling portion of its tonal pattern, has been called a grave accent.

What we have called close nexus is sometimes called accent à coupe forte, or stark geschnittener Akzent, and our loose nexus is then called accent à coupe faible, or schwach geschnittener Akzent. The terms accent frappé or Stosston refer to a type of intonation which falls on the onset of a vowel, or particularly of a diphthong, while the terms accent aiguisé, or geschleifter, or schleifender Akzent, or Schleifton, refer to a type of intonation in which the change falls on the middle of a prolonged vowel sound. These terms refer then to one aspect of accentuation, the pitch characteristics or intonation.

The reasons for the accentuation of any given syllable in an utterance may be various, but there seem to be two main classes of emphasis.[66] These have been aptly called the emphasis of prominence and the emphasis of intensity. Emphasis of prominence indicates that the word or phrase accented has greater importance than its neighbors. This emphasis results from rational or logical considerations. The emphasis of intensity reflects emotional intensity associated with some part or parts of the utterance. It has been called in French the accent affectif, and in German Affektbetonung.

Emphasis of prominence, while it is usually given to some word or phrase in every uttered sentence, is not indispensable to the intelligibility of that sentence. We rarely indicate the place of this emphasis when we write. Emphasis of intensity, on the other hand, must be marked in some way when it is to be given to some element of a sentence which we write; it cannot be inferred accurately from the form of the sentence or from the context. Such a sentence as *The book is not blue, it is black, and you will find it in his desk, not on it,* will be read with the appropriate accent of prominence on *blue, black, in,* and *on* by any native speaker of English who comes to read it. Emphasis of intensity of *very* in such a sentence as *His arithmetic is very good,* must be indicated by italics or small capitals, or in some other way, if the reader is to give this word the desired accentuation. This sentence with the accent of intensity on *very* is not synonymous with this sentence without accentuation of that adverb, and the difference may be important.

The phonetic means of accentuation comprise changes of stress, of pitch, of tempo, and of quality. The accentuation of prominence in English usually falls on syllables which have major stress in their contexts and it normally takes the form of a marked change of pitch, either a rise or a fall, from the pitch of its neighbors in the phrase. The accentuation of intensity may take any one of a number of quite different forms. It is by no means always achieved by increased stress. The accent of intensity on *undoubtedly* in such a sentence as *He is undoubtedly clever with his hands,* will be found to involve a displacement of the word stress, so that the syllable *un-* has quite as much stress as, or even more stress than the syllable *-doubt-*; it will also have a pitch a step or so higher than that of *-doubt-* and it may have much greater length than it has in the form which has the accent of prominence. The word *always* is frequently given an accent of intensity by the prolongation of both syllables and the increase of stress on the second syllable until the two are about level in both factors. Also the pitch of the two syllables may be level, but it will be higher than that of its neighbors in the context. On the other hand, intensity and vehemence are related and the accent of intensity sometimes involves the acceleration of the utterance of those syllables which are to be accentuated. Often this happens when the whole phrase rather than one of its components is emphasized.

Differences of quality contribute to the accentuation of intensity in the sense that any change from normal voice quality will add to the marking of the utterance. One may either squeal or whisper the form *wonderful* by way of accentuating the intensity of such an utterance as *That's wonderful!* Probably only civilized speakers whisper what they wish intensely to accentuate; in any case it is possible to put vast physical energy into such forms without appearing to shout.

Not infrequently emphasis of intensity falls upon a form which would have emphasis of prominence in any case. The result is apt to be an increase in the energy of the factors which produce emphasis of prominence, notably an increase in the range of the pitch change which is characteristic thereof. Often enough it is in the intensified forms of emphasis of prominence that we find circumflexion of intonation. What would have been a mere falling intonation in the accent of prominence becomes a rising-falling circumflexion if the accent of intensity is added to it, and what would have been a mere rising intonation becomes a falling-rising circumflexion. Individuals differ in their use of the emphasis of intensity. Some use it little, others use it much, and so some speakers rarely give a syllable a circumflex intonation; others do so much more frequently.

EPILOGUE

THE ESSENTIAL QUALITY OF A linguistic signal is its conventional nature: certain configurations of speech sounds come to serve as the conventional symbols of certain meanings. So too, certain patterns of accentuation become conventionalized in each linguistic group and serve as conventionalized symbols of certain attitudes or emotions which go with the words and phrases of an utterance. The proper speaking of any language requires, then, not only the proper articulation of its several speech sounds, but the proper fusion of these sounds in syllabic and larger forms, and finally the use of the proper accentual tune, with the right distribution of stress, melodic changes of pitch, duration, and quality. Each language requires to be analyzed with respect to each of these features, but none is likely to show phenomena which are not various combinations of the factors we have examined.

BIBLIOGRAPHICAL NOTES AND COMMENTARY

Books and periodicals in the following list are those to which repeated reference is made in the notes, where abridged citations are used. For titles referred to only once, full citation is made in the note where each occurs.

American Speech. New York: Columbia University Press.

Archiv für vergleichende Phonetik. Berlin: Metten.

Archives Neêrlandaise de phonétique experimentale. Société Internationale de Phonétique Experimentale. The Hague.

Beach, D. M. *The Phonetics of the Hottentot Language.* Cambridge: Heffer, 1938.

The Bell Laboratories Record. New York: The Bell Telephone Laboratories, Inc.

The Bell System Technical Journal. New York.

Bloomfield, Leonard. *Language.* New York: Henry Holt, 1933.

Boas, Franz. *Handbook of American Indian Languages.* Bureau of American Ethnology, Smithsonian Institution, Bulletin No. 40. Washington: Government Printing Office, 1911–1922. 2 vols.

Carmody, F. J. *X-Ray Studies of Speech Articulations. University Publications in Modern Philology,* Vol. XX, No. 4. Berkeley, 1937.

Cowan, Milton. *Pitch and Intensity Characteristics of Stage Speech.* Supplement to *Archives of Speech.* Iowa City, Dec., 1936.

Driver, G. D. *A Grammar of the Colloquial Arabic of Syria and Palestine.* London: Probsthain, 1925.

Festschrift für Wilhelm Viëtor. Die neueren Sprachen, Ergänzungsband. Marburg: Elwert, 1910.

Fletcher, Harvey. *Speech and Hearing.* New York: Van Nostrand, 1929.

Gairdner, W. H. T. *Egyptian Colloquial Arabic.* Cambridge: Heffer, 1917.

Grammont, Maurice. *Traité de phonétique.* Paris: Delagrave, 1930.

Grandgent, Charles Hall. *German and English Sounds.* Boston: Ginn and Co., 1892.

Jespersen, Otto. *Lehrbuch der Phonetik.* 5. Aufl., Leipzig: Teubner, 1933.

Jones, Daniel. *An Outline of English Phonetics.* 3d ed., New York: Dutton, 1932.

Joos, Martin. *Acoustic Phonetics.* Language Monographs, No. 23. Baltimore: Linguistic Society of America, 1948.

Journal of the Acoustical Society of America. Menasha, Wis.

Kenyon, J. S. *American Pronunciation.* 8th ed., Ann Arbor: Wahr, 1940.

Language. Journal of the Linguistic Society of America. Baltimore.

Le Maître phonétique. Organe de l'Association Phonétique Internationale, Troisiéme Serie. Paris.

Meinhof, Carl. *Grundriss einer Lautlehre der Bantusprachen.* 2. Aufl., Berlin: Reimer, 1910.

Miller, D. C. *The Science of Musical Sounds.* New York: Macmillan, 1916.

Miscellanea Phonetica. Paris: L'Association Phonétique Internationale, 1914. A volume to commemorate the twenty-fifth year of *Le Maître phonétique.*

Negus, V. E. *The Mechanism of the Larynx.* London: Heineman, 1929.

Die neueren Sprachen. Zeitschrift für den neusprachlichen Unterricht. Marburg in Hessen.

Paget, Richard. *Human Speech.* New York: Harcourt Brace, 1930.

Panconcelli-Calzia, G. *Experimentelle Phonetik.* (Sammlung Göschen, No. 884.) Berlin: de Gruyter, 1921.

——. *Die experimentelle Phonetik und ihre Anwendung auf die Sprachwissenschaft.* 2d ed., Berlin 1924.

Pflügers Archiv für die gesamte Physiologie. Bonn.

Proceedings of the Second International Congress of Phonetic Sciences. London: Cambridge University Press, 1936.

Russell, G. O. *Speech and Voice.* New York: Macmillan, 1931.

Ščerba, L. *Court exposé de la prononciation russe.* Paris: L'Association Phonétique Internationale, 1911.

Siebs, Theodor. *Deutsche Bühnenaussprache, Hochsprache.* 15. Aufl., Köln: Ahn, 1930.

Sievers, Eduard. *Grundzüge der Phonetik zur Einführung in das Studium der Lautlehre der indogermanischen Sprachen.* 5. Aufl., Leipzig: Breitkopf und Haertel, 1901.

Stetson, R. H. *Motor Phonetics: Archives Néerlandaises de phonétique expérimentale,* III (1928), 1–216.

Stumpf, Carl. *Die Sprachlaute.* Berlin: Springer, 1926.

Sweet, Henry. *A Handbook of Phonetics.* Oxford: Clarendon Press, 1877.

Trofimov, M. V., and Jones, D. *The Pronunciation of Russian.* Cambridge: University Press, 1923.

Tucker, A. N. *The Eastern Sudanic Languages.* London: Oxford University Press, 1940.

Viëtor, Wilhelm. *Elemente der Phonetik des Deutschen, Englischen und Französischen.* 7. Aufl., bes. von E. A. Meyer, Leipzig: Reisland, 1921.

Westermann, D., and Ward, Ida C. *Practical Phonetics for Students of African Languages.* London: Oxford University Press, 1933.

Wood, Alexander. *Acoustics.* London, Blackie and Son, Ltd. 1940.

Zwaardemaker, H., Cz., en Eijkman, L. P. H. *Leerboek der Phonetik.* Haarlem: Bohn, 1928.

NOTES TO CHAPTER I

1. We should eventually discern that the two *find*'s in our example are not wholly identical in their use and meaning, though the physical form of the two patterns is essentially the same.

2. Cf. Panconcelli-Calzia, *Experimentelle Phonetik,* p. 7: genetisch, "concerning the production" (ἡ γένεσις), gennemisch, "concerning the product" (τὸ γέννημα).

3. Unhappily, many writers have used this term, phoneme, with many meanings, so that its effective stimulus-response value is about as unimportant as that of the word romantic.

4. E. Sapir, "The Phonetics of Haida," *International Journal of American Linguistics,* II (1921–1923), 149.

5. I have assumed that phonetics as a science should proceed inductively from phenomena to generalizations about them, and I have started from the premise that phonetics is a part of linguistic science, not merely a form of physiology or acoustics. It is inconvenient, perhaps, but none the less imperative, that one who would understand phonetics must understand not only the principles of linguistic analysis but also the physiological and the physical aspects of phenomenal speech. The studies currently spoken of in America as "Phonemics" rest, consciously or otherwise, upon the premise of F. de Saussure, that "la langue n'est pas une fonction du sujet parlant, elle est le produit que l'individu enregistre passivement . . ."—*Cours de linguistique générale,* Paris, 1922, p. 30).

It is possible to evolve a hypothesis or a set of hypotheses concerning the production of speech sounds by examining the producing mechanism and postulating upon the basis of such observations all of the possible products of the mechanism. This procedure, eclectically applied, with liberal assistance from the inductive method, has given us, among other things, the discovery of the "bilabial lateral."

NOTES TO CHAPTER II

1. R. H. Stetson and C. V. Hudgins, "Functions of the breathing movements in the mechanism of speech," *Archives Néerl. Phon. Exp.*, V (1930), 1–30.

2. Cowan, *Pitch and Intensity Characteristics of Stage Speech.*

NOTES TO CHAPTER III

1. A readable and authoritative treatment of the pro blems involved may be found in Wood's *Acoustics;* especially pp. 332–65.

2. 10^{-8} cm. = 0.00000001 cm., 10^{-3} cm. = 0.001 cm.

3. Miller, *The Science of Musical Sounds*, pp. 194–201.

4. The frequency of such a resonator is given by the equation

$$f = \frac{c}{2\pi} \sqrt{\frac{S}{LV_0}}$$

where c = the velocity of wave motion, or frequency time wave length, S = area of a cross-section of the neck, L = the length of the neck, and V_0 = the volume of the resonator, Cf. Wood, *Acoustics*, p. 105.

5. The theory of resonators, particularly applied to the problems of vowel analysis is readably discussed by W. E. Benton in the first appendix of Paget's *Human Speech*, pp. 275–98.

6. Fletcher, *Speech and Hearing*, p. 67.

7. Joos, *Acoustic Phonetics.*

8. The score calls for the simultaneous sounding of the following fundamental tones, each with the overtones of the instruments which play it:

e^3 flat (1259) flute: b^2 flat (933) flute: g^2 flat (792) oboe, clarinet, violin I: e^2 flat (630) oboe, violin I: b^1 flat (466) violin I: g^1 (398) clarinet, horn, trumpet: e^1 flat (315) bassoon, violin I, violin II, viola: b-flat (233) horn: g (198) violin I, violin II, viola, horn, trumpet: e flat (157) bassoon, tympanum, violoncello: E flat (71) contrabass.

NOTES TO CHAPTER IV

1. I owe this expression and many of the ideas here set forth to extensive correspondence with Professor R. H. Stetson of Oberlin College and to his *Motor Phonetics*, yet it will be quite clear that particularly on the question of a norm we do not agree.

2. Except in Swiss and in Judeo-German, where [x] is used in both contexts.

3. Bloomfield, *Language*, p. 161.

4. Cf. Fr. Agostino Gemelli, "Variations significatives et variations individuelles des unités élémentaires phoniques du langage humain," *Proceedings of the Third International Congress of Phonetic Sciences* (Ghent, 1938), pp. 355–64.

5. Sweet, *Handbook of Phonetics.*

6. M. Heepe, *Lautzeichen und ihre Anwendung in verschiedenen Sprachgebieten* (Berlin, Reichsdruckerei, 1928).

6a. "The Principles of the International Phonetic Association," 1949, contains the most recent statement of transcriptional practice of this group. The pamphlet may be obtained from the Secretary of the I.P.A., University College, London W.C.1.

7. See note 81, Chapter IV.
8. The r-sounds: [r] trilled, apical, [ɪ] fricative, [ʀ] uvular, [r] single tap, apical
9. Cf. Bloomfield, *Language*, pp. 120–21.
10. Cf. J. Forchhammer, "Vokal und Konsonant," *Archiv für vergleichende Phonetik* (Berlin, Metten), IV (1940), 51–66.
11. Cf. E. W. Scripture, "Die Silbigkeit und die Silbe," *Archiv für das Studium der neueren Sprachen*, CLII (1927), 74; also G. Panconcelli-Calzia, *Die experimentelle Phonetik und ihre Anwendung*, 2. Aufl., p. 23.
12. Cf. Jespersen, *Lehrbuch der Phonetik*, p. 203.
13. Cf. Stetson, *Motor Phonetics*,
14. Cf. Fletcher, *Speech and Hearing*, p. 74.
15. Cf. Sievers, *Grundzüge der Phonetik*, §§528–35; Jespersen, *Lehrbuch*, p. 191.
16. Cf. Fletcher, *Speech and Hearing*, pp. 70–76.

NOTES TO CHAPTER V

1. Cf. Wheatstone (*i.e.* C. W.), *London and Westminster Review* (American Edition, New York, Lewer), 28 Oct. 1837. Hermann L. F. Helmholtz, *Die Lehre von den Tonempfindungen* (1. Aufl. Braunschweig, Vieweg, 1863). R. Willis, *Transactions of the Cambridge Philosophical Society*, (Cambridge: University Press, 1829). Ludimar Hermann, in *Pflügers Archiv*, 1889, 1890, 1891, and later.
2. Cf. Fletcher, *Speech and Hearing*, pp. 49.
3. Cf. for example, the plates in Fletcher's book, or in the work of Fr. Agostino Gemelli and G. Pastori, "Analyse électrique du langage," *Archives Néerl. Phon. Exp.*, X (1934), 1–29. A different technique is shown in the plates of Joos, *Acoustic Phonetics*.
4. Cf. J. C. Steinberg, in *Jour. Acoust. Soc. Amer.*, July, 1934, pp. 16–24.
5. Cf. L. Barszinski, and E. Thienhaus, in *Archives Néerl. Phon. Exp.*, XI (1935), 47–68; also Don Lewis, in *Jour. Acous. Soc. Amer.*, Oct. 1936, p. 95: "It would seem that each of the four vowel sounds [studied] was dependent upon the selective action of five simple resonators on the cord tone, some of these resonators being much more important than others."
6. E.g., E. W. Scripture, *Zeitschrift für Experimentalphonetik*, I (London, 1932), 101–9, and *Jour. Acous. Soc. Amer.*, Oct., 1933, pp. 148–52.
One fact requires to be stated here: not all differences in the contour of the records of sound-waves, as these are produced by our modern techniques, are due to differences of the component frequencies. The same component frequencies may produce the same quality of sound but very different wave-forms, because the wave-form is contingent not only upon the frequencies of the partial vibrations involved but also upon their relative phases, while the human ear appears to be wholly indifferent to most of the phase differences in speech sounds. It is quite clear from the records that the phase relationships of the several component frequencies often shift constantly as the sound is prolonged. Hence statements to the effect that no two periods of a wave-train have the same form *need not* mean that the component frequencies of each are different.
7. Cf. Fletcher, *Speech and Hearing*, pp. 52–53.
8. Lloyd's work is largely in the *Phonetische Studien* (Marburg, Elwert), or from Vol. VII onward, in the *Beiblatt* to *Die neueren Sprachen*, Vols. III, IV, V, XI, XIII (1890–1899). Paget's work is collected in his book, *Human Speech*.
9. Cf. E. W. Scripture, "Film Tracks of English Vowels," *Jour. Acous. Soc. Amer.*, V (1932), No. 3; A. Gemelli, in the *Archives Néerlandaises de Phonétique Expérimentale*, XIV (1938) 139.

10. Notably those of M. H. Liddell, Ferdinand Trendelenburg, Fr. A. Gemelli, and the studies of the Bell Laboratories by Crandall, Sacia, Fletcher, Steinberg, and many others.

11. Cf. *The Bell Laboratories Record*, XV (Dec., 1936), and XVII (Feb., 1939); *Proceedings of the National Academy of Sciences*, XXV (1939), 377–83; *Journal of the Franklin Institute*, CCXXVII (July, 1939), 739–64.

12. Homer Dudley, "The Carrier Nature of Speech," *Bell System Tech. Jour.*, XIX (Oct., 1940), 495–515.

13. Stetson, *Motor Phonetics*, p. 29.

14. E.g. the advertising for "Bromo-Selzer," for "Red-Heart," or the hideous noises articulated to say, "B-O." Cf. Dudley's statement (*Bell System Tech. Jour.*, XIX, 513), and F. A. Firestone, "An Artificial Larynx for Speaking and Choral Singing by One Person," *Jour. Acous. Soc. Amer.*, XI (1940), 357–61.

15. Data from Fletcher, *Speech and Hearing*, p. 58.

16. The relative phases of the components of the carrier wave are unimportant. The relative phases of the components of the modulating, or message, wave are all-important.

17. Cf. Don Lewis and C. Tuthill, *Jour. Acous. Soc. Amer.*, XI (1940), 451–56; but see also H. D. Bouman et P. Kucharski, in *Archives Néerl. Phon. Exp.*, IV (1929), 90–111.

18. Hence it cannot be defined by a Fourier Series, but at best by a Fourier Integral.

19. Cf. Paget, *Human Speech:* English vowels, pp. 86, 87, 89; French Vowels, p. 91; Russian vowels, p. 94. Cf. also Carl Stumpf, *Die Sprachlaute*, p. 113 for German vowels; and Zwaardemaker en Eijkman, *Leerboek der Phonetiek*, p. 103, for Dutch vowels.

20. Cf. *Archives Néerl. Phon. Exp.*, XI (1935), 47–68, especially p. 55.

21. Cf. Fletcher, *Speech and Hearing*, p. 58. The data for the four women speakers used by I. B. Crandall and C. F. Sacia, *Bell System Tech. Jour.*, III (1924), 232–37, show often three regions of reinforcement rather than two, as found for the four men speakers.

22. *Science*, CII, No. 2654 (Nov. 9, 1945), 463–70; *Life*, Nov. 26, 1945, pp. 91–94; R. K. Potter, G. H. Kopp, and Harriet C. Green, *Visible Speech* (New York, Van Nostrand, 1947); Joos, *Acoustic Phonetics*.

23. Cf. *De Nieuwe Taalgids*, XXV (1931), 234, and *Travaux du Cercle Linguistique de Prague*, IV (1931), 146.

24. *Human Speech*, pp. 86, 87, and 91, respectively.

25. *Bell System Tech. Jour.*, III (1924), 232–37.

26. Jones, *Outline of English Phonetics*, p. 36.

27. Viëtor, *Elemente der Phonetik*, pp. 46–47.

28. Negus, *The Mechanism of the Larynx*, pp. 428–30.

29. When helium is inhaled the frequencies of the formants are raised although the frequency of the fundamental is unchanged. Cf. J. C. Steinberg, in *Science Supplement*, XCI (1940), 8.

30. The Bell Telephone Laboratories film of high-speed motion pictures of the human vocal cords, with exposures at the rate of 4,000 per second, reveals the changes which occur as the pitch is raised, but for technical reasons the movements of the cords for the various vowel sounds were not recorded. This film has been available only in lecture-demonstrations, not for private study. Cf. D. W. Farnsworth, in *Bell Lab. Rec.*, XVIII (1940), 203–8; also R. L. Wegel, in *The Bell System Technical Journal*, IX (1930), 207–27.

31. Cf. L. P. H. Eijkman, "The area of the glottis in vowels," *English Studies*, XI (1929), 49; *Proceedings of the (first) International Congress of Phonetic Sciences* (Amsterdam, 1932), in the *Archives Néerl. Phon. Exp.*, VIII–IX (1933), 213–19; and *Archiv für vergleichende Phonetik*, I (1937), 76–89; also *Science Supplement*, 86 (Dec. 3, 1937), 12–13, and 91 (June 28, 1940), 8, and *Jour. Acous. Soc. Amer.*, 9 (1938), 274.

32. Cf. Westermann and Ward, *Practical Phonetics for Students of African Languages*, p. 204 and p. 210; A. N. Tucker, *The Eastern Sudanic Languages*, I, 94.

33. Cf. Fletcher, *Speech and Hearing*, pp. 76–80.

34. See note 4, Chapter II.

35. Jones, *Outline of English Phonetics*, p. 36.

36. Cf. for instance, K. Huber, *Archiv für Psychologie*, XCI (1934), 153–99; A. Gemelli, *Archives Néerl. Phon. Exp.*, XIV (1938), 126–64.

37. Cf. F. A. Firestone, *Jour. Acous. Soc. Amer.*, XI (1940), 357–61; W. W. Morrison, *Archives of Otolaryngology*, XIV (1931), 413–31; L. Kaiser, *Archives Néerlandaises de Physiologie*, X (1925), 468.

38. Cf. Negus, *The Mechanism of the Larynx*, p. 418; M. A. Goldstein, *Journal of Speech Disorders*, V (1940), 65–69; and *Laryngoscope*, L (1940), 164–88; Edward Twisleton, *The Tongue not Essential to Speech* (London: Murray, 1873).

39. Cf. Russell, *Speech and Voice*, Figs. 123 and 124 on p. 144, and his remarks about them, pp. 110–11; also cf. L. Kaiser, *Archives Néerlandaises de Physiologie*, IX (1924), 30; B. Dylewski, *Monatsschrift für Ohrenheilkunde*, 63 (1929), 538–59.

40. Cf. Carmody, *X-Ray Studies of Speech Articulations*, pp. 193–94.

41. Of the numerous studies available I have had before me Grandgent's *German and English Sounds*, together with some of his own drawings; a group of X-Ray negatives made by Professor R. T. Holbrook for Professor Grandgent, together with Carmody's *X-Ray Studies of Speech Articulations;* the plastographic studies made by E. A. Meyer, published in the *Festschrift für Viëtor*, pp. 173–74, the plates of Eijkman in Zwaardemaker en Eijkman, *Leerboek*, Russell, *Speech and Voice*, and Parmenter and Treviño, "Vowel Positions as shown by X-Ray," *Quarterly Journal of Speech*, XVIII (1932), 351–69. Also I have studied J. Schlumsky, A. Pauphilet, and B. Polland, *Radiografie francouzských samohlásek a polosamohlásek (Rozpravy Ceske Akademie ved a umeni*, 3, 75, V, 1938), with résumé in French and pictures which, while photographically excellent, were apparently not uniformly posed.

42. Cf. Benton in Paget's *Human Speech*, pp. 290–98.

43. The values involved may correspond approximately to the equation given by Benton, *ibid.*, p. 287:

$$N^4 - N^2(N_1^2 - N_2^2) + N_1^2 N_2^2 (1 - \frac{c_2}{(c_1 - c_2)} \cdot \frac{c_2}{(c_2 - c_3)} = 0$$

where N is the frequency of the double resonator as a whole, N_1 the frequency of the back cavity, N_2 the frequency of the front cavity, and c_1, c_2, c_3 the conductivities of the openings at the larynx, the junction between the two resonators, and at the mouth. The problem is a complex one and certain of its assumptions are subject to question.

44. Provided, as is likely in this instance, that the third, or transverse, dimensions are roughtly the same for each.

45. These values from Fletcher, *Speech and Hearing*, p. 58; cf. Paget, *Human Speech*, p. 317.

46. Cf. Benton, *ibid.*, pp. 290, 298.

47. In *The Science of Muscial Sounds*, pp. 226–27.

48. Cf. Fletcher, *Speech and Hearing*, p. 58.

49. Thomas H. Tarnoczy, "Resonanzdaten der Vokalresonantoren," *Akustische Zeitschrift*, VIII (1943), 22–31; "Untersuchungen mit künstlichen Vokalresonantoren," *ibid.*, pp. 169–75; "Über Eigenfrequenz und Dekrement der Vokalresonantoren der menschlichen Stimme," *Archiv für Sprach- und Stimmphysiologie*, VI (1942), 75–87.

50. Evidence in support of this statement is of three kinds: (1) evidence like that of Eijkman, gained from laryngoscopic study and the observation of the transilluminated larynx; (2) evidence as to the subglottal air pressures characteristic of the several vowel types; (3) evidence as to the volume and velocity of airflow found for the various types of vowel articulations. Cf. Eijkman, *Archives Néerl. Phon. Exp.*, IX (1933), 213–20; E. A. Meyer, in *Die neueren Sprachen*, XXI (1913–1914), 71–85, 146–54; H. Gutzmann and A. Loewy in *Pflügers Archiv*, CLXXX (1920), 111–37; P. Menzerath and E. Evertz in *Teuthonista*, IV (1927–1928), 114–24, 204–14. We need much more work on these problems.

51. Cf. Sweet, *A Handbook of Phonetics*, pp. 8–10.

52. Thus Sievers, *Grundzüge der Phonetik*, p. 98, §254.

53. In the *Festschrift für Viëtor*, pp. 168–248.

54. Cf. his *Handbook of Phonetics*, pp. 8–10.

55. Cf. *Festschrift für Viëtor*, p. 237.

56. Cf. Meyer's attempt in *Festschrift für Viëtor*, pp. 238–39.

57. Cf. *Handbook of Phonetics*, p. 10.

58. *Festschrift für Viëtor*, p. 238. I translate: "Der i-Laut geht in unbetonter Stellung im Satze infolge des damit verbundenen Nachlassens der Zungenspannung, d.h. Zungenhebung, und auch Nachlassens der Stimmbandpressung in [ɪ] über."

59. Siebs, *Deutsche Bühnenaussprache*, p. 51

60. Cf. Paget, *Human Speech*, p. 91. French uses a phonologic opposition between [a+] and [ɑ]; e.g., *patte* vs. *pâte*.

61. Cf. Jones, *Outline*, p. 74. This vowel is sometimes called Smart's Compromise, because of its advocacy by Benjamin H. Smart in his revision of *Walker's Pronouncing Dictionary of the English Language* (5th ed., London, 1846), p. v.

62. C. H. Grandgent, *German and English Sounds*, p. 15.

63. Cf. Kenyon, *American Pronunciation*, pp. 174–75; Jane D. Zimmerman; "Representative Radio Pronunciation in America," *Proc. Second Int. Cong. Phon. Sci.*, pp. 291–302.

64. Cf. Kenyon, *American Pronunciation*, p. 181.

65. Cf. Siebs, *Deutsche Bühnenaussprache*, p. 48.

66. Cf. Jones, *Outline*, pp. 77–78.

67. Cf. *Le Maître phonétique*, No. 48 (Dec., 1934), p. 103.

68. *Ibid.*, No. 56 (Dec., 1936), p. 60.

69. *Ibid.*, No. 68 (Dec., 1939), p. 67.

70. *Ibid.*, No. 21 (Mar., 1928), p. 3.

71. Cf. Martin Joos, *ibid.*, No. 43 (Sept., 1933), pp. 48–49; Kenyon, *American Pronunciation*, p. 201, §323.

72. Cf. Siebs, *Deutsche Bühnenaussprache*, p. 52.

73. Cf. *Le Maître phonétique*, No. 77 (June, 1942), pp. 6–7.

74. *Ibid.*, No. 59 (Sept., 1937), p. 45.

75. *Ibid.*, No. 58 (June, 1937), p. 21.

76. E. g., Jespersen, *Lehrbuch*, p. 153.

77. Cf. *Le Maître phonétique*, No. 60 (Dec., 1937), p. 66.

78. *Ibid.*, No. 47 (Sept., 1934), p. 77.

79. *Ibid.*, No. 56 (Dec., 1936), p. 60.

80. *Ibid.*, No. 69 (Feb., 1940), p. 11.

81. *Ibid.*, No. 72 (Dec., 1940), pp. 56–65. [ɜ] is accepted by the International Phonetic Association; [ɝ] is used in the journal, *American Speech;* and [r] has quite often been used by contributors to *Le Maître phonétique*. There is no compelling objection even to [ɜr] when [r] is pronounced.

82. Cf. J. S. Kenyon in *Le Maître phonétique*, No. 69 (Feb., 1940), pp. 3–4.

83. Cf. Jerpersen, *Lehrbuch*, p. 156.

84. If it were deemed desirable to discriminate between centralized front vowels and centralized back vowels in transcription, one might write [ï] and [ü] for the unrounded and [ï] and [ü] for the rounded vowels of the types [i] and [u] respectively.

85. Cf. Ščerba, *Court exposé de la prononciation russe*, p. 6; Trofimov and Jones, *The Pronunciation of Russian*, pp. 72–73.

86. E.g. by *Henry Sweet*, Handbook, pp. 66–69.

87. Cf. Kenyon, *American Pronunciation*, pp. 210–16.

88. By Harold E. Palmer; cf. Jones, *Outline*, p. 95.

89. Cf. Kenyon, *American Pronunciation*, pp. 217–18.

90. Sweet, *Handbook*, p. 66.

91. Cf. André Classe in *Le Maître phonétique*, No. 46 (June, 1934), pp. 46–47.

92. Cf. Paget, *Human Speech*, p. 93; Stumpf, *Die Sprachlaute*, p. 197.

93. Cf. Paget, *Human Speech*, p. 96; L.P.H. Eijkman in *Neophilologus*, XI (1926), 207–18; also *Neophilologus*, XX (1934), 25–30.

94. In the Congo, west of Lake Albert, cf. Tucker, *The Eastern Sudanic Languages*, p. 385.

95. Cf. Kenyon, *American Pronunciation*, pp. 59–60.

NOTES TO CHAPTER VI

1. Cf. §4.01, above. Bloomfield, *Language*, p. 121, uses the term *consonant* for sounds which occur only as nonsyllabics, *vowel* for sounds which occur only as syllabics, and *sonant* for sounds which may be either syllabic or nonsyllabic in function. I shall use the term *sonant* only in its functional sense, syllabic.

2. Cf. Grammont, *Traité de phonétique*, p. 40.

3. Cf. Beach, *The Phonetics of the Hottentot Language*, p. 74.

4. *Ibid.*, pp. 73–91.

5. Many English writers object to the use of the French terminology for these three phases, viz., *implosion, tenue, explosion*, because they wish to use the term *implosive* for suction stop and the term *explosive* for pressure stop.

6. Other terms which have been used for these sounds are: *surd*, French *sourde*, *breathed* (whether [brɛθt] or [briŏd], cf. *Le Maître phonétique*, No. 46, [June, 1934], p. 48) and *unvoiced*.

7. The voiced consonants have sometimes, I think wrongly, been called *sonants*. The French term is *les sonores*.

8. Cf. Paget, *Human Speech*, pp. 122–23.

9. I have substituted *by* here for Paget's *to*.

10. In the *Archives Néerl. Phon. Exp.*, XI (1935), 1–28.

11. Cf. Paget, *Human Speech*, p. 117.

12. Cf. J. C. Catford in *Le Maître phonétique*, No. 65 (Mar., 1939), p. 4.

13. Cf. Stumpf, *Die Sprachlaute*, p. 159; and Zwaardemaker en Eijkman, *Leerboek*, p. 202.

14. Cf. G. Panconcelli-Calzia, *Die Experimentelle Phonetik und ihre Anwendung* (2 Aufl.), pp. 35–45; and Paul Menzerath in *Le Maître phonétique*, No. 50 (June, 1935), pp. 24–25.

15. Cf. Jespersen, *Lehrbuch*, pp. 78–79.

16. The inclusion of French [g] and the exclusion of French [k] rest upon the assumption that the usual French [k] is a compound, rather than a simple, stop.

17. Cf. Beach, *Phonetics of Hottentot*, p. 66.

18. Cf. Alfred Götze, *Proben Hoch- und Niederdeutscher Mundarten*, (Bonn: Marcus & Weber, 1922), *passim*.

19. The International Phonetic Association classes these stops, I think improperly, as "uvular plosives." In any event, the uvula has nothing actively to do with their formation.

20. Observed long ago by Jespersen; cf. his *Lehrbuch*, p. 107.

21. Cf. Beach, *Phonetics of Hottentot*, p. 66.

22. Cf. *Le Maître phonétique*, No. 68 (Dec., 1939), pp. 67–68.

23. *Ibid.*, No. 48 (Dec., 1934), pp. 102–5.

24. *Ibid.*, No. 60 (Dec., 1937), pp. 66–67.

25. *Ibid.*, No. 39 (Sept., 1932), pp. 58–60.

26. Cf. William Dwight Whitney, *Sanskrit Grammar* (2d ed., Cambridge: Harvard University Press, 1931), §45.

27. Cf. Trofimov and Jones, *Pronunciation of Russian*, pp. 109–13.

28. Cf. Jespersen, *Lehrbuch*, p. 107.

29. E. g., Kenyon, *American Pronunciation*, pp. 122, 232.

30. V. A. Oswald, Jr., in *American Speech*, (Feb., 1943, pp. 18–25) has cited the important literature on this question. He tries to support the thesis that the sound is a "combinatory variant" not only of [t] but also of [d], and that it is heard equally in words like *plodding, hardy*, as in words like *plotting, hearty*.

31. Trofimov and Jones, *Pronunciation of Russian*, and Ščerba, *Court exposé*, who omits [dz].

32. Cf. *Le Maître phonétique*, No. 53 (Mar., 1936), p. 15, and No. 62 (Jan., 1938), p. 23.

33. Cf. Jespersen, *Lehrbuch*, p. 107.

34. Cf. Tucker, *Eastern Sudanic Languages*, I, 115.

35. Cf. Zwaardemaker en Eijkman, *Leerboek*, pp. 178–79.

36. The French term is *une consonne mouillée*.

37. Ščerba, *Court exposé*, p. 3. Trofimov and Jones (*Pronunciation of Russian*, pp. 84–88) observe that the velars are not fronted as much as the true prepalatal articulation requires.

38. Cf. *Le Maître phonétique*, No. 78 (Dec., 1942), p. 15.

39. Cf. Trofimov and Jones, *Pronunciation of Russian*, pp. 95–96.

40. Cf. Gairdner, *Egyptian Colloquial Arabic*, p. 2: "What one feels is as if the whole tongue was raised, and also expanded, in the mouth."

41. Cf. Sievers, *Grundzüge*, pp. 120–22; Jespersen, *Lehrbuch*, p. 73.

42. Cf. Tucker, *Eastern Sudanic Languages*, I, 101.

43. T. Navarro Tomás, *Manual de Pronunciación Española* (4th ed., Madrid: Hernando, 1932), p. 123.

44. Cf. *Le Maître phonétique*, No. 63 (Sept., 1938), p. 46.

45. Cf. Beach, *Phonetics of Hottentot*, p. 71, also *Le Maître phonétique*, No. 64, Dec. 1938, p. 63.

46. Cf. L'Abbé P.-J. Rousselot, *Principes de phonétique expérimentale* (Nouvelle édition, Paris: Didier, 1924), p. 607; Trofimov and Jones, *The Pronunciation of Russian*, p. 129.

47. Cf. *Le Maître phonétique*, No. 39 (Sept., 1932), p. 59.

48. *Ibid.*, No. 60 (Dec., 1937), p. 66.

49. An illuminating article on glottalized consonants is that of Edward Sapir, "Glottalized Continuants in Navaho, Nootka, and Kwakiutl," *Language*, XIV (1938), 248–74.

50. Cf. *Le Maître phonétique*, No. 78 (Dec., 1942), pp. 15–17.

51. *Ibid.*, No. 81 (June, 1944), pp. 5–6.

52. *Ibid.*, No. 56 (Dec., 1936), pp. 60–61.

53. *Ibid.*, No. 37 (Mar., 1932), p. 5.

54. Cf. Grammont, *Traité*, p. 40.

55. Cf. Viëtor, *Elemente der Phonetik*, pp. 278–79.

56. Cf. Beach, *Phonetics of Hottentot*, p. 74, and J. C. Catford in *Le Maître phonétique*, No. 65 (Mar., 1939), pp. 2–5.

57. Cf. Tucker, *Eastern Sudanic Languages*, I, 108.

58. *Ibid.*, p. 106.

59. Cf. Carl Meinhof, *Grundriß einer Lautlehre der Bantusprachen* (2. Aufl. Berlin, Reimer, 1910), p. 6.

60. Cf. Beach, *Phonetics of Hottentot*, p. 74; *Le Maître phonétique*, No. 64 (Dec., 1938), pp. 60–64; and Roman Stopa, in the *Archiv für vergleichende Phonetik* (Berlin, Metten), I. Abt, Bd. III, Heft 2, (1939), pp. 89–108.

61. Cf. Fletcher, *Speech and Hearing*, p. 59.

62. Cf. Meinhof, *Grundriß*, pp. 6–7, where a "velarlabiales m" is cited.

63. *Ibid.*, p. 11.

64. *Ibid.*

65. Cf. *Le Maître phonétique*, No. 47 (Sept., 1934), pp. 76–77.

66. Cf. Meinhof, *Grundiß*, p. 6.

67. Cf. *Le Maître phonétique*, No. 50 (June, 1935), pp. 27–28, and No. 65 (Mar., 1939), pp. 7–8.

68. *Ibid.*, No. 64 (Dec., 1938), pp. 60–64.

69. *Ibid.*, No. 78 (Dec., 1942), pp. 15–17.

70. Cf. Dozent Dr. Fröschels in *Wiener medizinische Wochenschrift*, No. 38 (1925), Sp. 2124; B. Karlgren, *Etudes sur la Phonologie Chinoise* (Leyde et Stockholm: Norstedt & Söner, 1913), p. 275; Franz Boas, *Handbook of American Indian Languages*, I, 16–17.

71. In Kolhapur, cf. *Le Maître phonétique*, No. 48 (Dec., 1934), p. 102.

72. In Ceylon, cf. *ibid.*, No. 60 (Dec., 1937), p. 66.

73. Cf. Trofimov and Jones, *Pronunciation of Russian*, pp. 121–23.

74. The classic introduction to the history of this sound in English is Charles Hall Grandgent's delightful essay, "The Dog's Letter," in his collection, *Old and New* (Cambridge: Harvard University Press, 1920), pp. 31–56.

75. Cf. C. K. Thomas in *American Speech*, X (1935), 106–12, 208–12.

76. Cf. M. Durand in *Revue de Phonétique* (Paris: Didier), VI (1930), 250–56.

77. So in Eskimo, cf. *Le Maître phonétique*, No. 47 (Sept., 1934), p. 77; in Pomo (California), *ibid.*, No. 37 (Mar., 1932), p. 5; and in Tagalog, *ibid.*, No. 63 (Sept., 1938), p. 46.

78. "Armenian [r] varies from fricative to fricative with one or two light taps, always fricative when final."—J. C. Catford in *Le Maître phonétique*, No. 80 (Dec., 1943), p. 23. Georgian [r] is "generally a single flap, but is fricative in final posi-

tion," D. Jones, *ibid.*, No. 81, p. 5. Albanian has an "r" which is a weak flapped apical [ᶜ], "hardly distinguishable from an English fricative 'r'...and a 'strong tongue-tip roll [r],'" the two being, according to J. T. Pring, separate phonemes. Cf. *ibid.*, No. 71 (Sept., 1940), pp. 45–46.

79. Cf. Driver, *Grammar of the Colloquial Arabic*, p. 5.

80. Cf. Zwaardemaker en Eijkman, *Leerboek*, p. 44.

81. Cf. Otto Bremer, *Deutsche Lautlehre.* (Leipzig: Quelle & Meyer, 1918), pp. 37–40.

82. Cf. E. A. Meyer, "Englische Lautdauer," *Skrifter utgifna af K. Humanistika Vetenskaps-Samfundet i Uppsala*, VIII, 3 (1903), p. 20; Jespersen, *Lehrbuch*, p. 92.

83. Cf. Gairdner, *Egyptian Colloquial Arabic*, p. 3.

84. Cf. *Le Maître phonétique*, No. 45 (Mar., 1934), pp. 8–9.

85. *Ibid.*, No. 80 (Dec., 1943), p. 23.

86. *Ibid.*, No. 78 (Dec., 1942), p. 15.

87. *Ibid.*, No. 47 (Sept., 1934), p. 77.

88. Cf. Daniel Jones and Ivar Dahl, *Fundamentos de Escritura Fonética* (London: University College, 1944), p. 9.

89. Cf. Trofimov and Jones, *Pronunciation of Russian*, p. 153.

90. Cf. Kenyon, *American Pronunciation*, p. 155.

91. Cf. Jespersen, *Lehrbuch*, pp. 45–47.

92. Cf. Fletcher, *Speech and Hearing*, p. 63.

93. Cf. *Le Maître phonétique*, No. 48 (Dec., 1934), pp. 102–105.

94. Cf. Jespersen, *Lehrbuch*, p. 34. He cites *vers, först.*

95. Cf. Meinhof, *Grundriß*, p. 7.

96. Cf. Driver, *Grammar of Colloquial Arabic*, p. 8, note 2.

97. Cf. Jespersen, *Lehrbuch*, p. 36.

98. Cf. S. Éliséév, in A. Meillet et M. Cohen, *Les Langues du monde* (Paris: Champion, 1924), p. 251; *Le Maître phonétique*, No. 68 (Dec., 1939), p. 66.

99. Cf. Zwaardemaker en Eijkman, *Leerboek*, p. 175.

100. Cf. Grammont, *Traité*, pp. 77–78.

NOTES TO CHAPTER VII

1. Stetson, *Motor Phonetics.*

2. Cf. Bloomfield, *Language*, p. 161.

3. Cf. E. Sapir, "The Phonetics of Haida," *International Journal of American Linguistics* (New York-Baltimore, Waverly Press), II (1921–1923), 149, and "Glottalized Continuants in Navaho, Nootka, and Kwakiutl," *Language*, XIV (1928), 248–74.

4. Cf. F. Boas, *Handbook of American Indian Languages* I, 743.

5. The basic study of this problem in our time is the monograph of R. H. Stetson, *Motor Phonetics.* 1928. A revision is in preparation.

6. Cf. Zwaardemaker en Eijkman, *Leerboek*, p. 41.

7. *Ibid.*, note 1.

8. Cf. Bloomfield, *Language*, p. 161.

9. Cf. Prince N. Troubetzkoy, "Die phonologischen Grenzsignale," *Proc. Second Int. Cong. Phon. Sci.*, pp. 45–49.

10. Cf. Stetson, *Motor Phonetics*, pp. 85, 99, for the demonstration of the effect of syllable rate upon releasing and arresting consonants.

11. English *apron* is a development of French *naperon* and resulted from the association of the initial [n] with the preceding indefinite article rather than with

the noun to which it etymologically belonged, so that *a napron* became *an apron*. The English suffix -ness is derived immediately from a general Germanic suffix *-nissi* or *-nassu*, which owes its [n] to the false analysis of such words as Gothic *skalkinassus, lêkinassus*, in which the [n] belongs to the stem of the basic word *skalkinon* or *lêkinon*, rather than to the suffix, which was originally *-assu*. This *-assu* should have given us the suffix *-es* or *-is*, but by acquiring the [n] from some of these compounds by false division it has evolved into our suffix *-ness*.

12. See note 24, below.

13. Cf. Stetson, *Motor Phonetics*, pp. 67–85.

14. Cf. J. S. Kenyon and T. A. Knott, *A Pronouncing Dictionary of American English* (Springfield, Mass.: Merriam, 1944), p. 214.

15. The fact that for some speakers this *o'* is [o] rather than [ə] means that for them the forms are not living contracted forms due to fusion in their own speech, but "spelling pronunciations" of more or less romantic advertisements.

16. Adequately in the sense of Weber's Law.

17. Henry Sweet, *A Handbook of Phonetics*.

18. Cf. *American Speech*, XVIII (1943), 208–15.

19. Cf. Jespersen, *Lehrbuch*, ρ. 202.

20. Cf. J. J. Salverda de Grave, *Homenaje a Menéndez Pidal* (Madrid: Hernando, 1925), p. 642.

21. Cf. Siebs, *Deutsche Bühnenaussprache*, p. 51.

22. Cf. Grandgent, *German and English Sounds*, p. 15.

23. Cf. *Science*, CII, No. 2654 (Nov. 9, 1945) pp. 463–70, and *Life*, Nov. 26, 1945. pp. 91–94; Potter, Kopp, and Green, *Visible Speech* (Van Nostrand, 1947); Martin Joos, *Acoustic Phonetics*.

24. It will probably be necessary to practice the analysis of speech forms in order to understand what is to follow here. It is suggested that a physiological description of phrases be worked at after something like the following scheme. Problem: analyze the phrase, "Step on it " Solution:

SOUND	POSITION OF LIPS	TONGUE	VELUM	VOCAL BANDS
[s]	spread	open, hole type alveolar constriction	raised	open
[t]	spread	stop, alveolar	raised	open
[ɛ]	spread	mid front lax vowel type [e]	raised	voicing
[p]	bilabial stop	indifferent	raised	open
[ɒ]	neutral	low back lax vowel type [a]	raised	voicing
[n]	neutral	stop, alveolar	lowered	voicing
[ɪ]	neutral	high front lax vowel type [i]	raised	voicing
[t]	neutral	stop, alveolar	raised	open

25. This example was suggested to me by my colleague W. F. Twaddell.

26. The traditional terms regressive and progressive when applied to assimilations regularly cause needless befuddlement of beginners. What is here called anticipative assimilation is traditionally called regressive assimilation, and what I have called continuative assimilation is traditionally called progressive assimilation.

27. Stetson, *Motor Phonetics*.

28. Cf. Tucker, *Eastern Sudanic Languages*, p. 93.

29. Cf. Hermann Grassmann, in *Zeitschrift für vergleichende Sprachforschung*, XII (1863), 81–138.

30. Other examples are cited by Jos. Schrijnen, *Einführung in das Studium der indogermanischen Sprachwissenschaft* (trans. by W. Fischer, Heidelberg, Winter, 1921), pp. 223–27. The most extensive treatment of the phenomena of dissimilation is still the monograph of Maurice Grammont, *La dissimilation consonantique* (Dijon, 1895); Cf. Hudgins and Di Carlo in *Journal of General Psychology*, XX (1939), 449–69.

31. Cf. Kenyon, *American Pronunciation*, pp. 102–10.

32. Cf. Parmenter and Treviño, *American Speech* X, (1935), 129–33.

33. Cf. *American Speech*, XVI (1941), 204–207, XVII, (1942), 42–48.

34. In RCA Victor Album C-10, Side 19.

35. Or fewer, if *you're*, which is one syllable, is counted one word. I have counted it two.

36. R. H. Stetson, *Bases of Phonology* (Oberlin College, 1945), p. 55.

37. Cf. *American Speech*, XVII (1942), 47–48.

38. Cf. Charles Hall Grandgent, "English in America," *Die neueren Sprachen*, II (1895), 443–67. Under "heavy" vowels he lists the stressed syllabics of *fast, hurt, hat, father, ride, out, hate, fair, eat, gloom, new, mope, hawk, oil*. Under "light" vowels he lists the stressed syllabics of *hut, bet, hit, music, port, whole, hot, full*, and the unstressed vowels of *sofa, rabbit*. He adds that the vowel of *hat* is generally "light" in eastern New England but "heavy" in the rest of the country, and that the vowels of *bet, hit, port*, and *full* may become heavy if they occur before [r].

39. *American Speech*, XII (1937), 128–34; XV (1940), 74–79, 377–80; XVI (1941), 205–7; XVII (1942), 42–48; XVIII (1943), 208–15.

40. Cf. P. Menzerath und A. de Lacerda, *Koartikulation, Steuerung und Lautabgrenzung* (Berlin: Dümmler, 1933), and the reviews of P. Meriggi in *Indogermanische Forschungen*, LIII (1935), 301–3 and E. Richter in *Literaturblatt für germanische und romanische Philologie*, LVII (1936), 1–6.

41. Cf. Oskar Vierling und Fritz Sennheiser, "Der spektrale Aufbau der langen und der kurzen Vokalen," *Akustische Zeitschrift*, II (1937), 93–106.

42. In much of American English the historic short [ɔ] of *hop* has been replaced by [ɑ].

43. Cf. *Grundzüge der Phonetik*, §694

44. Cf. Cf. *American Speech*, XII (1937), 128–34; XV (1940), 74–79, 377–80; XVI (1941), 205–7; XVII (1942), 42–48; XVIII (1943), 208–15.

45. Cf. E. Zwirner und K. Zwirner, "Phonometrischer Beitrag zur Frage der neuhochdeutschen Quantität, "*Archiv für vergleichende Phonetik*, I (1937), 96–113.

46. Cf. *American Speech*, X (1935), 129–33.

47. Beach (*Phonetics of Hottentot* p. 130), uses four categories: high, less high, mid, low.

48. Cf. *Language*, p. 116

49. Cf. Jones, *Outline*, p. 257, for five intonational patterns of "yes."

50. For this information I am indebted to my colleague Einar Haugen, who also spoke the recordings upon which it is based.

51. Another way of managing the transcription of tones is to write a symbol before the syllable, thus: ⁻ʃji high level tone, ⁄ʃji high rising, ⧵ʃji high falling, ₋ʃji low level. The starting point of the intonation is indicated by the level at which the mark begins, the direction of the tonal change is indicated by the direction of the line. A falling-rising tone which starts at a medium level would then be written v.

52. Cf. L. T. Wang, "Recherches expérimentales sur les tons du Pékinois," *Archives Néerl. Phon. Exp.*, XIII (1937), 1–38, and XIV (1938), 1–48.

53. Cf. "Monosyllabism in English," *Proceedings of the British Academy*, XIV. Separately printed in his *Linguistica* (London: Milford), pp. 384–408.

54. L. T. Wang, "Recherches expérimentales sur les tons du Pékinois," *Archives Néerl. Phon. Exp.*, XIII (1937), 1–38; IV (1938), 1–48.

55. An acute and very old observation on this point is that of Tobias Smollett in the letter of J. Melford, of July 13, in *The Expedition of Humphrey Clinker* (Saintsbury ed., II, 28–30):

"He said, the same observation would hold in all languages: that a Swiss talking French was more easily understood than a Parisian, by a foreigner who had not made himself master of the language, because every language had its peculiar recitative, and it would always require more pains, attention, and practice to acquire both the words and the music than to learn the words only; and yet nobody would deny, that the one was imperfect without the other. . . ."

56. Jones (*Outline*) gives a summary discussion of English intonation, with bibliographical references which will serve all ordinary purposes of orientation. There is a recent essay on American intonational problems by Kenneth L. Pike in *An Intensive Course in English for Latin-American Students* (Ann Arbor: English Language Institute, Univ. of Michigan, 1942), Vol. I; see also the same author's *The Intonation of American English*. Univ. of Michigan Publications in Linguistics (Ann Arbor, 1946), Vol. I.

57. Cf. Cowan, *Pitch and Intensity Characteristics of Stage Speech*.

58. Cf. H. O. Coleman, "Intonation and Emphasis," in *Miscellanea Phonetica*, pp. 6–26.

59. Jones, *Outline*, p. 36.

60. Cf. H. Klinghardt und P. Olbrich, *Französische Intonationsübung* (Leipzig, 1925), pp. 78–79.

61. *Ibid.*

62. Cf. E. Hoffmann-Krayer, "Grundsätzliches über Ursprung und Wirkung der Akzentuation," *Festschrift für Otto Behaghel* (1924), pp. 35–57.

63. In the *Archiv für vergleichende Phonetik* (Berlin: Metten), I (Jan., 1937), 51–52.

64. There is a brief reference to the same phenomenon in Westermann and Ward, *Practical Phonetics for Students of African Languages*, p. 203.

65. Cf. E. G. Boring, H. S. Langfeld, and H. P. Weld, *Psychology* (New York: Wiley, 1935), p. 256.

66. Coleman, in *Miscellanea Phonetica;* W. L. Schramm in *American Speech*, XII (1937), 49–56.

INDEX

Numbers refer to pages on which the discussion of the item begins.

J

[j] glide, 184
jaw movements, 35

K

Kieferwinkel, 36
Knarrstimme, 134

L

Labial, stops, 131; trill, 136
labialized, stops, 133; [r], 149
labiodental, stop, 132; [m], 142; open consonants, 159
labiovelar, 161
lack of nexus, 201
language, 1
laryngeal, articulation, 97, 100; open consonants, 150; pharynx, 25, Plate 10, p. 26; stop, 125; trill, 134; ventricle, 16
larynx, 15, Plates 4, 5, and 6, pp. 15, 17, and 18; artificial, 90; function of, 23; intrinsic muscles of, 19; lowering of, 91; nerves of, 41; range of movement, 25
lateral consonants, 141, 143
lateral cricoarytenoid muscles, 20, 21
lateral release, 191
lateral [s], [z], 144
lax vowels, 96
lenis, 120, 194
lenition, 192
lento forms, 202
level stress, 227
lexical forms, 202
lexical pronunciation, 63
light [l], 144
light vowels, 207
linguistic forms, 173
linguistics, 1
linking, 184, 186; [n], 187; [r], 186; [t], 186
lip opening, types of, 38
lip rounding, 104, 105; horizontal, 98; vertical, 98
lips, 37; nerves of, 41
lisped [s], 157
long and short sounds, 207, 210
long consonants, 176, 210

loose nexus, 183, 229
loudness, 51
low vowels, 95; back vowels, 103; front vowels, 102
lower teeth, 156
Luftfüllung, 97
lungs, 9, 10, Plate 1, p. 10

M

Mandible, 34, 38, Plate 15, p. 35
masseter muscle, 35, Plate 16, p. 39
maxillae, 34
maxillary sinuses, 30
maximum rate, 206
mediopalatal [r], 148
mediopalatal, region, 37; stops, 126
mentalis muscles, 38, Plate 16, p. 39
metaphonie, 197
mid vowels, 95; back, 104; front, 101
mimic musculature, 224
mixed double consonants, 194
modifications in context, 165
molar teeth, 36
monophthongization, 196
morpheme, 165, 173; delimitation of, 201
motor context, 63, 66, 163
motor nerves, 41
motor unit, 39
mouillé, 133
mouth, 34, Plate 13, p. 31
murmur, 86
muscle, 39; contraction of, 40
mylohyoid muscle, 25, 34, Plate 11, p. 27

N

Nares, posterior, 29
narrow transcription, 68
narrow vowels, 96
nasal, cavity, 29, Plate 10, p. 26; pharynx, 29; sinuses, 30
nasal conchae, 29
nasal consonants, 141
nasal vowels, 112
nasality, 31, 112
nasalization, 193
natural length of vowels, 210
negative pressure, 11

repetition time, 199, 206
resonance, 45, 49; resonance frequency (fR), 50; of cavity, 88
retroflex [t], 128; [d] 128; [r], 108, 115, 147, 148; [l], 144, 145; [s], 157
reversible reduction, 202
rhythm, 227, 228
rib cage, Plate 2, p. 11
risorius muscle, Plate 16, p. 39
rounded vowels, 98
rounding, 193

S

[s] glide, 185
sandhi, 165, 174
scala tympani, 55
scala vestibuli, 55
Schleifton, 229
schwa, 108
selective transmission, 87
semiconsonants, 73
semivowels, 73, 154
Semitic gain, 153
shortening, effect of, 212
significant duration, 209
simple stops, 118
sinus, Plate 10, p. 26
sinus glossoepiglotticus, 19
slit type articulation, 155, 156; fricatives, 158, 160
soft palate, Plate 10, p. 26
soft [s], 155
sonant, 73, 116
sonority, 74
sotto voce, 86
sound, speed of propagation, 46
sound interchange, 197
sound waves, 42; measurement of, 52
speech, measure, 173, 200; melody, 213; power, 50; sensory basis of, 9; sound defined, 2; sounds as events, 64; sounds classified, 72; sounds identified, 65; stumbling, 189; units, 173
spelling, 67
sphenoidal sinuses, 30
spirant, 146
spontaneous sound changes, 192
Sprechtakt, 173
staccato, 215
standing waves, 87

statistical method, 91
Steigton, 229
sternum, 11
sternohyoid muscle, 25, 35
sternothyroid muscle, 25
stimulus-response, 62; unit, 64
stød, 125, 170
stop consonants, 117; criteria of description, 123
stopped beginning, of consonants, 167; of vowels, 166
stopped release, of open consonants, 172; of stops, 173
stopped vowel attack, 151, 166
stopped vowel release, 170
Stosston, 229
stress, 224; and duration, 206; secondary stress, 226
stressed vs. unstressed, 203
styloglossus muscles, 33, Plate 14, p. 33
stylohyoid muscles, 25, 33, Plates 11 and 14, pp. 27 and 33
stylopharyngeus muscles, 31
stylothyroid muscles, 33, Plate 14, p. 33
styloid processes, 25
subglottal pressure, 86, 97
substitutions, as a means of identifying speech sounds, 2
suction stops, 119
superior lingualis muscle, 32
supersonic waves, 46
svarabhakti vowel, 185
syllable, 73, 76, 174
syllabics, 72, 114
synaeresis, 178
synchronic, 4, 187
synchronization, 166, 167
syncope, 179
synezesis, 178
swallowing, 17, 19
Swedish tones, 229

T

Tapped [r], 135
teeth, 36
tempo, 174, 204
temporal muscles, 35
tense vowels, 96
tetanus, 40
thoracic cavity, 11